Interchange Fees

The Economics and Regulation of What Merchants Pay for Cards

By David S. Evans

© 2011 Competition Policy International (CPI)

Competition Policy International (CPI) provides comprehensive resources and continuing education for the global antitrust and competition policy community. Created and managed by leaders in the competition policy community, CPI delivers timely commentary and analysis on antitrust and global competition policy matters through a variety of media and applications.

www.competitionpolicyinternational.com

CONTENTS

Acknowledgments iv

Introduction v

chapter 1 The Economics of Interchange Fees and Their Regulation: An Overview 1

chapter 2 The Economic Principles for Establishing Reasonable Regulation of 34
Debit-Card Interchange Fees that Could Improve Consumer Welfare

chapter 3 The Effect of Regulatory Intervention in Two-Sided Markets: 57
An Assessment of Interchange-Fee Capping in Australia

chapter 4 Economic Analysis of the Effects of the Federal Reserve 86
Board's Proposed Debit Card Interchange Fee Regulations
on Consumers and Small Businesses

chapter 5 How Changes in Payment Card Interchange Fees Affect Consumers 131
Fees and Merchant Prices: An Economic Analysis with Applications
to the European Union

chapter 6 Payments Innovation and Interchange Fee Regulation: 164
How Inverting the Merchant-Pays Business Model Would Affect
the Extent and Direction of Innovation

chapter 7 Economic Analysis of Claims in Support of the 185
"Durbin Amendment" to Regulate Debit Card Interchange Fees

Conclusion 206

Contributors 207

About the Author 208

Bibliography 209

ACKNOWLEDGMENTS

This volume collects a series of articles I have written, with various collaborators, over the last decade concerning interchange fees. Many of the pieces were written in 2011 in connection with initiatives to regulate interchange fees in the United States (as a result of federal legislation) and the European Union (as a result of antitrust cases brought by the European Commission). My research for these articles was funded by a variety of large financial institutions in the US and Europe. The opinions do not necessarily reflect the views of anyone other than me and the other authors of the articles.

I would like to extend my appreciation to all of my co-authors for these articles. But in particular I thank Howard Chang and Richard Schmalensee with whom I have collaborated on this topic closely since the middle 1990s and from whom I have learned a great deal.

Finally, I would like to thank Lauren Chiang, Managing Editor of Competition Policy International, who has assembled this volume, and Dean Whitney of Aericon for the book design.

INTRODUCTION

By David S. Evans

Payment cards differ along several dimensions.

- When do you have to pay? Roughly speaking there are credit cards that allow you to pay later (after you get your monthly bill) if you want; there are debit cards that often pull money out of your checking account right away; and there are prepaid cards where someone has already committed money.

- Where you can pay? There are store cards that consumers can only use at the stores that issued the card and there are general-purpose cards—most cards today in terms of dollar volume—that can be used at many unaffiliated merchants.

- Whether a single firm works with both the cardholder and merchant or whether different entities do that? Some payment card networks such as American Express work directly with both the merchant and the cardholder; these are called three-party systems. Others such as Visa work with banks that issue cards to consumers and as well as banks and other parties that handle card payments for merchants; these are called four-party systems.

With the exception of store cards, merchants usually have to pay a fee whenever a consumer pays with a card. That fee generally gets deducted from the charge that the consumer puts on the card and is called the merchant discount. The merchant discount goes directly to the company that stands between the merchant and consumer in the case of three-party systems. For the four-party systems the merchant discount includes a fee that goes to the bank or other company that works with the merchant and an "interchange fee" that goes to the bank that issued the card with which the consumer paid. (Sometimes the "merchant discount" refers to the fee net of the interchange fee, and other times it refers to the fee inclusive of the interchange fee.) The interchange fee is set by the network, which stands between the cardholder's bank and the merchant's bank.

Interchange fees have become increasingly controversial. These fees constitute the bulk of the cost that merchants incur for taking cards because most consumers pay with a card from a four-party system that assesses these fees. The total interchange fees paid by merchants have increased dramatically as consumers have switched to electronic payments. Merchants have complained, have filed lawsuits, and have lobbied governments to do something about this. Meanwhile governments around the world have intensified their examination of these fees. For example, the US Congress passed legislation in 2010 that required the Federal Reserve Board to regulate debit card interchange fees; the Reserve Bank of Australia decided to regulate credit card interchange fees in 2002 after concluding that a market failure had resulted in merchants paying fees that were too high; and in 2007 the European Commission ruled that MasterCard's interchange fees violated the EU's antitrust laws.

The controversy raises two broad issues. The first relates to how payment card systems decide how much merchants should pay for taking cards either through the interchange fee for four-party systems or the merchant discount for three party systems. The second concerns whether the setting of interchange fees by private businesses results in a market failure and if so what if any regulation should be adopted to correct this market failure.

This interchange fee debate helped stimulate a new literature on multi-sided platforms or what are sometimes called two-sided markets. Payment card systems serve as intermediaries between merchants and consumers and operate a platform that enables these two different kinds of customers to interact. It turns out that there are many other businesses that have similar features including software platforms like the iPhone OS, shopping malls, search engines, and exchanges. Economists have developed general models of multi-sided businesses and applied them to payment cards.

This volume consists of seven articles on the economics and regulation of interchange fees. All rely on the multi-sided platform framework. The first two chapters examine whether there is a market failure in setting interchange fees and present principles for considering correction to a market failure. One of the themes of these articles is that regulating one side of a two-sided market necessarily has effects on the other side of the market: lower prices for merchants means higher prices for consumers. Chapters 3-5 address that tradeoff which is sometimes called a "waterbed effect". Chapter 3 presents an empirical study of what happened following the imposition of price controls on interchange fees in Australia in the mid 2000s. Chapters 4 and 5 estimate the prospective impact on consumers in the US and EU of interchange fee caps. These chapters rely heavily on the economic concept of pass-through, which concerns the extent to which business change their prices in response to changes in costs. The net impact of reductions in interchange fees on consumers depends on the extent to which issuing banks raise fees and merchants lower prices in response to a reduction in interchange fees which are revenues to banks and ultimately costs to merchants. Chapter 6 examines a related question: how do interchange fee price caps affect investment and innovation for payment systems. Chapter 7 examines arguments that merchant representatives have made concerning debit card interchange fee regulation. That is followed by a short chapter with a few concluding thoughts.

chapter 1

THE ECONOMICS OF INTERCHANGE FEES AND THEIR REGULATION: AN OVERVIEW

By

David S. Evans and Richard Schmalensee

I. INTRODUCTION

In 1958, Bank of America began operating the BankAmericard credit card system, the predecessor of Visa, as a *unitary* system.[1] It performed both the issuing function (dealing with cardholders) and the acquiring function (dealing with merchants) itself. Similarly, it set the fees charged to both these customer classes—the annual fee, interest rate, late fees, and other fees charged to cardholders and the per-transaction fee to merchants known as the merchant discount. It was therefore able to determine both the overall level of fees (which might be measured as total fees per dollar of transactions) and their structure (which might be measured by the shares of total fees paid by merchants and cardholders).

In 1966, the Bank of America began to bring other banks into the system as franchisees. Individual banks within the system were free then, as now, to determine the fees they charged merchants and cardholders. When a consumer holding a card issued by bank A made a purchase at a merchant that had bank A as its acquirer, bank A could, if it wished, have the same fee structure as Bank of America. But what if this same consumer made a purchase from a merchant acquired by bank B? Bank of America required the acquiring bank to pass the full merchant discount to the issuing bank. Acquiring banks had incentives to lie about their merchant discounts under this rule, as issuing banks were well aware. More importantly, this rule meant that acquiring banks received zero revenue for transactions for which they provided the merchant but had not issued the card being used. The rule therefore blunted the incentives for all banks to sign up merchants, to the obvious determent of the system as a whole.

In 1970 the BankAmericard system was converted into a membership corporation, a *multi-party* system. This cooperative association established an *interchange fee* in 1971 to deal with transactions in which issuing and acquiring banks were different. This fee was paid by the acquiring bank to the issuing bank and initially set at 1.95 percent. It was not linked to any individual bank's merchant discount. The interchange fee thus became a revenue source on the issuing side of the credit card business and a cost element on the acquiring side. Acquiring banks had to charge a merchant discount that was greater than the interchange fee to recover this cost. The interchange fee was an element of a standard contract that the multi-party system established for its members; other terms of the contract defined who bore the risk of fraud or nonpayment, as well as how disputes would be resolved.

This essay surveys the economic literature on interchange fees and the debate over whether interchange should be regulated and, if so, how.

---

[1] This discussion in this paragraph and the next two follows Evans and Schmalensee (2005, pp. 153-156).

A. What's Interesting About Interchange?

Until 1979, few outside the Visa and MasterCard systems had any idea what an interchange fee was. In that year, the National Bancard Corp. (*NaBanco*) filed a lawsuit contending that when the Visa member banks determined the interchange fee those banks engaged in illegal price-fixing, which, it was claimed, had damaged NaBanco.[2] An appeals court found in favor of Visa in 1986, holding that the interchange fee had potential efficiency benefits for a two-sided system:

> *Another justification for evaluating the [interchange fee] under the rule of reason is because it is a potentially efficiency creating agreement among members of a joint enterprise. There are two possible sources of revenue in the VISA system: the cardholders and the merchants. As a practical matter, the card-issuing and merchant-signing members have a mutually dependent relationship. If the revenue produced by the cardholders is insufficient to cover the card-issuers' costs, the service will be cut back or eliminated. The result would be a decline in card use and a concomitant reduction in merchant-signing banks' revenues. In short, the cardholder cannot use his card unless the merchant accepts it and the merchant cannot accept the card unless the cardholder uses one. Hence, the [interchange fee] accompanies "the coordination of other productive or distributive efforts of the parties" that is "capable of increasing the integration's efficiency and no broader than required for that purpose."*[3]

In 1983, William Baxter, a leading antitrust scholar who had worked for Visa on the case, published an important paper on the economic rationale for interchange fees.[4] But after the *NaBanco* decision, interchange fees faded from view in academic and policy circles and was a topic of interest mainly to industry insiders.

A few academic papers in the 1990s mentioned interchange fees,[5] but for the most part, this topic languished in obscurity until around the turn of this century. And then, as the dates on most of the entries in this essay's list of references indicate, interest in interchange fees increased dramatically among academics, banking regulators, and competition authorities around the world.

Two developments caught the attention of policymakers. Cards had become an increasingly important part of the payment system in many countries. The share of consumer expenditures in the United States paid for with cards had increased from about 3 percent in 1986, the year of the *NaBanco* decision, to 25 percent in 2000.[6] Similar increases occurred in other countries. For example, in 2000, cards accounted for 30 percent of consumer expenditures in Australia and 35 percent

---

[2] National Bancard Corporation v. Visa U.S.A., Inc. (1984, 1986a, and 1986b).
[3] National Bancard Corp. v. Visa U.S.A., Inc. (1986a, p. 602).
[4] Baxter (1983). We discuss this paper below.
[5] These include Carlton and Frankel (1995a and 1995b), Evans and Schmalensee (1995), and Frankel (1998).
[6] HSN Consultants (1987, 1991, 1992, 2001a, and 2001b), and United States Department of Commerce (2003).

in the United Kingdom.[7] While American Express played a significant role in the United States, globally most cards were associated with multi-party systems that had interchange fees. In the United Kingdom, for example, an influential report on the banking industry issued in 2000—the "Cruickshank Report"—addressed interchange fees in multi-party systems, concluding that "[t]here is a strong case for reform of the interchange fee system."[8]

For retailers, merchant discounts (which included interchange fees in the bank card systems) had become a growing portion of their costs, as more people paid with cards. Some retailers had periodically complained about merchant discounts; hotels had gone so far as to create their own card system in the United States in the mid-1950s to avoid the merchant discount of Diners Club (a unitary system). However, with increases in interchange fees and perhaps other legal and political developments, various organizations of retailers around the world sought regulatory relief from the fees. For example, EuroCommerce, a retailer association, filed a complaint with the European Commission in 1997. This led to an investigation of Visa Europe and ultimately a settlement in which Visa Europe agreed to lower the interchange fees. Interchange fee levels have also been under active attack and/or regulated in a number of other countries, including Australia and the United Kingdom.[9]

Why has interest in interchange fees surged among economists in recent years? Some, including us, were exposed to the topic through their involvement in litigation and/or regulatory proceedings. But the same could be said for many other legal and regulatory issues that have spawned much smaller literatures over longer periods of time. The large volume of theoretical literature on interchange fees has arisen for the simplest of reasons: understanding their determination and effect is intellectually challenging. As the discussion below indicates, this is not necessarily good news for policy-makers.

B. This Essay

The remainder of this essay is organized as follows. The next section provides context by considering the operation of unitary payment systems, such as American Express, in the context of the recent economic literature on two-sided markets, in which businesses cater to two interdependent groups of customers. The main focus is on the determination of price structure. We then discuss the basic economics of multi-party payment systems and the role of interchange in the operation of such systems under some standard, though unrealistic, simplifying assumptions. The key point of this discussion is that the interchange fee is not an ordinary price; its most direct effect is on price structure, not price level. While it is clear that an unregulated monopolist or a cartel in a one-sided

---

[7] Visa International (2001). Measures of consumer expenditures may not be entirely consistent across countries but are sufficiently comparable to provide a rough sense of importance. See also Weiner and Wright (2005).
[8] Cruickshank (2000, p. 272).
[9] See Reserve Bank of Australia (2002), European Commission (2002 and 2003), Office of Fair Trading (2003), and Gandal (2005). Weiner and Wright (2005) provide a useful overview of government involvement.

market, like electricity generation, would set a price that is higher than would be socially optimal, no such presumption exists for the interchange fee set by a monopoly card system.

We then consider implications for privately determined interchange fees of some of the relevant market imperfections that have been discussed in the economic literature. While some studies suggest that privately determined interchange fees are inefficiently high, others point to fees being inefficiently low. Moreover, there is a consensus among economists that, as a matter of theory, it is not possible to arrive, except by happenstance, at the socially optimal interchange fee through any regulatory system that considers only costs. This distinguishes the market imperfections at issue here for multi-party systems from the more familiar area of public utility regulation, where setting price equal to marginal cost is theoretically ideal.

The penultimate section examines the implications of the results of the previous sections for policymakers. Since there is so much uncertainty about the relation between privately and socially optimal interchange fees, the outcome of a policy debate can depend critically on who bears the burden of proof under whatever set of institutions and laws the deliberation takes place. There is no apparent basis in today's economics—at a theoretical or empirical level—for concluding that it is generally possible to improve social welfare by a noticeable reduction in privately set interchange fees. Thus, if antitrust or other regulators had to show that such intervention would improve welfare, they could not do so. This, again, is quite unlike public utility regulation or many areas of antitrust including, in particular, ordinary cartels. By the same token, there is no basis in economics for concluding that the privately set interchange fee is just right. Thus, if card associations had to bear the burden of proof—for example to obtain a comfort or clearance letter from authorities for engaging in presumptively illegal coordinated behavior—it would be difficult for them to demonstrate that they set socially optimal fees.

We take a pragmatic approach by suggesting two fact-based inquiries that we believe policymakers should undertake before intervening to affect interchange. These inquiries are premised on the view, which we believe is now widely held, that the government should intervene in markets only when there is a sound basis for believing that it can devise policies that will improve social welfare significantly. First, policymakers should establish that there is a significant market failure that needs to be addressed. To do so, they would need to examine the marginal social benefits and costs of alternative payment systems, as they vary among transactions; we suggest that there is highly incomplete information available on these benefits and costs, so that any inference from the current data is, at best, problematic. Second, policymakers should establish that it is possible to correct a serious market imperfection, assuming one exists, by whatever intervention they are considering (such as cost-based regulation of interchange fee levels) and thereby to increase social welfare significantly, after taking into account other distortions that the intervention may create. We illustrate both of these points by examining the recent Australian experience.

The final section summarizes our conclusions. Many of the results of the economic literature necessarily depend on various simplifying assumptions. In this last section, we highlight those that we believe are robust, in the sense that they are likely to hold generally. Our main focus throughout is on conceptual issues; the companion paper by Weiner and Wright provides a good deal of useful factual material.[10]

II. PAYMENT SYSTEMS AS TWO-SIDED PLATFORMS

In the last few years, economists have come to understand that payment systems have much in common with auction houses, exchanges, shopping malls, and video game consoles. All are examples of two-sided (or, more generally, multi-sided) platform businesses. Such businesses are intermediaries that add value if and only if they can appropriately coordinate the demands of two distinct groups of customers. Beauty salons may attract both men and women, for instance, but heterosexual singles bars *must* attract both men and women—and in the right proportions. Similarly, shopping malls must attract both retailers and shoppers, auction houses need both buyers and sellers to stay in business, sellers of video games need both game players and game creators—and payment systems need both consumers and merchants.

The earliest use of the term "two-sided" in this sense of which we are aware is in a 1998 paper considering a match-making intermediary that adds value by bringing individuals of two different types together.[11] The authors find that, under plausible conditions, one of the types will not pay for the service, and they note that this highly asymmetric pricing is descriptive of some real two-sided markets, such as real estate agents in the United States and some dating services.

The reason why skewed pricing can happen is central to the analysis of two-sided markets in general: there are typically positive indirect network externalities between the two groups.[12] For example, the more men (women) who use a particular dating service, the more attractive the service is to women (men). If the service cannot attract both in the right proportions and sufficient numbers, it will fail. If it needs to serve men for free to accomplish this, it is rational for it to do so. Giving the service away to men, even though serving them involves positive marginal costs, can be profitable if it attracts sufficient fee-paying women.

The recent general literature on two-sided platform markets began around 2002 with early versions of a seminal contribution by Jean-Charles Rochet and Jean Tirole.[13] Early versions of an important related paper by Mark Armstrong appeared shortly thereafter.[14] These papers pointed out that many businesses or markets can usefully be thought of as two-sided, and they developed

---

[10] Weiner and Wright (2005).
[11] Van Raalte and Webers (1998). While he used different terminology, Baxter (1983) did the first two-sided analysis, as we discuss below.
[12] See Ackerberg and Gowrisankaran (2003) for an attempt to quantify these externalities in a payments context.
[13] Rochet and Tirole (2003b).
[14] Armstrong (2004).

some general implications of the importance of balanced participation from the involved customer groups (or, as it is more commonly put, "getting both sides on board"). Since then, the literature on two-sided platform markets has grown explosively.[15] This literature generally considers one or more vendors dealing directly with both (or all) involved customer groups, and it is thus most directly relevant in our context to the analysis of unitary payment systems.

A. Pricing by Two-Sided Platforms

Almost all theoretical analyses of pricing by two-sided platforms assume that they either charge only an access or membership fee (following Armstrong) or that they charge only a variable or per-transaction fee (following Rochet and Tirole). While this simplification generally facilitates understanding of basic principles, it is problematic in some cases. Newspapers, for example, typically charge an access fee to readers (a fixed cost for the newspaper regardless of what is read), while advertisers pay a variable fee based on the number of readers. In the payment card context, for instance, merchants incur small fixed access (terminal) costs of card acceptance as well as per transaction merchant discounts. On the other side of that market, consumers sometimes pay membership fees, but variable fees are typically slightly negative as a result of free float and sometimes noticeably negative as a result of transaction-based reward programs.[16]

The literature on pricing by two-sided platforms distinguishes between the level of prices and the structure of prices. The profit-maximizing *price level*—the price paid by men plus the price paid by women in the dating service example, for instance—depends on the costs of serving both groups, on the sensitivities of both demands to price, and on the indirect network effects between the two customer groups. The price sensitivities depend in the usual way on the price and quality of available substitutes and other factors, including, in some models, the presence of two-sided competitors.

The profit-maximizing *price structure*—the ratio of the price paid by men to the price paid by women, for instance—also depends in general on costs, price sensitivities, and the way participation by the members of each group affects the demand of the other group.[17] In addition, all general models of two-sided platform markets imply that profits may be maximized by highly asymmetric

---

[15] Contributions that look beyond payment systems include Armstrong (2005), Armstrong and Wright (2004), Bolt and Tieman (2004a and 2004b), Caillaud and Jullien (2003), Gabszewicz and Wauthy (2004), Hagiu (2004a and 2004b), Jullien (2004), Rochet and Tirole (2004a and 2004b), and Schiff (2003). Evans (2003a) and (2003b) and Wright (2004b) provide accessible discussions of the implications of some of this work as well as empirical support; Rochet and Tirole (2004b) provide a more technical overview.

[16] As we note below, the payment card industry has followed this pricing structure since its birth, as a two-sided platform, in 1950.

[17] In the Rochet-Tirole model, which is based on particular assumptions about the structure of demand, the price structure is completely independent of the relative costs of serving the two groups (there are no fixed costs on either side in their formulation). See Rochet and Tirole (2003b, pp. 996-997).

pricing in which one group is served at a price close to or even below marginal cost, and most or all gross margin is earned by serving the other group.[18]

It is important to note that many, if not most two-sided markets exhibit this sort of asymmetry in pricing and gross margin generation.[19] Shopping malls, for instance, often provide free parking to consumers, sometimes in expensive parking structures, and make all their money by charging rent to merchants. Yellow Pages and competing telephone directories of merchants in the United States are given away to consumers; all the revenue is provided by merchants.[20] Similarly, Microsoft and Apple do not charge applications software developers anything for the highly valuable software services (sometime called APIs) included in their software platforms. Both these firms make almost all of their money from end-users of computer systems. (In Microsoft's case, Windows is usually licensed to computer makers that in turn license it to end-users.) On the other hand, makers of video game consoles sell them to end users at or below cost and make most or all of their gross margin from license fees paid by game developers.[21]

B. Unitary Payment Systems

The general literature on multi-sided markets has immediate application to the analysis of unitary payment systems—for instance the BankAmericard system before franchising, the American Express system today (ignoring recent franchise-like bank deals), or the store-specific cards offered by such merchants as Neiman-Marcus. Neglecting for the moment the distinction between access and variable prices, the price structure here can be described by the ratio of fees paid by merchants, typically in the form of the merchant discount, to transaction-related fees paid by consumers, in the form of annual and other fees.[22] Using this measure, the available evidence indicates that unitary systems have generally adopted asymmetric pricing structures and earned the bulk of their revenue from merchants, rather than consumers.

---

[18] We define gross margin here and below as revenues minus direct, side-specific variable costs, such as the manufacturing costs of video game consoles. Attributing profits to one side or another is strictly incorrect, since both sides must be on board for profits to be earned, and many costs in platform businesses, like the cost of developing the Windows operating system, are properly thought of as joint between the two sides.

[19] Bolt and Tieman (2003) offer an explanation based on the fact that some demand functions that are well-behaved in an ordinary one-sided context yield non-concave profit functions in some two-sided models, thus making corner solutions (for example, prices of zero) optimal.

[20] In the payment card context, Vickers (2005) has argued that one might find "a distortion of competition" when one side of the market is charged "more than all the costs" of providing services to both sides. There is no theoretical basis for this test of which we are aware, and this sort of pricing is not uncommon. It occurs whenever, as in the two examples in the text, one side of a profitable two-sided business pays nothing, so the other side must be charged "more than all the costs" if the enterprise is to be profitable.

[21] See Evans and others (2004).

[22] By "transaction-related," we mean that we are here following almost the entire literature and focusing on the payment function of credit, charge, and debit cards, putting to one side the credit function that only credit cards perform and the associated revenue flow from consumers.

Before 1950, payment cards were issued by retailers for use in their stores. Then, as now, cardholders who paid their bills within a specified amount of time (usually a bit less than a month) did not pay any fee for charging and in fact benefited from the float. Those who financed their store card charges paid interest, of course. But to our knowledge, then as now, retailers did not cancel cards held by customers who chronically did not finance. Although we would not want to push this point too far, given that store cards are one-sided and are bundled with finance services, store card transaction services have what might be thought of as a slight negative variable price and a zero access price.[23] Merchants with retail cards presumably find that this is the optimal pricing scheme.

Diners Club introduced the first two-sided payment platform—that is, a general purpose payment card that could be used by cardholders at many retailers—in 1950. After initially offering the cards for no fee to consumers, Diners Club settled on a business model in which cardholders paid an annual fee of $3 (over $18 in 2004 dollars) and a slightly negative transaction fee in the form of float, while merchants paid a variable fee of seven percent of each transaction. During the 1950s and into the early 1960s, based on available data, Diners Club earned about 70 percent of its revenues—and probably most of its gross margin—from the merchant side of the business.[24]

American Express entered the card business in 1958. It adopted a similar business model, though it eventually settled on slightly lower merchant fees and slightly higher cardholder fees than Diners Club. But available data indicate that for the last four plus decades, American Express has earned upwards of 65 percent of its transaction-related revenues from merchant fees (in later years, some American Express cards began to bundle borrowing with transaction services, which makes clean comparisons more difficult).[25] Bank of America also entered in 1958, with a card that did not charge consumers a fee, although there were finance charges (and associated costs of funds and default risk) from consumers who chose to revolve. Their merchant fee was 5 percent of each transaction.[26]

Even though transactions-related costs on the acquiring side of the business seem to be lower than those on the issuing side,[27] these unitary systems apparently concluded that the profit-

---

[23] Store cards may increase purchases by relaxing short-run liquidity constraints. As we note below, this argument has been advanced as a motivation for retailer acceptance of general purpose payment cards (particularly credit cards) by Chakravorti and To (2003). See also Chakravorti and Emmons (2003) and Wright (2000). However, again note that we would expect that retailers would take efforts to weed out transactors if that were the entire motivation.

[24] Evans and Schmalensee (2005, pp. 54-55). Annual fee converted to real 2004 dollars using the GDP implicit price deflator from United States Department of Commerce (2004).

[25] Evans and Schmalensee (2005, pp. 57-59, 150). In 2004, about 84 percent of American Express's card transaction-related revenues came from merchants, excluding finance revenues from cardholders. The proportion is about 63 percent when net finance revenues are included and using American Express's card revenues on a "managed" basis (which includes revenues for card loans that have been securitized); this same measure is 71 percent on a GAAP basis (which excludes finance charges on securitized card loans). Figures calculated using data from American Express (2005, pp. 45-49).

[26] Wolters (2000, p. 331).

[27] The portion of the merchant discount retained by acquirers on MasterCard and Visa transactions in the United States averages about 0.4 percent, which goes to cover acquirers' costs. This compares to an average interchange fee of about 1.7 percent, which, in combination with additional cardholder fees, goes to cover issuers' costs. Evans and Schmalensee (2005, pp. 11, 262).

maximizing price structure for the system—the price structure that gets and keeps both sets of customers on board and permits both issuers and acquirers to be profitable—is one that obtains the bulk of the revenue from the merchant side of the business.

These unitary systems instituted these pricing schemes in their early years, when they would appear to have had little market power. We think it is fair to conclude that the "competitive"—certainly in the sense of non-collusive and non-monopolistic—pricing structure for payment cards is (or at least was for some time) one in which merchants pay a relatively high transaction price and cardholders pay zero or possibly slightly negative transaction prices plus modest fixed fees, and in which the bulk of the profits, loosely speaking, thus flow from the merchant side. Being the competitive pricing structure does not necessarily mean that it is socially optimal, however, and it is to that issue we turn next.

C. Profit versus Welfare

How do prices charged in two-sided markets compare with socially optimal prices? Most theoretical analysis of this question considers a single firm with some market power (in other words, it faces demand curves that slope down—though they may be highly price-elastic) selling to two customer groups in an otherwise perfectly competitive economy. Under these assumptions it is clear that the price level will be too high because of the exercise of market power—a conclusion that, of course, applies to most firms in real economies.

In fact, the monopoly pricing problem is even more serious than usual: Even if marginal costs are constant and there are no fixed costs, the first-best social optimum requires setting prices that do not cover total cost, just as is the case with natural monopoly.[28] The intuition is straightforward. In an ordinary, one-sided market under the usual assumptions, buyers' willingness to pay for incremental units of output provides a measure of the social value of that output. Thus the social optimum in such markets occurs at the output level at which price is equal to marginal cost, since at lower levels of output buyers are willing to pay more than marginal cost for incremental output, while at higher levels of output they are willing to pay less than marginal cost. In a two-sided market, however, increases in output on side A of the market provide positive benefits to buyers on side B that are not reflected in the side A demand curve. Thus, if price equals marginal cost to customer group A, it is nonetheless socially beneficial to increase output to A because of the (externality) benefits that would thereby be conferred on members of group B.

What about price structure? In general single-firm models of two-sided markets in otherwise perfectly competitive economies, one can compare the conditions defining profit-maximizing

---

[28] This is explicitly shown in Armstrong (2004) and Bolt and Tieman (2004b). It is implicit in Rochet and Tirole (2003b), since their analysis of socially optimal pricing imposes the binding constraint that the firm just break even.

pricing, welfare-maximizing pricing (which involves the seller losing money and, presumably, being subsidized by the government), and Ramsey pricing (which involves maximizing social welfare subject to the constraint that the firm does not lose money). Comparing these conditions in various models yields two general observations that appear to be robust to modeling assumptions. First, neither welfare-maximizing pricing nor Ramsey pricing is ever purely cost-based. In both cases, the optimal price structure also depends on price sensitivities and externalities on both sides of the market.[29] Second, there is no simple, general description of the relations among the profit-maximizing and Ramey price structures. They are rarely identical, but the sign and magnitude of the difference between them depends on essentially all the demand, cost, and externality parameters in the model.

III. INTERCHANGE FEES IN MULTI-PARTY SYSTEMS

Multi-party systems emerged in the mid 1960s.[30] One was the BankAmericard franchise system that we mentioned earlier. Others were cooperatives of banks that agreed to collaborate on a card brand and, in effect, pool the merchants they had signed up so that any individual with a card from a member of the cooperative could use their card at any merchant also signed up by any member of the cooperative. The predecessor of MasterCard emerged during this period as a national cooperative of banks. BankAmericard adopted a cooperative structure a few years later.

These banks initially had a purely practical problem to solve. When a cardholder serviced by bank A presented her card to a merchant serviced by bank B, the two banks had to have agreement on many issues in order to execute the transaction, even if that meant following custom or a default rule. One set of issues concerned which party bore various risks—of nonpayment by the cardholder; non-delivery of goods by the merchant; bankruptcy of the merchant or, for that matter, of the merchant's bank. Another issue was how much the issuer and acquirer were compensated for executing a transaction that could not take place without participation by both of them.

As noted above, when Bank of America began franchising, its first response to this problem was a rule stipulating that whenever acquiring bank A and issuing bank B were different, A was to send the full amount of its merchant discount to B (and, of course, B was to reciprocate when one of its merchants dealt with one of A's cardholders). Presumably, the idea was that if all banks adopted similar price structures, then to a first approximation, typical bank A's merchant/consumer revenue mix would not depend on whether its cardholders dealt with its

---

[29] In fact, in the Rochet-Tirole model, which assumes a particular demand structure, the Ramsey price structure, like the profit-maximizing price structure, is completely independent of group-specific marginal costs. See Rochet and Tirole (2003b, pp. 997-998).

[30] This discussion in this section is based on Evans and Schmalensee (2005, pp. 153-156).

merchants or with those acquired by other banks. If this had worked, the system could have maintained a merchant-centered (or any other) price structure. But, as we observed above, this device failed—both because it reduced everyone's incentives to sign up merchants and because it invited deception.

In the early cooperatives, some banks entered into bilateral agreements with each other; this was possible when the systems had few members. But ultimately the cooperatives decided to develop a default set of rules, or contracts, that defined the allocation of risks and payments. In NBI—the cooperative that evolved from the BankAmericard franchise system and was the predecessor of Visa—as long as an acquirer's merchant met certain terms, such as properly authorizing transactions and checking card numbers against a list of known fraudulent accounts, it was guaranteed payment. If a transaction turned out to be fraudulent or a consumer failed to pay, the issuer was responsible. Various procedures also were set up to resolve disputes between merchants and cardholders as to the validity of particular charges. MasterCharge—MasterCard's predecessor—developed a similar contract with a similar interchange fee.

Both contracts were presumably the result of a bargain struck within the cooperative organizations between members with different stakes in acquiring and issuing (although back then there was less specialization on this dimension than there later came to be). Given the payment card industry at the time, the price structure that resulted from these interchange fees was similar to that of the unitary systems, although the price levels were lower. Since the interchange fee was a cost to the acquirer, it was passed on to merchants as part of merchant discounts. The resulting merchant discounts were lower, however, than those charged by American Express at the time. The issuers then chose to issue cards with modest access fees and slightly negative transaction fees for cardholders.[31] Unlike the charge-card systems, of course, the credit cards came bundled with longer-term financing. For transactions, the resulting percentages of revenue that the multi-party systems earned from the merchant side were similar to those of American Express and Diners Club, if not higher.

A. Alternatives to Interchange

What might the early multi-lateral card systems have done instead? Some have argued that for competition policy reasons, bilateral negotiations should have been used to set the terms of two-bank transactions rather than collective action.[32] This argument seems farfetched for the early cooperatives. They had no collective market power by any measure, and it seems more plausible that the interchange fee was, as advertised, devised to reduce the transactions costs of entering into bilateral negotiations. Moreover, as we noted above, the *NaBanco* court found that bilateral negotiations were not a practical solution in systems with many banks, both because of transactions

---

[31] At least through most of the 1970s, annual fees for Visa and MasterCard cards were relatively uncommon. National Bancard Corporation v. Visa U.S.A., Inc., (1984, p. 27).

[32] E.g., this was one of the remedies proposed by NaBanco. National Bancard Corporation v. Visa U.S.A., Inc. (1984, p. 1241).

costs and because the honor-all-cards rule gave issuers substantial leverage over acquirers.[33] As long as an honor-all-cards rule is in effect, so that merchants are required to accept all cards of a given brand, an acquirer is at a significant disadvantage in negotiations with other issuing banks, since its merchant is required to accept their cards, but it has no guarantee of payment by the card issuer. A guarantee of payment is possible only when the terms of payment, including the interchange fee, if any, are specified. Because of this asymmetry, there is no reason to believe that bilateral negotiation would generally lead to lower average interchange fees or merchant discounts than multilateral action at the association level.

Others have argued that the interchange fee should simply have been set at zero by competition authorities or some agency. Credit card paper would then exchange "at par," like checks in the United States.[34] One can raise several questions about this proposal. First, a zero interchange fee would result in lower prices for merchants (since acquirers would not have the interchange fee cost) and higher prices for cardholders (since issuers would not have this source of revenue). Although this might seem "fair" in a philosophical sense, there is no basis in the economics of two-sided industries for presuming that this pricing structure is more—or less—efficient that one that, similar to the structures adopted by the unitary systems, imposes higher prices on merchants. That is, without further information, there is nothing economically special about an interchange fee of "0"; there is no economic basis for concluding that an interchange fee of "0" is better or worse for society than any randomly chosen positive or negative percentage.[35]

Second, setting the interchange fee at zero imposes a particular price structure on the system, one in which side-specific prices are tightly linked to side-specific costs. For example, had the predecessors of MasterCard and Visa had a zero interchange fee in the early 1970s, they would have had to raise card fees by $4.88 per account (or about $18 in 2004 dollars) to compensate for the loss of interchange fee revenues.[36] Imposing less pricing flexibility on the emerging cooperative card systems in the early 1970s would have necessarily placed them at a competitive disadvantage

---

[33] A recent analysis (Small and Wright 2000) concludes that, at least under certain somewhat special assumptions, even if transactions costs were low enough to make bilateral negotiations practical in large systems, banks' strategic behavior would undermine the system's viability. It is worth noting, though, that the terms of two-bank transactions in the Australian EFTPOS system (a PIN-based debit card system) are set exclusively by bilateral negotiation; see Reserve Bank of Australia (2004). There are only 11 acquirers and 150 issuers in the EFTPOS system; these numbers, while nontrivial, are orders of magnitude lower than the thousands of issuers and (at least) hundreds of acquirers in, e.g., the Visa system in the United States. See Reserve Bank of Australia (2005a, pp. 4, 40-45). Wright and Weiner (2005) report that interchange fees are also set by bilateral negotiation in Sweden. Banking concentration is quite high in Sweden, with the top four banks accounting for over 80 percent of total assets in 2003. See Swedish Bankers' Association (2004). By contrast, the top four banks in the United States accounted for only a 24 percent share in 2002. See United States Census Bureau (2004).

[34] See, e.g., Frankel (1998) and Balto (2000) and, for a rebuttal, Ahlborn et al. (2001).

[35] Interchange payments in the Australian EFTPOS system flow from issuers to acquirers; see Reserve Bank of Australia (2004). Negative interchange fees of this sort existed in some online debit card systems in the United States until 1997 and remain the norm in U.S. ATM systems; see Hayashi et al. (2003).

[36] Calculated from data provided by Visa U.S.A. Card fee converted to real 2004 dollars using the GDP implicit price deflator from United States Department of Commerce (2004).

relative to the more established unitary systems, which could choose their price structures without constraints. This distortion in competition between unitary and multi-party systems would need to be weighed against whatever benefits policymakers believe would arise from mandating exchange at par.

One also has to consider what other changes might result from a zero interchange fee. It is possible that a multi-party system is not even viable with the pricing structure that would result from a zero interchange fee.[37] In their early days, the viability of these systems was very much an open question. Even today, large numbers of issuers might move to other card systems (possibly new ones) that are organized so as to be able to replace interchange revenue without regulatory or antitrust scrutiny. (Consider, for instance, franchise arrangements with for-profit unitary systems in which merchant discounts and payments to issuers are set unilaterally by the system.) It is not clear that the pricing structure from such systems would be more favorable to merchants. Another possible effect of a zero interchange fee would be to change the other terms of the contract among member banks. For example, rules governing disputes among issuers and acquirers might be made more favorable toward issuers in order to avoid issuer defections. Or the circumstances under which payment is guaranteed to acquirers might become more limited.

B. The Baxter Analysis

William Baxter addressed the issue of system viability in his pioneering analysis of interchange fees.[38] His was also the first paper of which we are aware that showed an understanding of the two-sided nature of payment systems—or, indeed, of any market. As we will see, although his model is special and unrealistic in some respects, it provides important insights.

Baxter assumed perfect competition among issuers, among acquirers, and everywhere else in the economy, and, as in almost all the subsequent literature, he assumed away all fixed costs and access prices. Under these conditions, collective determination of the interchange fee cannot be an exercise of market power, since there is no market power anywhere in the economy. It is simply a payment from one set of perfectly competitive firms, which will have to raise their (variable) prices to cover it, to another set of perfectly competitive firms, which will lower their (variable) prices so as to compete it away completely. The interchange fee thus can only affect the price structure, not the price level. Baxter assumed that consumers and merchants would use a particular payment card if and only if the per-transaction price charged to them was less than the per-transaction benefit from using the card rather than cash or check.

To see the role of the interchange fee in ensuring system viability in this setup, suppose for simplicity that all consumers have the same per-transaction benefits and that so do all merchants. Let the per-transaction prices charged by the card system to consumers and merchants be Pc and

---

[37] We illustrate this point in a simple model immediately below.
[38] Baxter (1983).

Pm, respectively; let the corresponding per-transaction benefits relative to cash or check be Bc and Bm; and suppose the constant per-transaction marginal cost of serving a consumer is Cc and of serving a merchant is Cm. Under these assumptions, it is efficient to use the card for all transactions if and only if

$$(Bc + Bm) \geq (Cc + Cm). \qquad (1)$$

With a zero interchange fee and perfect competition, consumers will agree to use the card and issuers will break even if

$$Bc \geq Pc = Cc, \qquad (2)$$

And merchants will agree to accept the card and acquirers will break even if

$$Bm \geq Pm = Cm. \qquad (3)$$

For a zero-interchange system to be viable, both (2) and (3) must be satisfied. It is easy to find numerical examples in which (1) is satisfied, but either (2) or (3) is not. Suppose, for instance:[39]

$$Bc = 1, Bm = 8, Cc = 3, \text{ and } Cm = 2. \qquad (4)$$

Here, total per-transaction benefits from using the card are almost double the corresponding cost, but there is no price to consumers that satisfies (2). In this example, retailers receive the most benefits if the card is used, and it would be logical for them to cover most of the system's costs. But there is no way to accomplish this with a zero interchange fee. An interchange fee of 2 solves the problem. This raises the acquirer's cost and (because of perfect competition among acquirers) the merchant discount, Pm, to 4, and it lowers the issuer's cost and (because of perfect competition among issuers) the consumers' fee to 1. Merchants contribute 80 percent of the system's revenue but are better off by 4 per transaction, while consumers are just indifferent to the card's existence even though the positive interchange fee has reduced their fees substantially.

By assumption, the costs incurred by both sides are necessary to execute a transaction. If this assumption is correct, it makes no sense to think of either side as providing particular services to the other; both must incur all the costs stated for either to benefit. Moreover, there is no way for regulators to look only at cost conditions and conclude that an interchange fee of 2 is appropriate. Even in this simplest possible example, demand conditions must be considered. It could happen, of course, that some cost-based formula produced an interchange fee of 2. But this could only happen by chance.

In Baxter's model, the interchange fee is not set to maximize profits, since there are no profits earned anywhere in the payment system. He argued that its level was determined uniquely by the

---

[39] This example is from Rochet (2003), where this model is instructively explored in more detail.

need to balance the supply and demand of card transactions. This seems somewhat artificial, since as long as some merchants have agreed to accept a card, the volume of transactions is determined unilaterally by card-carrying consumers' deciding whether or not to use the card for particular transactions. Nonetheless, the proposition that at some interchange fee levels the system would not be viable is likely to hold in more general models. The important—and robust—insight from Baxter's analysis, although it is not framed precisely this way, is that the interchange fee helps internalize an externality between the two customer groups and, in so doing, has the potential of making both customer groups better off.

C. Imperfect Competition in Issuing and Acquiring

The assumption of perfect competition between homogeneous issuers and acquirers is not realistic and leads to most interesting questions having indeterminate answers—since there are no profits to be had, there is no motivation for doing anything. The next logical step was taken by Richard Schmalensee.[40] He made the standard assumption that, except for the payment system under study, the economy was perfectly competitive.[41] This implies that the demand system facing the system, which Schmalensee took as given and did not derive from first principles, could be used for standard welfare analysis. Schmalensee allowed for imperfect competition among issuers and/or among acquirers and made a particular assumption about the functional form of the demand system and, thus, about the structure of indirect network effects. As in the Baxter analysis, the system itself was assumed to operate like the Visa and MasterCard systems operate in fact, on a break-even basis, and fixed costs and access prices were again assumed away. Thus, as in the numerical example above, the interchange fee simply shifts costs between issuers and acquirers, raising costs on one side of the market by exactly as much as it lowers costs on the other side.

In this model, the level of the interchange fee can affect the profits earned by issuing and acquiring banks whenever competition among them is imperfect, making it possible to compare profit-maximizing and welfare-maximizing fees. Under some special assumptions, the comparison is simple: when there is a single issuer and a single acquirer and demand curves are linear, for instance, Schmalensee shows that the profit-maximizing interchange fee also maximizes system output and economic welfare. In this case, regulation could only reduce overall performance. In general, however, these three fees may be different even under the particular demand structure Schmalensee assumed, and even when the further assumption of linear demand is imposed. Thus, even under strong assumptions about demands and costs, the relations among

---

[40] Schmalensee (2002).
[41] Much of the subsequent literature has persuasively called that standard assumption into question in this context, as we discuss in the next section. Nonetheless, it is instructive to see its implications before considering how it might be altered in the direction of greater realism.

these quantities is complex and depends on demand parameters, cost conditions, and (an element not present in analysis of unitary two-sided platforms) the nature of competition among issuers and among acquirers.

In the Schmalensee model, the interchange fee is not an ordinary market price – it is a balancing device for shifting costs between issuers and acquirers and, thus, shifting charges between consumers and merchants.[42] Fixing the interchange fee is quite unlike fixing a price in a typical one-sided market. The first-order effect of ordinary price-fixing is to harm consumers by restricting output. The first-order effect of collective determination of interchange fees in this model is generally to enhance the value of the system by balancing participation of the two customer groups, thus internalizing indirect externalities. This is illustrated most clearly by the existence of a special case, noted above, in which collective determination of the interchange fee in order to maximize profit also maximizes output and economic welfare. And even in Schmalensee's simple model, the socially optimal interchange fee depends on costs, demand conditions, competition among issuers and among acquirers, and externalities between merchants and consumers. Thus as a practical matter, there is no rule for regulatory determination of the interchange fee that could be relied on to improve overall system performance and thus enhance economic efficiency.

IV. SECOND-BEST INTERCHANGE FEE ANALYSIS

Except for Schmalensee, most writers on interchange assume some market distortion in addition to imperfect competition among issuers and/or acquirers. In these models, social welfare analysis cannot generally be based on the demand system facing issuers and acquirers, and that demand system is derived from more fundamental assumptions rather than assumed as in the Schmalensee paper. These authors then generally examine how the additional distortion they consider affects the relation between the profit-maximizing and welfare-maximizing interchange fees. Almost all assume away fixed costs and access pricing and assume that all revenues flow from variable prices. When used to consider regulatory policy, these models become exercises in the economics of the second best.[43] That is, they consider policy in the presence of multiple, interacting departures from the competitive ideal. In general, such exercises rarely yield tractable rules that can be used to design practical policies. The interchange literature, which points to many additional distortions but typically considers them one at a time, provides no exceptions.[44]

---

[42] In addition, the interchange fee can be used to shift profits between issuers and acquirers, though when it is used for that purpose total system profit is necessarily reduced.

[43] Lipsey and Lancaster (1956).

[44] For surveys of some of the literature discussed here, see Chakravorti 2003, Hunt 2003, Rochet 2003, Rochet and Tirole (2003a), and Schmalensee (2003).

A. Imperfect Competition Among Merchants

In a very influential paper that was the first analysis of interchange to derive system demand functions from first principles, Jean-Charles Rochet and Jean Tirole allowed for imperfect competition among merchants.[45] They assumed perfect competition among acquirers and, for simplicity, identical merchants. They also assumed that some fraction of consumers was more likely to patronize merchants who accepted cards, so that merchants had a strategic incentive to accept cards in order to avoid losing the economic profits they would earn from selling to those consumers. Thus, in contrast to Baxter's model, because of this strategic, rent-seeking incentive, merchants would find it optimal to accept cards even if transactions using them were somewhat more expensive than transactions using cash.

Since all profits in this model system are earned by issuers, the profit-maximizing interchange fee is the highest fee consistent with all merchants accepting the card. This may be equal to the socially optimal fee, but it may be higher because competition forces merchants to internalize part of the benefits of cardholders. In the former case, card usage is welfare-maximizing, but in the latter case it is excessive, since an interchange fee that is too high drives consumer variable fees too low and thus stimulates excessive card usage by consumers.[46] No cost-based or other simple rule for regulating the interchange fee reliably solves this problem, however, even in this bare-bones model.

The result that a profit-maximizing system never sets an interchange fee below the welfare-maximizing level in the Rochet-Tirole model, which seems to underpin some current regulatory initiatives, depends critically on the very strong assumption that merchants are identical. Julian Wright shows that if this assumption is relaxed and even if consumers know which merchants accept cards (so merchants' rent-seeking incentive to take cards is maximized), the profit-maximizing interchange fee may be above or below the welfare-maximizing level, and there may thus be too many card transactions or too few.[47] The relation between profit-maximizing and welfare-maximizing fee levels in this more general model is complex and depends on details of demand and competitive conditions as well as costs.

B. Reducing the Transactions Costs of Borrowing

Credit cards bundle the provision of credit with transaction processing. In so doing, they reduce the transactions costs of borrowing on the part of cardholders, so that cardholders can buy on credit more easily. Through the development of sophisticated risk scoring methods, credit cards may also

---

[45] In an influential review of the literature undertaken for the Reserve Bank of Australia, Katz 2001 stressed the effects of such competition. See also Wright (2003c) and Hayashi (2004).
[46] It is worth noting that De Grauwe and Rinaldi (2002) have developed a model involving rent-seeking by merchants in which the level of card usage is below the welfare-maximizing level. They treat merchants' decisions to accept or not accept cards as exogenous, however.
[47] (Wright 2004a).

have relaxed the overall liquidity constraints that many consumers face. In addition, charge cards provide short-term liquidity, albeit only for a couple of weeks on average, and debit and charge cards reduce the transaction costs of obtaining funds from alternative sources. If a merchant's decision to accept cards induces consumers sometimes to spend more than they otherwise would because of these reductions in consumers' transactions costs, merchants have another incentive to accept payment cards, over and above their own transaction cost savings and the rent-seeking incentive discussed above.[48] There is also at least anecdotal evidence that these are benefits that merchants receive at lower cost from general purpose payment cards than they could have provided themselves through store card programs. Many smaller retailers dropped store cards as credit cards became more widely held, and few retailers steer customers to their own store cards anymore.

It is hard to evaluate the welfare implications of providing increased liquidity. Relaxing liquidity constraints and reducing transaction costs clearly benefit consumers. The more merchants that accept cards, the larger these benefits. A rigorous analysis also would need to consider the sources of both liquidity constraints and transaction costs, however, and we are not aware of any empirical or theoretical analysis that even attempts to do this.

C. Competition Among Payment Systems

In the United States, payment card systems compete against cash and checks as well as each other. The production of cash is a government activity, subsidized through the Federal budget. And cash users do not fully internalize some of the social costs of using it, such as crime against merchants. The check system in the US is run by the Federal Reserve, which essentially forced banks early in the last century to exchange checks at par—that is, to have a zero interchange fee in the checking system.[49] The price structure in this competing system is thus not fully market-determined. Similarly, outside the United States, governments have commonly influenced the evolution of Giro (a payment system in which a bank or a post office transfers money from one account to another when it receives authorization to do so) and related transactional systems.

There is no rigorous analysis of which we are aware of the effects of government-determined pricing in these competing systems on pricing in payment card systems. It is worth noting, for instance, that a large fraction of consumers in the United States and Western Europe pay no variable fees for writing checks, primarily as a result of the decision by banks to bundle this service (and ATM/debit cards) with the general banking relationship. This might explain why credit and charge card systems have generally not imposed transaction-specific variable fees on consumers. Similarly, there has been no analysis of which we are aware that considers the impact of this sort of competition on the relationship between profit-maximizing and welfare-optimizing interchange fee levels.

---

[48] Chakravorti and To (2003). See also Chakravorti and Emmons (2003) and Wright (2000).
[49] Chang and Evans (2000); for an alternative view, see Frankel (1998).

The existing literature does contain a number of (generally complex) analyses of competition between payment systems or between two-sided platforms in general.[50] It is fair to say that this work is at an early stage. It seems clear that the nature of consumer and merchant behavior shapes the competitive price structure, and that there is no general tendency for competition between platforms to make the price structure closer or farther from the social optimum, though competition will generally tend to lower the price level. Suppose, for instance, that consumers all have multiple cards (this is termed "multi-homing" in the literature) and are indifferent among them, and that merchants can effectively persuade consumers which card to use. In this case, competing systems will have an extra incentive to compete for merchants' favor, and this will cause a tilt in the price structure against consumers that may or may not improve performance. Similarly, if consumers tend to use only one card (to "single-home") while merchants find it easy to accept all cards, competing systems will have an extra incentive to attract consumers, and the price structure will be tilted in their favor accordingly. These aspects of consumer and retailer behavior have received little empirical study, however.[51]

D. Barriers to Surcharging

In the United States and, at least until recently, elsewhere, payment card systems generally seem to have required merchants that accept their cards to agree not to impose a surcharge on consumers who use those cards. At first blush, this no-surcharge rule (NSR) would appear to be an artificial distortion likely to reduce performance. Dennis Carlton and Alan Frankel were the first to observe that, in a fully competitive system (*a la* Baxter), if there is no NSR, and if it costs merchants nothing to charge different prices to consumers depending on what payment system they use, the interchange fee will be irrelevant and card usage will be efficient.[52] If acquirers are perfectly competitive, an increase in the interchange fee is passed along dollar for dollar to the merchant discount, and perfect competition among merchants means that the merchant discount is passed along dollar for dollar to card-using consumers (and not at all to those who pay with cash). On the other side of the market, competition among issuers means that the increase in interchange is passed to card-users, dollar for dollar, in reduced fees. Thus, card-using consumers pay the full cost of the system regardless of the interchange fee, and, if they also bear the full costs of all other payment systems, they will use payment cards if and only if they are socially less costly. Accordingly, Carlton and Frankel advocate abolishing NSRs.

---

[50] See Armstrong (2004 and 2005), Armstrong and Wright (2004), Chakravorti and Rosson (2004), Gabszewicz and Wauthy (2004), Guthrie and Wright (2003), Manenti and Somma (2003), Rochet and Tirole (2002) and (2003b),

[51] Rysman (2004) finds that most U.S. consumers carry multiple cards but tend to concentrate their purchases on only one, suggesting a weak form of single-homing. It is unclear what combination of preferences, costs, and merchant behavior this finding reflects, however, or how much a typical consumer prefers her primary card over others she carries.

[52] Carlton and Frankel (1995a and 1995b); see also Evans and Schmalensee (1995).

It turns out that the Carlton-Frankel assumptions are stronger than necessary for the interchange fee to be irrelevant in the absence of an NSR. What is required is only costless surcharging—i.e., the ability of merchants at no cost to charge different prices depending on the means of payment used.[53] But without perfect competition everywhere, abolishing an NSR generally does not lead to an efficient outcome. In particular, imperfect competition among issuers then tends to lead to under-provision of card services, and merchants could use surcharges as a mechanism for price discrimination. Economic welfare may be lower than at the profit-maximizing equilibrium with an NSR—even if card usage is excessive in the latter case. In the murky realm of the second-best, this sort of ambiguity is not uncommon.

Moreover, it is clear that the assumption of costless surcharging is unrealistically strong; most merchants do not discriminate among people using different means of payment even when they are not prevented from doing so. For instance, it has generally been permissible for U.S. merchants to give a discount for cash purchases, and, though this was done for a time at gasoline stations, it is now extremely rare.[54] In the Netherlands, about 10 percent of merchants imposed surcharges when they were allowed.[55] In the United Kingdom, surcharges are permitted for credit and charge cards but surcharging is uncommon.[56] And when NSRs were abolished in Sweden, only about 5 percent of merchants imposed surcharges.[57] Although we are not aware of any concrete data yet from the elimination of NSRs in Australia,[58] our understanding from colleagues there is that the prevalence of surcharging, at least to date, is likely in line with these other experiences. The one instance we are aware of with a somewhat higher incidence of surcharging, although still far from pervasive, was in Denmark, where earlier this year, 19 percent of merchants (primarily grocery retailers) passed a new 0.55 Kroner debit card surcharge through to consumers.[59]

We suspect merchants are reluctant to impose surcharges for two reasons. The first is that there are transaction costs of imposing different prices based on payment methods. The second is that consumers may prefer to patronize stores that do not surcharge. No analysis of which we are aware has considered or attempted to measure these costs and preferences. There is nothing unusual here, of course: there are many things that merchants could surcharge for—because they entail specific costs that are caused by particular customers—and do not.[60] Parking in shopping malls is an obvious example.

---

[53] See Rochet and Tirole (2002), Wright (2003a), and, especially, Gans and King (2003b). Schwartz and Vincent 2004 provide a related analysis for a unitary system.
[54] Chakravorti (2003, p. 55).
[55] ITM Research (2000).
[56] Office of Fair Trading (2003b, pp. 114-115).
[57] IMA Market Development AB (2000, p. 18); but see Katz (2001, p. 44).
[58] For example, the Reserve Bank of Australia notes that "some merchants" have started surcharging but that "there are no comprehensive data." Reserve Bank of Australia (2004, p. 11).
[59] The Danish competition authority had announced that it was going to investigate whether there had been any collective action by grocery stores. Konkurrencestyrelsen (2005).
[60] See, for example, Evans and Schmalensee (2005, p. 131).

E. Implications

The quantity of recent theoretical literature discussed in this section makes it clear that economists find interchange fees fascinating. Almost all of these papers find that profit-maximizing interchange fees are unlikely to be socially optimal, but none yields workable rules for welfare-improving regulatory intervention. (In particular, none points to the optimality of any rule that is purely cost-based.) Moreover, these models are highly stylized. A variety of market imperfections are considered one at a time; not only are some visible imperfections not considered at all (for example, government-determined zero interchange in U.S. checking), no analyst has even attempted to consider them all together. Most papers assume consumers are faced with variable (i.e., transaction-specific) charges, even though most systems do not impose such charges and rely instead on annual fees and other access charges. Finally, there has been essentially no empirical work devoted to testing any of these models or to measuring the importance of any of the effects they predict. This literature, in short, is not very useful for either rationalizing or designing a system of interchange fee regulation. Of course, for exactly the same reasons, it is not capable of proving that the interchange fees determined by the card associations are exactly or approximately socially optimal.

It is useful to compare the results for interchange fees for payment cards with some other business practices that economists have analyzed. In many ways, the theoretical results surveyed here are similar to those for advertising, research and development, product design, product variety, location decisions, firm entry in the presence of fixed costs, bundling, and price discrimination.[61] In all these cases, economic models show that the profit-maximizing result under imperfect competition may deviate from the social welfare-maximizing result. However, in most cases, the bias can go in either direction, and in all cases, determining the socially optimal result depends on complex factors that cannot be measured in practice. Based on our review of the theoretical literature on interchange fees to date, there does not seem to be any basis for concluding that the potential distortions caused by collective determination of interchange fees are any more—or any less—significant than the potential distortions caused by these other deviations from the ideal model of perfect competition.

V. GOVERNMENT DETERMINATION OF INTERCHANGE FEES

Traditionally, government control of prices and conditions of service—either via government ownership or economic regulation—has been most prevalent in network public utility sectors, such as water, electricity, telephone, and gas. Firms in these sectors were traditionally local monopolists. The stated purpose of regulation or government ownership in these sectors was to protect consumers from prices that would otherwise reflect the exercise of monopoly power and

---
[61] See, generally, Tirole (1988).

thus, as every student of basic economics should be able to explain, would be too high. As all of those students also should know, efficient prices in these sectors are based on marginal costs, with socially optimal markups above marginal cost depending on demand conditions. However, the global movement toward privatization, deregulation, and incentive regulation reflected an emerging consensus that even in these near-textbook cases, economic welfare was in practice not reliably improved by government ownership or price regulation.[62] Politics inevitably intrudes into government price-setting, for instance, and limitations on profit rates tend to lead to waste and inefficiency.

Experience with government control of prices has taught analysts that a persuasive economic case for price regulation requires a positive answer to two questions:

1. Is the performance of the market or markets being considered substantially sub-optimal?
2. Is there a practical regulatory policy that is reasonably certain to improve market performance substantially?

Since regulation is a blunt policy instrument in practice, unless there is a substantial market failure, there is scant chance that regulation will reliably improve matters. And unless there is a known, practical regulatory rule that, if followed, is reasonably certain to improve performance, it is likely that regulation will be on balance harmful. At least in theory, there is no economic point to interfering with even imperfect markets unless those imperfections are serious and capable of correction by known methods.

A. The First Question: Is There a Significant Market Failure?

As we have discussed, the growing body of theoretical writing on interchange fees establishes that privately optimal fees are unlikely to be socially optimal, but it does not indicate whether they will be systematically too high or too low. This literature does not and, in the absence of evidence, cannot indicate whether non-optimal interchange fees have a significant or trivial effect on overall performance. The related literature on pricing structures for two-sided markets reaches a similar result.[63] There is no reason to presume that even competing two-sided platforms will settle on a price

---

[62] See, for instance, Armstrong et al. (1994), Megginson and Netter (2001), and Littlechild (2003). In the United States, price cap regulation has been used as an alternative to rate of return regulation by the FCC and some states in regulating telephone companies starting in the (1980s). Viscusi et al. (2000), Chapter 12. This approach has been very widely used outside the United States. Winston and Morrison 1986 document some of the adverse effects of airline regulation in the United States.

[63] It is worth noting one difference explicitly. Both profit- and welfare-maximizing interchange fees depend in general on the nature of competition among issuers and among acquirers, and this additional complexity is not present in the analysis of ordinary, unitary two-sided platform businesses.

structure that is socially optimal. And, for this reason, there is no reason to presume that unitary systems have pricing structures near the social optimum.

Empirical evidence, not theory, therefore must play the leading role in assessing whether interchange fees—and the resulting prices to cardholders and merchants—lead to significant underprovision or overprovision of payment card services relative to the social optimum. In a recent discussion of the rationale for regulation of interchange in Australia, Ian J. Macfarlane, Governor of the Reserve Bank of Australia, similarly stresses the results of a factual inquiry rather than the deductions of economic theorists:[64]

> ...we saw that credit cards were growing faster than the other means of payment. This was initially somewhat surprising as credit card transactions are more expensive than most other means of payment—that is, they involve a larger payment from the users of the payments system to the providers of the payments system. ... Why was this possible?

Governor Macfarlane poses *almost* the right question: Are payment system usage patterns significantly inconsistent with system costs—and, it is essential to add, benefits? There is nothing unusual about a high-cost product driving out cheaper competition if the high-cost product is much better. U.S. drivers generally prefer automatic to manual transmissions in their automobiles, for instance, even though automatic transmissions cost more and are more expensive to maintain. Drivers seem to believe the difference in benefits outweighs the difference in cost.[65]

In our context, U.S. banks typically charge consumers the same variable price for handling a check as for handling a signature-based debit card payment: zero. Debit cards are nonetheless rapidly replacing checks because consumers find them more convenient.

An approach that is based on careful measurement of costs and benefits has the potential to distinguish what is important from what is only a theoretical possibility. Dealing with quantitative evidence rather than qualitative possibilities can also inform regulatory policies if regulation is deemed appropriate. Since the objective of interchange-fee regulation, where it is warranted, should be to correct the effects of a distortion of price signals, it is important to get a quantitative sense of the importance of those effects. Let us, accordingly, turn to the available evidence.

Some studies have argued that payment cards are used too much, based on the observation that they are more expensive on average for merchants than cash and checks but are nevertheless increasing in use at the expense of cash and checks.[66] While this is intuitively appealing, it ignores both cardholders and the role of benefits in determining the social optimum.

---

[64] Macfarlane (2005).

[65] Similarly, as Joanna Stavins pointed out in a paper on electronic check truncation and presentment, bicycles may be cheaper than cars but that does not mean that society would necessarily be better off if bicycles replaced cars. Stavins (1997, p. 28).

[66] See, for example, Balto (2000) and Reserve Bank of Australia (2002).

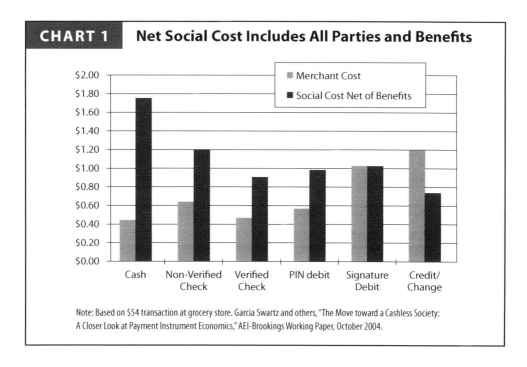

Note: Based on $54 transaction at grocery store. Garcia Swartz and others, "The Move toward a Cashless Society: A Closer Look at Payment Instrument Economics," AEI-Brookings Working Paper, October 2004.

To see this, consider a simple economy with only cash and cards and with a fixed set of transactions to be executed, as illustrated in Chart 1.

For each transaction, one can compute in principle the social marginal cost of executing the transaction using cash—the sum of the marginal costs to the merchant and consumer involved, as well as the net costs to all other involved parties, including governments and commercial banks. One can similarly compute the social marginal cost of executing each transaction using cards, along with the social marginal benefit of using cards as opposed to cash—the sum of the marginal benefits to consumers, merchants, governments, and commercial banks.[67] The marginal benefit in any of these cases may be negative, of course; consumers may find cards less convenient than cash for very small transactions, for instance. In this simple case, the efficient outcome is clearly for cash to be used for transactions for which the social marginal cost of using cash is less than the <u>net</u> social marginal cost of using cards—the social marginal cost of using cards minus the social marginal benefit of using cards rather than cash— and for cards to be used for the others. Transactions-specific marginal costs and benefits in principle are necessary to assess the importance (in other words, the net social cost) of any deviation from this ideal. Considering only costs and only one of the parties involved cannot be very informative.

To our knowledge, there are no empirical studies in the literature that consider the marginal social costs and benefits for merchants and cardholders, and, thus, there are no comparisons of actual versus optimal use of alternative payment systems that have even approximate economic

---

[67] For consumers, benefits would be measured by changes in consumers' surplus; for the other entities the measure would generally be changes in rents.

validity. There is some evidence on marginal costs for merchants, some highly incomplete evidence on marginal benefits for merchants, and essentially nothing on marginal costs or benefits for cardholders or other parties.[68]

Garcia Swartz, Hahn, and Layne-Farrar provide a useful overview of much of the available evidence, examine some of the issues one would need to consider in evaluating whether an economy has roughly the socially optimal use of payment cards, and present some rough calculations based on available data and some plausible assumptions about consumer benefits for a few transactions sizes and types.[69] They take the merchant-based cost surveys as a point of departure, but then proceed to make three types of adjustments. First, merchant-based surveys of costs usually compare payment instruments at different transaction sizes, typically the average transaction size for each payment instrument. The authors depart from this norm and compare payment instruments at a set of fixed transaction sizes, small and large, to assess the sensitivity of their results. Second, by combining plausible assumptions with available data, they attempt to incorporate all other parties to the transaction—consumers, the government, and commercial banks—into the calculation of cost and benefits. Finally, they consider the benefits received by the cardholder and merchants; as a result, they compare the "net" cost of payment methods. Garcia Swartz, Hahn, and Layne-Farrar present rough estimates of these magnitudes and find that the optimal payment method (considering quantifiable costs and benefits) varies by transaction size, store type, and other circumstances. For many transactions, it appears that credit and debit cards do not have higher "net costs" than cash or checks. While this work is instructive, however, it falls well short of a rigorous overall assessment of payment system performance.

B. The Second Question: Will Interchange Regulation Help?

Let us assume that one has shown that it would be socially optimal to reduce the use of payment cards in favor of other payment systems. Two further questions would then need to be considered. (1) Is the interchange fee the appropriate method for trying to achieve this improvement? (A related question is whether the source of the distortion is the collective setting of the interchange fee.) (2) If the answer to that question is affirmative, then do we have a method for regulating the interchange fee that is likely to increase social welfare? Since we know that interchange fees can be too high or too low, and either case can lead to a distortion, the issue is whether regulators can estimate the optimal interchange fee precisely enough to have confidence that they will improve social welfare.

The first question is more problematic than it might seem at first. As we noted earlier, card issuers charge merchants mainly variable fees and charge cardholders both access (fixed) and variable (transaction-specific) fees. The claim has been that cards are over-used because issuers—benefiting from and competing away to some extent interchange fee revenue—impose too low (possibly

---

[68] Compare, for instance, Humphrey et al. (2003), which argues that electronic payments systems are inherently socially more efficient, and Food Marketing Institute (1998), which argues that payment cards impose excessive costs on grocers.
[69] Garcia Swartz et al. (2004).

negative) variable fees on cardholders. Cardholders, who do not bear the costs imposed on the merchant by their choice of payment method, it is thus argued, use their cards too much.

A regulation-mandated reduction in the interchange fee tends to reduce the variable fees faced by merchants; if competition in acquiring is sufficiently intense, this reduction is one-for-one. However, reducing the interchange fee does not necessarily raise the variable fee paid by cardholders one-for-one—or, indeed, at all. Issuers can respond to the loss of interchange fee revenue by varying either fixed or variable fees, or both. The extent to which they vary each will depend on a variety of factors, including the elasticity of demand for access to cards and the elasticity of demand for transactions. In addition, there are likely to be one-time costs of various sorts (including costs of changing accounting and billing systems) caused by moving from the traditional regime of zero variable charges to a regime with positive variable charges. The one-time costs of making reward programs less generous are likely to be less significant, if they exist at all.

Suppose, for instance, that issuers increased annual fees but did not reduce variable fees at all. In that extreme case, the regulation of the interchange fee would not alter consumer incentives to use cards, although it might reduce the average number of cards that people carry. (Since it is hard to function in modern economies without at least one payment card, we doubt that the fraction of households with zero cards would rise noticeably.)

As shown in Chart 2, preliminary data from Australia suggests that even though interchange fees were reduced by nearly half in late 2003, the marginal price to cardholders of using credit

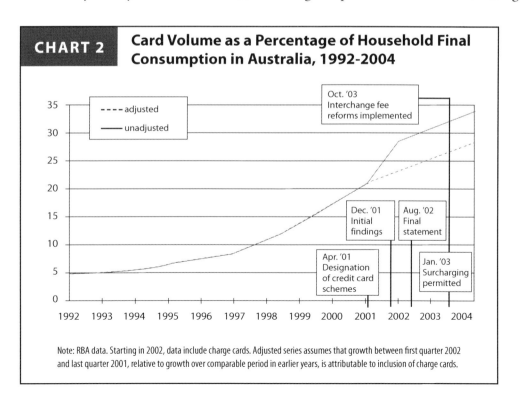

cards has not changed much. While some reward programs were made somewhat less generous, these cover only a fraction of consumers and card transactions,[70] and we have not seen widespread evidence of surcharging by merchants or the imposition of fees by issuers that increase with card usage.[71] So while available data suggest that interchange fee reductions were passed through more or less completely to reductions in merchant discounts, it does not seem that the stated objective of the RBA to make consumers face the "right" variable prices for different payment methods was realized to any appreciable extent.[72] Consistent with this, the data do not reveal much, if any, impact of the reforms on the use of credit cards.[73]

All this is not to say that dramatic reductions in the interchange fee had no economic effects. Because retailing in Australia is relatively concentrated and thus competition is likely to be imperfect,[74] it is reasonable to expect that only a fraction of the fall in merchant discounts was passed on to consumers in the form of lower prices, and the remainder went to increasing retailers' profits. When consumers use cash or credit cards without rewards, they are better off as a result; when they

---

[70] Industry estimates suggest that reward cards constitute about one third to one half of all credit cards in the United States; we lack comparable data for Australia. Bayot (2003).

[71] Making some reward programs less generous moved some negative variable prices toward zero. Many of these changes were in the form of caps on the total number of rewards points that can be earned each year. These limits have been set at relatively high levels, over AUS$40,000 (approximately US$31,000 at the time of this writing) a year, and likely have not been a binding constraint for many cardholders. See Reserve Bank of Australia (2004, p. 11). There were also some reductions in the marginal reward per dollar spent in some cases. There is no reason to think that this would have a big effect on card volume. In fact, if one is accumulating points in a rewards program to take a trip, and the rewards program is made less generous so that more purchases are required to earn the trip, one might use the card more rather than less intensively. There would be costs of various sorts associated with imposing positive transaction fees on non-reward cards, so it is not surprising that this does not seem to have been done.

[72] The RBA stated that its reforms were in line with the principle that "consumers should face prices that take into account the relative costs of producing goods and services, as well as demand conditions." Reserve Bank of Australia (2002, p. 34).

[73] Credit card dollar volume grew significantly in Australia in the late 1990s. The rate of growth started declining following 1999. The rate of decline in the growth rate leveled off in 2003 and 2004, in contrast to an acceleration in the rate of decline that would be expected were the reforms to have had a substantial impact. Nonetheless, the real dollar volume of credit card purchases role 20.0 percent between 2002 and 2004, about four times as rapidly as real household consumption. Interestingly, the number of credit card accounts grew by 11.1 percent over this period, compared to a growth of only 2.6% in population. See Reserve Bank of Australia (2005b).

[74] Government statistics on firm concentration are not available. We have identified what data we could find from a range of sources. Many merchant categories appear to have significant levels of concentration. For example, within their respective categories, the top department store had a 71 percent share (and the top two had an 83 percent share) in 2003; the top two supermarket and grocery stores (excluding convenience, specialty and miscellaneous food stores) had a 75 percent share in 2003; the top two mobile telephone operators had a 78 percent share in 2005; the top land-line telephone operator had a 75 percent share in 2005; and the top two airlines had an 83 percent share in 2005. In contrast, the four-firm concentration index for these categories is significantly lower in the United States based on 2002 U.S. Census data: 65 percent for department stores, 33 percent for supermarkets and grocery stores, 61 percent for mobile telephone operators, and 60 percent for land-line telephone operators. The U.S. Bureau of Transportation Statistics reports the top two firms accounting for 32 percent of enplaned passengers among major U.S. airlines in 2000. The one merchant category that we found with lower concentration was for warehouse clubs and superstores, for which the four-firm concentration index in Australia was 41 percent, compared to 92 percent in the United States. See Euromonitor (2005a), Euromonitor (2005b), Euromonitor (2005c), United States Census Bureau (2004), Bureau of Transportation Statistics (2000), Maxwell (2005), and McFarland (2005).

use cards with reward schemes, they are likely worse off. We have seen no evidence that these effects can be associated with distinct groups of consumers – different income quintiles, for instance.

On the other side of the market, the best evidence we have been able to obtain indicates that issuers have recovered between a third and a half of the fall in interchange revenue through increased fees to consumers.[75] Thus, issuers' profits have been reduced, and consumers with credit cards of all sorts have been directly harmed, particularly if they use reward cards. In order to mitigate reductions in MasterCard and Visa interchange revenues, three of the top four Australian banks have signed agreements to issue American Express or Diners Club cards, which can provide greater, unregulated transaction-related revenues to issuing banks.[76] In part as a consequence, the shares of these unitary systems have risen, though from initially low levels.[77]

All in all, it seems that in the short time since interchange fee reductions were imposed, retailers have been made better off, issuers have been made worse off, and some consumers have been made better off (particularly those who tend to use cash a lot) and others have been make worse off (particularly those who use credit cards with reward schemes). In the long run, some of these effects are likely to be undone as consumers and issuing banks move toward American Express and Diners Club, as these schemes have substantially higher average merchant discounts than the bank card systems.[78]

The apparent ineffectiveness of the fairly dramatic Australian regulatory intervention in terms of its stated goals may result from the particular competitive environment in that country and the types of cards used by consumers. However, it would appear to be generally the case that the interchange fee is a highly imprecise instrument for affecting the volume of transactions on cards and thus for correcting any perceived market distortion. That is because a there is only a loose connection between interchange fees and transactions prices to cardholders.

Let us suppose for the sake of argument that regulators went further than any have gone in fact and banned the use of consumer access fees. Interchange fee regulations would then necessarily affect the transaction price paid by consumers, as they are assumed to do in the theoretical literature. (This ban, of course, would likely impose a new set of costs and distortions on the system.)

---

[75] See Chang, Evans and Garcia Swartz (2005).
[76] See, e.g., Cornell (2004 and 2005).
[77] Reserve Bank of Australia (2004, p. 13).
[78] Some have argued that reducing the interchange fees of the multi-party systems will put pressure on unitary systems to follow suit, but this is not persuasive. To the extent that interchange regulation disadvantages the multi-party systems, it reduces competitive pressure on the unitary systems. (We are indebted to Michael Katz for this point.) The Reserve Bank of Australia suggests that there has been some downward pressure on merchant discounts for American Express and Diners Club in Australia, with a decline of 13 basis points over the 12 months ending June 2004 (although it does not discuss whether other factors might have been responsible for this), but expresses concern that the gap between the merchant discount for the unitary versus multi-party systems had widened by 30 basis points. See Reserve Bank of Australia (2004, pp. 12-13). Given that the merchant discounts for the unitary systems were, according to one account, about 100 basis points higher than for the multi-party systems (Reserve Bank of Australia 2001, Figure 2.2), even if there is a modest decrease in the merchant discounts for multi-party systems attributable to the reforms, the post-reform unitary merchant discount would still exceed the pre-reform multi-party merchant discount. And the merchant discount paid on volume shifted from the multi-party to the unitary systems would increase.

There would still be the question whether it is possible to estimate the optimal interchange fee with sufficient precision that policymakers could expect to increase rather than decrease social welfare. A robust conclusion from the theoretical literature is that an estimate of the optimal interchange fee would depend on a host of factors: estimates of the price responsiveness of cardholders and merchants, indirect network effects between cardholders and merchants, competition in issuing and acquiring and among merchants, price distortions in competing payment systems, transactions costs and liquidity constraints, and marginal costs of serving cardholders and merchants. It would also depend on how competing systems—some of which may be unitary—would respond to changes in prices to cardholders and merchants. Because of the difficulty of the task, there are no serious attempts of which we are aware to estimate the socially optimal interchange fee for any real payment system. Given currently available data and estimation methods, we believe that any such attempt could at best yield highly imprecise estimates.

This task would require far more empirical information than classic public utility regulation. Most public utilities have historically been monopolies, so the strategic interaction with competitors could be ignored, unregulated prices can be safely presumed to be too high, and reducing prices until the utility just breaks even will generally increase economic welfare – at least as long as impacts on the utility's incentives for efficiency are ignored. Although sometimes present, network effects rarely played an important role in the analysis, and the calculation of optimal (Ramsey) prices required only estimates of marginal costs and demand elasticities. However, even in the public utility context it has proved difficult to calculate precise estimates of the relevant parameters, and the determination of optimal prices has often led to considerable controversy among economists and policymakers.

A robust conclusion of the economic literature on interchange fees and two-sided markets is that cost-based interchange fees are generally not socially optimal.[79] Even if one were convinced, as some regulators seem to be, that current interchange fees are too high, unlike the public utility case, there is no guarantee that lowering them toward any particular target will improve welfare. In particular, there is no basis for believing that any particular cost-based formula for determining interchange fees would even provide a first approximation to the socially optimal interchange fee. Nor is there any basis at the moment for believing that moving from the collectively determined interchange fee to a fee based on any formula that considers only costs would be likely to improve social welfare. Unlike the public utility situation, therefore, there is no basis in economic theory or fact for cost-based regulation of interchange fees such as the regime adopted in Australia or by the European Commission.[80]

---

[79] The economic literature appears to be unanimous on this point; examples include Bergman (2005), Gans and King (2003a and 2003c) (who accept for the purpose of argument the assumption that externalities between merchants and consumers are unimportant in mature card systems) and Wright (2003b).

[80] These regulatory schemes have the further peculiarity from an economic standpoint that the merchant discount charged by unitary systems is left unregulated while the merchant discount for cooperative systems is regulated through cost-based interchange fees. This favors the unitary systems and thus leads to a further economic distortion whose effects would need to be considered in evaluating the net social benefits from moving to cost-based interchange fees.

In both Australia and Europe, the regulators (or at least their economic consultants) recognized that socially optimal interchange fees also depend on demand factors or network effects but, presumably, decided not to incorporate those factors because of the difficulty of doing so, citing instead the "objectivity" and "transparency" benefits of a cost-based measure.[81] Objectivity and transparency may have benefits, of course, but by themselves they do not, necessarily lead to greater economic efficiency.

Although cost-based interchange fee regulation could by happenstance improve the efficiency of the payment system, there are two fundamental reasons to doubt that it would regularly do so in practice. The first is that regulating the interchange fee will not necessarily have a significant effect on the variable prices paid by cardholders and therefore will not necessarily have a significant effect on the volume of transactions—generally the putative target of the intervention. The second is that even if regulating the interchange fee could affect the variable prices paid by both merchants and cardholders, cost-based regulation is not capable of achieving the optimal prices except by happenstance. Whether cost-based regulation in practice would increase efficiency is unknown given the current state of theoretical and empirical knowledge.

C. Competition Policy and Interchange Fee Determination

Relatively early in the development of the payment card industry, the *NaBanco* court recognized the complexity of the role played by the interchange fee and the differences between that role and the role of an ordinary price in deciding that interchange fees should be evaluated under the rule of reason rather than be subject to the *per se* condemnation of price-fixing under U.S. law. We believe the recent theoretical literature supports this approach. There is a strong economic presumption that collective determination of ordinary prices harms consumers, relative to uncoordinated, competitive pricing, but there is *no* economic presumption that collectively setting interchange fees reduces output or consumer welfare as compared to any other feasible regime.

Under U.S. law, to evaluate whether the pro-competitive benefits of collectively set interchange fees outweigh the anti-competitive costs (the test under the rule of reason), one would presumably have to compare collectively set interchange fees with the results of bilateral negotiations among acquirers and issuers.[82] As we have discussed, bilateral negotiation would at the very least involve high transactions costs in systems, like those in the United States, with large numbers of issuers and acquirers, and it may not be feasible in such systems. But assume it is feasible, and assume away the associated transactions costs. Then one would have to examine whether bilateral negotiations would lead to lower prices and higher output than collectively set interchange fees. Existing theory does not provide much help in predicting the outcome of such bilateral negotiations,[83] and, of course, the

---

[81] Reserve Bank of Australia (2002, p. 12); Katz (2001, p. 29); European Commission (2002).
[82] That is the remedy that was sought by the plaintiff in *NaBanco*.
[83] As we noted above, Small and Wright (2000) conclude bilateral negotiation would threaten system viability, but it is unclear how robust this result is.

arguments in favor of interchange regulation imply that the output of credit card systems is already too high. Thus, there is no reason at all to believe that bilateral negotiations would result in an interchange fee that would be closer to the social optimum than the collectively set interchange fee.

VI. CONCLUSIONS

Economists have only scratched the surface of the theoretical and empirical work that will be needed to understand pricing in two-sided markets in general and the determination of interchange fees in particular. Like much work in economics, many of the existing theoretical models are based on highly simplified representations of the industries in question and employ highly special assumptions concerning relevant economic relationships in order to isolate individual aspects of interest. Nevertheless, several results have emerged from the literature that seem robust enough for policymakers to rely on:

1. The socially optimal prices for customer groups in multi-sided industries depend on price elasticities of demand, indirect network effects between the customer groups, marginal costs for providing goods or services to each group, and other factors.

2. Although socially optimal prices in the payment card industry depend on the same set of factors, the socially optimal interchange fee also depends on other characteristics of these industries that affect the relationship between the interchange fee and final prices. Those factors include the use of fixed and variable fees; competitive conditions among merchants, issuers, acquirers; and the nature of competition from cash, checks, and unitary payment systems.

3. Thus the socially optimal interchange fee is not, in general, equal to any interchange fee based on cost considerations alone.

4. One cannot presume on the basis of theory alone that the interchange fee set collectively by an association is greater than, less than, or equal to the socially optimal interchange fee.

5. One cannot presume on the basis of theory alone that movements from the collectively set interchange fee to any particular cost-based interchange fee will increase or decrease social welfare.

6. One cannot presume on the basis of theory alone that the collectively set interchange fee is greater than, less than, or equal to the interchange fee that would be set by bilateral negotiations.[84]

---

[84] As we noted above, in the one example of bilateral interchange negotiation on which we have seen data, the Australian EFTPOS debit card system, the fee is negative, flowing from issuers to acquirers. And the Reserve Bank of Australia is considering raising EFTPOS interchange, shifting costs from consumers to merchants. See Macfarlane (2005).

If regulators have concluded that multi-party payment systems have exhibited significantly sub-optimal economic performance, the current state of theoretical and empirical research leaves them with three serious challenges if they try to increase payment system performance overall and thereby raise economic welfare:

1. There is no empirical research that reliably addresses whether payment cards or any other payment mechanism is used too much or too little. Such research would need to consider the social costs and benefits of alternative payment systems and consider the effect of other market distortions.

2. Although it is possible that economists will be able to estimate the quantities necessary for determining optimal interchange fees, very little empirical work has been done thus far on most of the relevant quantities.

3. It is not clear that interchange fee regulation is the appropriate intervention for correcting distortions in payment systems. The interchange fee is a blunt instrument for affecting the prices faced by consumers if issuers assess fixed fees as well as variable fees.

chapter 2

THE ECONOMIC PRINCIPLES FOR ESTABLISHING REASONABLE REGULATION OF DEBIT-CARD INTERCHANGE FEES THAT COULD IMPROVE CONSUMER WELFARE

By

David S. Evans, Robert E. Litan, Richard Schmalensee

I. INTRODUCTION AND OVERVIEW

Over the last century economists have developed a three-step process for designing regulations that are in the public interest.[1]

- Identify if there is a market failure that needs to be fixed, and, if so, what that failure is. If there is no significant market failure, the process ends because any regulation is more likely to be harmful than beneficial.

- Determine the best feasible method for correcting that failure.

- Ensure that after considering costs and the risk of unintended consequences the public is likely to be better off with regulation than with the results of an unregulated, inevitably imperfect market. If the proposed regulation does not make the public better off it should be either replaced by one that does, or the market should be left alone.

This framework is analogous to that used by physicians. The physician asks: is there an illness, and, if so, what is it; what's the best medicine for the illness; and, after taking side effects into account, is the patient going to be better off with the medicine? If not, would the patient be better off with a different medicine or no medicine at all? A cardinal rule for the physician, as for the regulator, is "to do good or to do no harm."[2]

We apply this framework to the regulation of debit card interchange fees by the Board of Governors of the Federal Reserve System ("Board") as required by Section 1075 of the Dodd-Frank Wall Street Reform and Consumer Protection Act ("Dodd-Frank"). The Board considered proposals for regulating debit cards on December 16, 2010 and agreed to release those proposals for comment.

We conclude that the proposals the Board released with respect to interchange fee regulation are not economically sound at least in part because they did not emerge from the three-step process above. The Board:

- did not clearly identify a significant market failure;

- did not take into account the virtually unanimous conclusion in the economics literature and the work of its own economists that purely cost-based regulation, which the Board proposed, is inappropriate in this setting;

---

[1] Kenneth Arrow, Robert W. Hahn, Richard Schmalensee, et al. (1996), "Is There a Role for Benefit-Cost Analysis in Environmental, Health, and Safety Regulation," Science, 272, pp. 221-222.

[2] Hippocrates, "Of the Epidemics," Translated by Francis Adams, available at http://classics.mit.edu/Hippocrates/epidemics.1.i.html.

- did not ensure that the proposal would be in the interest of consumers; and,
- should withdraw the proposal and revise it so that it would at least not harm consumers.[3]
- This introduction summarizes our basis for these findings.

A. Has There Been a Proper Diagnosis of the Problem to be Fixed?

The debit card market seems to have worked very well for consumers. Debit cards compete with other means of payment for merchant acceptance and consumer use. And they have competed effectively: the number of debit card transactions grew from 8.4 billion in 2000, to 21.6 billion in 2005, to 36.6 billion in 2009.[4] The total dollar value of transactions charged on debit cards increased from $311 billion in 2000, to $869 billion in 2005, to $1,421 billion in 2009.[5] In terms of numbers of transactions, debit cards are the favorite noncash method of payment for consumers.[6] Debit cards have improved the efficiency of the payment system by displacing checks.[7]

This (and other evidence of effective competition and social benefit) on its face argues that regulation, with all its attendant costs, is not called for. This evidence begs the critical question that regulators must answer before prescribing a remedy that overrules the market: what is the problem? At the hearing, Chairman Bernanke asked the staff to identify the problem, or market failure, that justified government regulation.[8] The staff suggested that a problem could result from the fact that consumers usually make the decision on how to pay.[9] In theory, consumers might overuse debit cards because they do not bear the total costs caused by their decision, since they do not see the costs they impose on merchants when they pay with a debit card. But, of course, consumers

---

[3] We focus on consumer welfare in our analysis for several reasons. First, the broad purpose the Dodd-Frank Act articulates in its preamble is "to protect consumers from abusive financial services practices." Second, advocates of reducing interchange fees often argue that doing so would benefit consumers by lowering retail prices, so the ultimate effect on consumers would appear to be a key test. Third, more broadly, the statute instructs the Board to ensure that interchange fees are "reasonable," and regulations that harm consumers are not generally considered "reasonable" in public policy discussions. Finally, Section 904 of the Electronic Fund Transfer Act, which Section 1075 of Dodd-Frank amends, also requires that the Board consider the impact of regulations on consumers, as we discuss further below.

[4] The Nilson Report.

[5] Ibid.

[6] "The 2010 Federal Reserve Payments Study: Noncash Payment Trends in the United States: 2006 – 2009," *The Federal Reserve System*, December 2010, at p. 4.

[7] Ibid., at p. 5.

[8] "There's a presumption that prices will be set by market competition, generally, but then, of course there are counter examples such as electric utilities, for example, where the government intervention can be justified … for various reasons. Can you … help us thin[k] about … what are the arguments for and against allowing interchange fees to be determined in the market versus having a regulatory intervention when we think about the economics?" Board December 16, 2010 Open Meeting, at p. 8 of 28. And as Governor Warsh noted, Chairman Bernanke's question referred to what the "market failure" was. Board December 16, 2010 Open Meeting, at p. 13 of 28.

[9] Board December 16, 2010 Open Meeting, at pp. 8-9 of 28.

do not bear the full costs of paying with cash, checks, or credit cards either. The increased use of debit cards in recent years has been in large part a switch away from checks. In releasing the 2010 study of the use of noncash payments in the United States, the Federal Reserve System's Financial Services Policy Committee noted that,

"The number of noncash payments in the United States grew more slowly between 2006 and 2009 than in prior periods and the total value of noncash payments declined. As in previous years, check payments continued to decline and were eclipsed by debit cards as the most used noncash instrument in the United States."[10]

In this release, Richard Oliver, executive vice president of the Federal Reserve Bank of Atlanta and the manager of the Federal Reserve System's check and ACH business nationwide, also noted that, "The results of the study clearly underscore this nation's efforts to move toward a more efficient electronic clearing system for all types of retail payments."[11]

Unsurprisingly, there does not appear to be any evidence that consumers have used debit cards excessively and, despite extensive study and monitoring of the growth of electronic payments by the Federal Reserve System, we have found no statement by any official of the Federal Reserve that has suggested that the growth of debit cards was not in the public interest.

There is a large theoretical literature in economics that suggests that the private market may not choose the socially efficient interchange fee, but that literature does not find that the market interchange fee should necessarily be lowered. In a comprehensive survey paper that accurately summarized that literature as of mid-2009, Board economists Robin Prager, Mark Manuszak, Elizabeth Kiser and Ron Borzekowski concluded:

"In theory, privately-set interchange fees can **be either too high or too low relative to the efficient interchange fee**, depending on a number of factors, including the cost and demand considerations underlying the merchant decision to accept cards and the extent of competition among issuing and acquiring banks."[12] (emphasis added)

The draft regulations the Board has put out for comment do not appear to reflect any of the factors identified by these staff economists. The Notice of Proposed Rulemaking in the Federal Register does not identify any market failure or suggest any analysis to determine the problem for which the Board is seeking a reasonable solution.

B. Has the Best Solution to the Problem Been Selected?

The Board was presented with proposed rules that would base debit card interchange fees on the average variable costs of certain tasks that issuers undertake for debit card transactions. It is

---

[10] "Federal Reserve Study Shows More Than Three-Quarters of Noncash Payments Are Now Electronic," *Federal Reserve Financial Services Policy Committee,* December 8, 2010, available at http://www.federalreserve.gov/newsevents/press/other/20101208a.htm.
[11] Ibid.
[12] The Fed Economists (2009), at p. 4.

striking that while the theoretical literature in economics describes a variety of possible market failures that might affect interchange rates, there is broad agreement that cost-based regulation is not an appropriate response to *any* of them. Again, the Fed Economists summarized this consensus well:

"[T]he determination of which costs should be included in a cost-based fee is necessarily arbitrary, and measuring those costs is nontrivial, particularly if frequent re-estimation of costs is necessary. More importantly, the **economic theory underlying the efficient interchange fee provides no rationale for either a strictly cost-based interchange fee** or an interchange fee of zero."[13] (emphasis added)

As Professor Calvano makes clear in his accompanying submission, more recent studies have only strengthened this conclusion: in striking contrast to most regulatory environments, the literature is unanimous that it is not efficient for interchange fees to be equal to any measure of any entity's marginal, incremental, or average cost.[14] The proposal to base regulation on cost alone in this case is like a physician, unsure of the right diagnosis, nonetheless prescribing a remedy that the medical literature agrees is inappropriate for any plausible illness considered.

C. Is the Regulation Likely to Make Consumers Better Off?

Section 904 of the Electronic Fund Transfer Act requires the Board, to the extent practicable, "demonstrate that the consumer protections of the proposed regulations outweigh the compliance costs imposed on consumers and financial institutions."[15] Perhaps the most obvious and most serious problem with the proposals that were presented to the Board is that there was no finding that they would benefit consumers. In fact, the Board was informed by a Board staff economist that, "[O]verall it's hard to anticipate what the overall [e]ffect on consumers will be."[16]

The Board was told that consumers could pay higher fees for their checking accounts and for using debit cards, that consumers *might* obtain benefits from lower prices at merchants, but that it was not possible to predict whether consumers would, on balance, be better or worse off as a result of the regulations.[17] In other words the staff felt it was possible that the proposed regulations would make consumers worse off. It is hard to imagine a physician recommending that a patient take a particular medicine even though its effects are "hard to anticipate."

---

[13] The Fed Economists (2009), at p. 48. Also, see The Fed Economists (2009), at p. 62.
[14] Emilo Calvano, "Note on the Economic Theory of Interchange," Submission to the Board of Governors of the Federal Reserve System, February 22, 2011, at pp. 4-8 ("Calvano Report").
[15] 15 U.S.C. § 1693b(a) (3).
[16] Board December 16, 2010 Open Meeting, at p. 11 of 28.
[17] Ibid. Board economist, Mark Manuszak, stated, "[A]ny savings that consumers might realize at point of sale could be offset by fee increases at their banks, as well as changes in terms that debit cardholders face for card use and deposit accounts. So, specifically, account holders at covered institutions may face higher fees for debit card use or additional account fees, and they couldn't foresee if less favorable terms for their debit -- for their deposit accounts and related services.... [O]verall it's hard to anticipate what the overall [e]ffect on consumers will be."

In fact, research and analysis we have conducted shows that consumers are likely to be harmed on balance by the proposed regulation, because the higher costs they would face on their checking accounts would likely exceed any price reductions they would receive from merchants, at least over the first 24 months of the regulation.[18] Even after 24 months, there is no economic basis for concluding that the cost-based interchange limits set by the Board would necessarily produce net benefits for consumers. Consumers may continue to get less back from merchants in lower prices than they pay in higher retail banking fees. More importantly, consumers would likely suffer harm from reduced innovation, weakened efficiency incentives, and other well-known consequences of government price regulation. The Board's proposal violates the cardinal rule of regulation: "do no harm." As we discuss below, the Board could follow the Congressional mandate and devise interchange fee standards that are "reasonable and proportional to cost" without harming consumers.

D. Is There a Better Approach to Regulation?

We understand that the Board is required by Congress to promulgate standards for assessing debit card interchange fees by April 21, 2011 and that these must be implemented by July 21, 2011. We have several suggestions for what the Board should do – and not do – at this point:

First, the Board should begin now to conduct the serious empirical research and analysis necessary to determine what restrictions on interchange fees, if any, would best serve the public interest. That involves identifying what the market failure is, if any; finding the best solution for whatever market failure is found; and making sure the regulated solution will benefit consumers. In conducting this analysis the Board and its staff can rely on extensive economic research into two-sided platform businesses generally and payments systems in particular, as well as its own expertise and experience with the banking industry.[19] The literature is unanimous that a proper analysis must consider factors other than cost in order to determine rates that are "reasonable and proportional to cost."

Second, the Board should not promulgate regulations that are likely to harm consumers materially. Regulations that harm consumers would not generally be considered reasonable, particularly if sound and thorough economic analysis does not support them. The greater the cut in interchange fees, the greater the likelihood of substantial harm to consumers and the greater the disruption to their depository account relationships.

Third, the Board should seriously consider finding that market-set interchange fees are "reasonable and proportional to cost," at least until the research and analysis described above can be

---

[18] See generally, Consumer Impact Study, at pp 6-8.
[19] For recent contributions to this literature see Marc Rysman (2009), "The Economics of Two-Sided Markets," *Journal of Economic Perspectives,* 23:3, pp. 125-143 ("Rysman 2009"); Julian Wright (2004), "The Determinants of Optimal Interchange Fees in Payment Systems," *Journal of Industrial Economics*, 52:1, pp. 1–26 ("Wright 2004"); and Özlem Bedre-Defolie and Emilio Calvano (2009), "Pricing Payment Cards," ECB Working Paper No. 1139. Available at SSRN: http://ssrn.com/abstract=1522026 ("Bedre-Defolie and Calvano 2009").

completed. Without additional empirical work, the Fed Economists concluded that regulation was risky: "[T]he possible effects of any intervention are highly uncertain. Although economic models can provide some insights regarding the qualitative effects of a policy intervention, they typically have little to say about the quantitative magnitudes of these effects."[20]

We are not aware of any empirical analysis showing that the efficient interchange fee is below the market-determined rate, let alone substantially below. In what follows we briefly discuss some recent theoretical work that seems broadly consistent with Dr. Prager's answer to Chairman Bernanke concerning the possible market failure. This work, which is based on a number of assumptions, suggests that the efficient rate may be equal to or below the market-set rate but that the gap, if any, is likely to be small. In light of all this, market-set interchange fees seem reasonable given the current state of knowledge, and, as costs vary substantially among issuers, they are more reasonable and no less "reasonable and proportional to cost" than the safe harbor and ceiling proposed by the Board.

E. Organization of This Report

The remainder of this report has six sections that present the basis for the conclusions summarized above.

Section II examines the likelihood that the proposed regulation will harm consumers, contrary to the intent of Dodd-Frank.

Section III considers the overall economic impact of the recent growth in debit card usage and concludes that this is a story of market success, not market failure.

Section IV shows in more detail that the Board has not identified a market failure that its proposed regulation is designed to correct.

Section V demonstrates that the proposed regulation is not justified by any of the possible market failures discussed in the theoretical literature.

Section VI considers the implications of some recent theoretical work for the empirical research and analysis the Board needs to do in order to estimate the gap, if any, between socially efficient and market-set interchange fees. We argue both that it is possible to estimate this gap and that the gap is most likely small, perhaps small enough, in light of the inevitable costs of price regulation, to justify a finding that market-set fees are reasonable and proportional to cost.

Section VII considers what the Board should do now to meet its statutory deadline in the absence of an estimate of the difference between market-set and socially-efficient interchange fees. We argue, as above, that the Board should avoid what may well prove to be unjustified disruption of an industry that has served consumers well and should, therefore, require, at most, a small reduction in interchange fees.

---

[20] The Fed Economists (2009), at p. 42.

II. THE FED'S PROPOSED REGULATION WILL LIKELY HARM CONSUMERS

In a separate submission we have documented that the Board's proposed interchange fee cap of between 7 and 12 cents for debit-card issuers would result in substantial, direct, and immediate harm to individuals and small businesses that currently have checking accounts.[21] Almost all households and small business in the United States would likely be affected.[22] The Board's proposal would reduce the debit card interchange fee revenues that banks and credit unions earn on consumer and small business checking accounts by $33.4-$38.6 billion in the 24 months immediately following July 21, 2011, the date the proposed regulations will become effective.[23] We have found that banks and credit unions will pass on much of the revenues lost from merchants (and merchant acquirers) to consumers in the form of higher fees and reduced services and will do so quickly.[24]

Our research and analysis indicates that consumers are unlikely to receive significant savings in the form of lower prices from merchants during the 24 month period after the proposed regulations become effective. Most large merchants would not go to the trouble of reducing prices in the near term in response to the tiny cost reductions they would receive: about 10 cents on an average $59.89 transaction and less than 2 cents on a $10 purchase.[25] Many small and medium sized merchants would not receive any cost reductions in the near term from the acquirers or from the agents for these acquirers.[26] They would thus have no savings to pass on in the near term. As discussed above, it is generally accepted that the government should replace market-set prices with regulator-determined prices only when doing so is likely to benefit consumers. Such benefits are likely only when regulation is squarely aimed at correcting a significant market failure. Because price regulation often has unanticipated costs and rarely, if ever, has unanticipated benefits, regulation is likely

---

[21] Consumer Impact Study.
[22] Based on 2007 data, 89.7 percent of households had a checking account. See "Changes in U.S. Family Finances from 2004 to 2007: Evidence from the Survey of Consumer Finances," *Federal Reserve Bulletin*, February 2009, at p. A20.
[23] Consumer Impact Study, at pp. 14-15. As discussed there we believe that it is likely that banks and credit unions with less than $10 billion in assets would not receive debit card interchange fees significantly higher than those received by larger institutions despite the fact that these smaller institutions are technically exempt from the interchange fee regulations.
[24] While the Board staff did not quantify these losses they also concluded that demand depository account customers could be harmed by the debit card interchange fee proposals. Board economist Mark Manuszak stated, "…any savings that consumers might realize at point of sale could be offset by fee increases at their banks, as well as changes in terms that debit cardholders face for card use and deposit accounts." See Board December 16, 2010 Open Meeting, at p. 10 of 28.
[25] There is extensive evidence that prices are do not change quickly in response to small changes in costs and in particular do not adjust downwards quickly in response to reductions in costs. For further discussion see the Consumer Impact Study, at pp. 48-51.
[26] As we describe more fully in the Consumer Impact Study, the smaller merchants that account for about 75 percent of all merchants that accept cards usually have contracts specifying a single "blended" merchant discount rate across multiple brands and card types, and these rates would probably not change substantially in the short term in response to the reductions in debit card interchange fees.

to be beneficial after the fact only when estimated benefits are well above estimated costs before the fact.[27]

There is accordingly no sound basis for adopting a regulation that before the fact seems as likely to harm consumers as to benefit them. Therefore, it is not reasonable for the Board to implement the proposed rules given that it cannot support a prediction that the rules would make consumers better off and that its own staff acknowledges that it is possible that the rules would make consumers worse off.

Our analysis indicates that imposing the proposed rules would not be the coin toss between "consumers win and consumers lose," as the staff's conclusion that it was "hard to anticipate" might suggest. In fact, consumers and small businesses who use checking accounts would likely lose tens of billions of dollars in the 24 months after these rules would take effect.

III. DEBIT CARDS LOOK LIKE A MARKET SUCCESS, NOT A MARKET FAILURE

Debit cards have been embraced by both merchants and consumers and look like a real success story for the American economy. They have enabled consumers to reduce the number of paper checks they write. Debit cards have provided a convenient payment method for physical and online transactions that does not require the use of credit. As former Board Vice Chairman Donald Kohn noted in 2006, "[c]onsumers seem to view debit cards as a natural progression from cash and checks because they are a convenient electronic means of making payments without incurring the additional debt often associated with credit card use."[28]

Consumers use debit cards in part to help manage their budgets,[29] as they tend to use these cards to pay for daily necessities such as groceries, gasoline, and drugstore purchases.[30] Debit cards have enabled consumers to conveniently pay for these items electronically, without using cumbersome paper checks. Virtually all depository accounts now come with a debit card. According to the Federal Reserve's 2009 Survey of Consumer Payment Choice, 77.6 percent of consumers had a debit card.[31] Consumers surveyed by Federal Reserve that year also reported that debit cards are

---

[27] See, generally, A.E. Kahn, *The Economics of Regulation*, II (New York: Wiley, 1971), ch. 7 and W.K. Viscusi, J.E. Harrington, and J. M. Vernon, *Economics of Regulation and Antitrust*, 4th Ed (Cambridge: MIT Press, 2005), ch. 10 ("Viscusi et al. 2005").

[28] Donald L. Kohn , "Evolution of Retail Payments and the Role of the Federal Reserve," presentation At the Western Payments Alliance 2006 Payments Symposium, Las Vegas, Nevada, September 11, 2006, available at http://www.federalreserve.gov/newsevents/speech/kohn20060911a.htm

[29] Drazen Prelec and George Loewenstein (1998),"The Red and Black: Mental Accounting of Savings and Debit," *Marketing Science*, 17:1.

[30] Kevin Foster, Erik Meijer, Scott Schuh, and Michael A. Zabek (2010), "The 2008 Survey of Consumer Payment Choice," Federal Reserve Bank of Boston, Public Policy Discussion Papers, at table 23 ("Foster et al 2010").

[31] Schuh, Scott, "Basic Facts about U.S. Consumer Payment Choice," Presented at the MPD Payments Innovation Institute, Harvard Faculty Club, Cambridge, MA, November 5, 2010 ("Schuh November 2010 Presentation").

more widely accepted than checks by merchants.[32] As indicated previously, in 2009, consumers made 36.6 billion debit card transactions, with a total value of $1.421 trillion.

Merchants have also embraced debit cards. Many merchants have installed PIN pads so that consumers who wanted to pay with their PIN codes could do so. According to the acquirers who responded to the Board's survey conducted in late 2010, 22 percent of merchant locations are able to accept PIN debit transactions and it is our understanding from knowledgeable sources in the industry that these account for about 80 percent of volume.[33] Since May 2003, retailers have been able to choose whether or not they wanted to take signature debit cards in addition to credit cards.[34] It is our understanding from conversations with knowledgeable industry observers that virtually no merchants accepting credit cards have decided to forgo debit cards. Because fewer people are pulling out their checkbooks to pay, checkout lines move faster for everyone.

Competition authorities, courts, and economists often look at output, prices, innovation, and quality of service to assess how well a market is working.[35] On all these metrics it appears that the debit card business has performed well.[36]

Debit card output has increased dramatically. The number of transactions on debit cards grew at an average rate of 17.8 percent per year between 2000 and 2009, while the dollar value of transactions increased at an average annual rate of 18.4 percent during that decade. The fraction of households that use a debit card increased from 17.6 percent in 1995 to 67 percent in 2007 based on the Board's Survey of Consumer Finance.[37] More recently, the Survey of Consumer Payment Choice conducted by the Federal Reserve Bank of Boston found that 77.6 percent of consumers had debit cards in 2009.[38]

Debit card prices have fallen for consumers. At the beginning of the 2000s many banks charged consumers fees for using their debit cards. By the end of the 2000s few consumers paid for using their debit cards, and about two-thirds of debit cards came with rewards that provided consumers with value for using their cards.[39]

Debit card features and services have expanded for consumers. Introduced to most US consumers in the mid-1990s, debit cards began to acquire a range of value-added services beginning

---

[32] Foster et al 2010, at table 27.
[33] The Proposed Rules, at p. 81725.
[34] Prior to that date MasterCard and Visa required merchants that entered into contract to accept their cards to honor all cards that consumers presented with their brands on them regardless of whether they were debit or credit cards. Wal-Mart and other merchants wanted to be able to take credit cards but not signature debit cards. The card networks agreed to this as part of a settlement of the lawsuit.
[35] We are not suggesting that any of these metrics provides definitive evidence about whether there is or is not a market failure of some sort. They are often used, however, as indicators of market performance along with other metrics.
[36] In addition published signature debit card interchange rates for merchants have been roughly constant since mid-2004 and for most networks published PIN debit card interchange fee rates have changed much since mid 2005. See The Fed Economists (2009), at figure 3.
[37] Loretta J. Mester (2009), "Changes in the Use of Electronic Means of Payment: 1995-2007," *Business Review*, pp. 29-37.
[38] Schuh November 2010 Presentation.
[39] "2009 Debit Card Rewards – Consumer Insights," Consumer Loyalty Study, First Data, April 2009.

in the 2000s. Multiple fraud and risk management offerings were introduced to reduce consumer liability for fraud, and enhance the intrinsic fraud prevention characteristics of the debit card. "Swipe and go" solutions allowing fast payment (with neither signature nor PIN) for low value purchases were introduced in the mid-2000s. In addition, debit rewards, from points programs to savings booster solutions, became standard by the late 2000s.

Debit cards have resulted in significant innovations in payments. The introduction of debit cards in the mid-1990s tapped into a broad consumer preference for using payment solutions that drew from a consumer's "funds at hand." This in turn led to a host of innovations around prepaid card solutions, including "open loop" prepaid cards that enabled debit transactions anywhere Visa or MasterCard were accepted. These open loop cards became available in many forms, including gift cards, electronic benefits transfer (EBT) card programs, payroll cards, and many other solutions. Particularly useful for populations with minimal access to other card solutions (e.g. youth, government benefits recipients), these solutions extended electronic payments to areas previously dominated by cash.

From the standpoint of overall economic efficiency, debit cards have been instrumental in finally moving the American payment system into the digital era. In an August 2006 speech, the President of the Federal Reserve Bank of Atlanta noted that "[w]ith rapid growth in the use of credit cards, debit cards and point-of-purchase check conversion, our vision of an efficient, predominantly electronic system [for payments] is in sight."[40] As the former Chief Operating Office of the Federal Reserve Bank of St. Louis noted in a 2003 article,

Nationwide, we know consumers are choosing the efficiency of electronic payments, such as ACH and debit cards, over checks. One of the Fed's objectives is to promote an efficient payment system, so we endorse these trends.[41]

As of 2004, the percentage of transactions made by paper check in the United States was considerably higher than in virtually every industrialized country, as shown in Table 1 on next page. Check use in the United States fell dramatically over the latter part of the 2000s even though merchants were increasingly able to scan checks and process them electronically.

The use of debit cards by consumers is one of the leading factors in the declining use of checks. Debit cards were initially introduced as a substitute for writing checks. The value for the consumer was that she did not have to present identification and go through the time-consuming process of having a check accepted. The value for the merchant was use of debit cards could reduce checkout lines and waiting time at the cash register while reducing check fraud and the cost of returned checks.[42] Over time the value of debit cards to consumers and

---

[40] "Guynn Reflects on Changes in Banking and Economics and Addresses Future Concerns," The Federal Reserve Bank of Atlanta, August 22, 2006, available at http://www.frbatlanta.org/news/pressreleases/atlantafed/press_release_guynn_reflects_on_changes_in_banking_and_economics.cfm.

[41] W. LeGrande Rives (2003), "The Check Re-engineering Initiative: It Really Is Business as Usual," Central Banker, available at http://www.stlouisfed.org/publications/cb/articles/?id=899.

[42] Elizabeth Klee (2006), "Paper or Plastic? The Effect of Time on the use of Checks and Debit Cards at Grocery Stores," Finance and Economics Discussion Series, Board of Governors of the Federal Reserve System, 2006-02.

TABLE 1: Percent of All Transactions Made by Check for Selected Industrialized Countries					
	2004	2005	2006	2007	2008
United States	41.3	37.0	32.6	28.6	26.0
France	29.7	27.8	25.8	23.8	22.1
Canada	18.9	17.2	15.8	14.5	13.0
Italy	15.7	14.6	13.9	12.5	11.1
United Kingdom	15.9	13.9	12.3	10.7	9.2
Singapore	4.6	4.5	4.2	4.3	3.8
Germany	0.8	0.7	0.6	0.5	0.4
Belgium	1.1	0.8	0.7	0.5	0.4
Switzerland	0.3	0.2	0.1	0.1	0.1
Sweden	0.1	0.1	0.0	0.0	0.0
Japan	3.5	3.4	2.2	1.5	NA

Source: Bank of International Settlements, Country Statistics of Payment Settlements 2008
Notes: Excludes checks written by banks. Germany has different methodology and data collection since 2007

merchants increased as banks and networks provided more features such as improved fraud control, processing times, and cash back.

All in all, observers who are innocent of interchange fee disputes would almost certainly find it hard to see how this performance would signal the need for regulation rather than applause.

IV. THE BOARD HAS NOT IDENTIFIED A MARKET FAILURE

In the open meeting in which the proposed rule was discussed, Chairman Bernanke asked the staff to explain the basis for price regulation of the debit card business:

"There's a presumption that prices will be set by market competition, generally, but then, of course, there are counterexamples such as, electric utilities, for example, where the government intervention can be justified by various -- for various reasons. Can you ... help us thin[k] about ... what are the arguments for and against allowing interchange fees to be determined in the market versus having a regulatory intervention ...?"[43]

---

[43] Board December 16, 2010 Open Meeting, at p. 8 of 28.

Staff economist Dr. Robin Prager answered at length:

"[I]n most markets increased competition leads to lower prices. However, in payment card markets, competition between networks tends to drive interchange fees higher. And the reason for this is that in these markets the party that decides what method of payment will be used at the point-of-sale, that is, the customer, is different from the party that incurs the costs associated with that decision, the merchant. And in general, customers don't tend to take into account the costs incurred by merchants as a result of their decisions. The networks want banks to issue their cards, and they want customers to hold and use their cards. And they provide an incentive to the banks to issue cards by offering higher interchange fees. The banks use the revenues from these interchange fees to offer more attractive deposit account terms to their customers, including, in some cases, rewards for making payments with debit cards. Meanwhile, the merchants, who ultimately foot the bill for their customers' payment choices, have little or no ability to influence the customer's decision with regard to what payment method to use. In addition, given the near ubiquity of card acceptance and the expectations of customers, many merchants believe that they really don't have the option of refusing to accept card payments. So even though merchants would prefer lower interchange fees, unless the fees are extremely high, they're likely to continue to accept cards. And as a result competition in these markets tends to focus on the issuers and the cardholders who prefer higher interchange."[44]

Dr. Prager's description of debit card competition is broadly accurate, but economists do not generally recognize most of the features that she emphasizes as symptoms of market failure. Rather, they are understood to occur in a wide variety of markets that are generally thought to perform well and are not candidates for price regulation.

Free television stations are a good example. Consumers decide which television station to watch at any particular time. An advertiser that wants to reach a particular set of viewers does not have any ability to get viewers to watch shows for which advertising is cheap. Television stations and the networks with which they are affiliated compete to get viewers by offering free programming. They spend a great deal of money on this. To recover this money they charge advertisers. Of course, advertisers would prefer that stations spent less money on programming so they could offer cheaper advertising rates, so long as the stations still delivered the viewers. The advertisers pass the cost of advertising onto all customers, not just the ones who happened to watch their advertising. These same features apply to the internet-search business, magazines, newspapers, radio, social networking and other advertising-supported businesses.

Shopping malls are another example. Shoppers decide which shopping mall to visit. If a store wants to benefit from the foot traffic at a mall, then it has to pay – typically an annual rent and often a percentage of its transaction volume as well. Shopping malls compete for shoppers by securing good locations, building malls that shoppers want to visit, and recruiting an appealing group of merchants that shoppers can patronize when they come to the mall. They

---

[44] Ibid., at pp. 8-9 of 28.

also compete by offering free amenities like parking and perhaps even music and upscale decor. Shoppers typically do not pay to patronize shopping malls, so they bear none of the costs incurred to attract them. Merchants bear all of those costs and more, and they would, of course, benefit if malls delivered foot traffic but if the shoppers paid the mall instead of them. If any single mall tried to do this, of course, its traffic would decline and its merchants would not be happy. Online shopping malls and aggregators have the same basic business model: Amazon and eBay charge sellers but not buyers.

Advertising-supported media and shopping malls are two examples of businesses that are in "two-sided markets." In these markets businesses usually provide a service that brings two different kinds of customers together for the purpose of a value-creating interaction.[45] A significant portion of the economy is based on two-sided markets.[46] Many of the leading companies in the United States operate "multi-sided platforms" that have become global brands. These include Apple, eBay, Facebook, Google, Microsoft, NYSE, and Yahoo.

The recognition that the economics of these businesses was different than the standard one-sided business treated in classic textbooks occurred around 2000.[47] In one-sided businesses, economists have long known that the socially efficient prices are equal to marginal costs inclusive of a fair rate of return on capital and that competition drives prices to this level. Two-sided businesses must generally attract sufficient numbers of both groups to be viable, so the terms offered to both sides must involve a price *level* that generates at least a fair rate of return and a price *structure* that induces balanced participation. It is possible in theory that the efficient price structure for a two-sided business has one price above the corresponding marginal cost and one price well below marginal cost. Such price structures are in fact common in practice. For example, free content to television viewers (in effect a subsidy for watching at a particular time) builds an audience that advertisers value because they can present messages to them. In many two-sided businesses, as in television stations and shopping malls, one "side" covers most or all of both variable and fixed costs, and the other "side" pays little or nothing.[48]

The economics literature has also found as a general matter that the market prices established by two-sided businesses can deviate from socially efficient prices for a variety of complicated reasons. In practice, of course, the prices set by ordinary one-sided businesses are rarely socially efficient: perfect competition exists only in textbooks, and departures from perfect competition lead to

---

[45] In the case of advertising-supported media consumers in particular need to be bribed with content to come to a place where they are exposed to advertising.

[46] Thomas Eisenmann, Geoffrey Parker, and Marshall W. Van Alstyne (2006), "Strategies for Two-Sided Markets," *Harvard Business Review*.

[47] Jean-Charles Rochet and Jean Tirole (2006), "Two-Sided Markets: A Progress Report," *The RAND Journal of Economics*, 37:3, pp. 645-667 ("Rochet and Tirole 2006"). David S. Evans (2010), "Introduction," Essays on the Economics of Two-Sided Markets: Economics, Antitrust and Strategy. Available at SSRN: http://ssrn.com/abstract=1714254.

[48] It is worth noting that every successful payment system of which we are aware began with a pricing structure in which merchants, not consumers, contributed the bulk of revenues. Thus this pattern emerged well before charge, credit or debit cards became ubiquitous.

prices that are too high. Nonetheless, economists and policy makers generally prescribe price regulation only when substantial departures from perfect competition are essentially unavoidable – in what are commonly called natural monopoly businesses, such as the distribution of electric power mentioned by Chairman Bernanke. A large literature has documented the adverse effects of regulation, particularly on productive efficiency and innovation.[49]

In two-sided industries, as in all industries, market power can also lead to price levels that are too high relative to the perfectly competitive ideal. But the price level is not at issue here, since regulating only interchange fees does not directly affect the price level. Interchange fees are transfers from one side (merchants and acquiring banks) of payment system businesses to the other side (consumers and issuing banks) and thus do not directly affect the net per-transaction revenue. Interchange fee regulation is regulation of the price structure, not the price level. As noted above and well summarized by the Fed Economists, the theoretical literature has shown that a variety of fairly subtle factors could lead market-set interchange fees – and thus the market-set price structure – to deviate from the social ideal:

"In theory, privately-set interchange fees can be either too high or too low relative to the efficient interchange fee, depending on a number of factors, including the cost and demand considerations underlying the merchant decision to accept cards and the extent of competition among issuing and acquiring banks."[50]

The problem here is that, in her response to Chairman Bernanke, Dr. Prager did not provide evidence on any of those factors or any of the others mentioned in the economic literature, nor did she suggest that a particular model in that literature both described the U.S. debit card market and showed that the market-set interchange fee was too high. Thus she did not in fact provide the complete answer to his question on market failure that the situation would seem to warrant. Her answer mainly described the process of competition in a particular two-sided market. Unfortunately, her short answer at the hearing is the only analysis of market failure that we have seen from the Board at this point.[51]

The full problem is, however, even more serious than this. Just as regulation of the price level of single-sided businesses is only justified in extreme cases, regulation of the price structure of a two-sided business is only appropriate if that structure deviates substantially and persistently from the social optimum. Consistent with the views of most economists who have written on this subject, Dr. Prager did not assert that there is a substantial deviation here or suggest there was any evidence that would support such an assertion. Just as few single-sided businesses operate in perfectly competitive markets, the theoretical literature suggests that few

---

[49] See Paul L. Joskow and Nancy L. Rose (1982), "The Effects of Economic Regulation," *Handbook of Industrial Organization*, 2, pp. 1449 – 1506 and the extensive literature they discuss; and Viscusi et al. 2005.

[50] The Fed Economists (2009), at p. 4.

[51] Our point, of course, is not that Dr. Prager should have given a long comprehensive answer at the hearing but rather that her short answer is all there is in the record we have seen on a very critical issue.

if any two-sided businesses have exactly the socially optimal price structures that theoretical models imply.

If the general market features discussed in Dr. Prager's response, with no supporting empirical analysis, were found to be sufficient to justify the proposed regulation here, then those same general features would also justify regulation that would shift most of the costs of other merchant-supported products – including newspapers, radio, television, search engines, social networks, shopping malls, and others – from merchants to consumers. As an economic matter, however, there is simply no justification for such regulation of two-sided markets just because they are two-sided.

Neither the Notice of Proposed Rulemaking in the Federal Register nor any other document linked to this proceeding provides a discussion of market failure that might either replace or clarify that given by Dr. Prager. As the Board has thus not identified a problem in the debit card market that prevents interchange fees from being "reasonable," it lacks any economic basis for asserting that its proposed regulation makes it likely that they will become "reasonable."

V. THE PROPOSED COST-BASED REGULATION IS PLAINLY THE WRONG REMEDY

In fact, there is a consensus among economists, including those at the Board who have studied this issue, that the cost-based approach proposed by the Board is not an economically reasonable and sound solution to *any* theoretically plausible market failure involving interchange fees. As we noted above, the Fed Economists published a survey of the theoretical literature on interchange fees in May 2009. That literature considers a variety of factors that could in principle lead market-set interchange fees not to be socially efficient, though it contains no empirical work demonstrating the existence or estimating the importance of any of these factors. That literature is also essentially unanimous in concluding that even if one or more of these factors leads market-set interchange fees to be socially inefficient, cost-based regulation is not the answer. The Fed Economists provide a clear and succinct summary:

"… [T]he economic theory underlying the efficient interchange fee provides no rationale for either a strictly cost-based interchange fee or an interchange fee of zero."[52]

Professor Calvano's accompanying submission summarizes the key papers by economists that have examined the economics of interchange fees, including papers written too recently to be included in the Fed Economists' survey.[53] As he shows, all of the relevant papers conclude that there is no economic basis for assuming that it would be socially efficient, or would raise consumer

---

[52] The Fed Economists (2009), at p. 48.
[53] Calvano Report, at pp. 4-8.

welfare, to set the interchange fee based only on consideration of costs.[54] That is to say, if there is any substantial market failure that has seemed to be even a theoretical possibility, the one clear message from the literature is that an appropriate remedy cannot be devised without considering more than costs. Thus if the debit card market is suffering from any market failure disease that has so far been imagined, then it is essentially certain that the Board's proposed cost-based medicine would not cure it.

The reason is straightforward: as noted above, the purpose and effect of the interchange fee is to shift costs from one set of a payment system's customers – acquirers and the merchants they serve – to another set – issuers and the consumers they serve. It is not surprising that economic theory makes clear that knowing only the costs involved can tell one nothing about what fraction of those costs each side should bear. A very similar problem arises in the regulation of multi-product single-sided firms with fixed costs, like electric distribution companies. In these situations setting all prices equal to marginal costs does not cover fixed costs. Knowledge of costs alone can tell one nothing about how prices should optimally depart from marginal cost in order to cover total cost. In both settings one must have information on demand conditions.

The Board clearly recognized that it could consider factors other than cost in designing a reasonable remedy and that it was not required to focus only on issuers' costs. At the hearing, Dr. Manuszak noted that the 12 cent cap was higher than actual costs for some issuers but argued that "we're not required … to disallow all profit that might come along."[55] And in discussing the "proportional to cost" language in the statute, Dr. Prager asserted that, "The statute doesn't require the proportion to be the same for every issuer."[56] Thus the Board did not believe it needed to make interchange fees equal to issuers' individual costs or even strictly proportional to issuer-specific costs. Under the same approach the Board could have explicitly considered non-cost factors, including merchant and consumer demand functions, to determine an upper bound on reasonable fees. To put it in the terms of the statute, a rule that considered merchant and consumer demand functions in addition to costs would be an appropriate response to a statute calling for a price that is "reasonable and proportional" to a subset of the costs issuers incur.

The Board's implementation of cost-based regulation departs from good regulatory practice in other settings. In classic public utility regulation, where the argument for cost-based regulation (to mitigate market power coming from a natural monopoly) is strongest, prices are not based on only

---

[54] Economist Alan Frankel has argued that interchange fees should be zero. He argues that privately and jointly set interchange fees may permit the exercise of market power. He does not, however, attempt to demonstrate that an interchange fee of zero is optimal. His papers contain no formal economic analysis and are inconsistent with the formal models of interchange that have been published in peer-reviewed economics journals. See Alan Frankel, "Towards a Competitive Card Payments Marketplace," in Reserve Bank of Australia, Payments System Review Conference, Proceedings of a Conference held in Sydney on November 29, 2007; Alan Frankel and Allan Shampine (2006), "Economic Effects of Interchange Fees," Antitrust Law Journal.

[55] Board December 16, 2010 Open Meeting, at p. 19 of 28.

[56] Ibid.

a subset of variable costs, and fixed costs are not ignored.[57] Here we see no economic justification for considering only some of the variable costs of providing debit cards and for ignoring the associated fixed costs that must somehow be covered.

In fact, whether interchange fee regulation is to be based only on costs or to consider other factors, as even public utility regulation generally does, it should logically take into account all costs incurred by both issuers and acquirers to provide debit card services to merchants and consumers. The difficult issue is how those costs should be covered—that is, who should bear them. Moreover, as debit cards are provided along with other services as features of depository account relationships, there is no obvious economic argument for ignoring account-specific costs that are not specific to debit cards. In short, the Board's implementation of cost-based regulation, even as an interim measure until informative empirical work on other relevant factors can be done, is not economically sound.

VI. ESTIMATING SOCIALLY EFFICIENT INTERCHANGE FEES

In their survey of the theoretical literature, the Fed Economists list some of the non-cost factors that must be studied empirically in order to estimate the gap, if any, between the market-set interchange fee and the socially efficient fee:

"At a minimum, calculation of the efficient interchange fee requires estimation of the demand curves for card services for heterogeneous consumers and merchants, in addition to precise cost data for acquirers, issuers, merchants, and consumers."[58]

Some models imply that additional demand-related factors must also be estimated.

We share the Fed Economists' view that such estimation must be done if interchange fee regulation is to be placed on a sound basis. While such estimation will not be a simple task, we do not believe that it is beyond the capacity of the Board's able staff. After all, the antitrust enforcement agencies – the U.S. Federal Trade Commission and the Antitrust Division of the Department of Justice, as well as their counterparts in the European Union and elsewhere – make decisions on proposed mergers in a variety of industries that are based on estimates of own-price and cross-price elasticities of demand. And they are generally not able to bring to bear anything like the extensive data or the deep experience and expertise that the Board staff can employ to study banking in general and debit card services in particular.

In order to estimate the socially efficient interchange fee, it will be necessary first to determine which of the various models in the literature, or which combination of them, best describes this market. Then that model can be used, perhaps after estimating all its parameters,

---

[57] Viscusi et al. 2005.
[58] The Fed Economists (2009), at p. 18.

to determine whether there is a substantial gap between the market-set interchange fee and the socially efficient fee.

In order to shed some light on the issues involved in such estimation, we have worked with the recently developed model of Bedre-Defolie and Calvano ("BC").[59] The BC analysis, in contrast to most other models in this literature, turns on the fact that consumers choose whether to pay with cards or cash, a feature of this market that Dr. Prager emphasized in her response to Chairman Bernanke.[60] The BC model implies that the socially efficient interchange fee is never above the privately optimal fee and is typically below it. It therefore seems the best readily available theoretical framework for dealing with the market failure that the Board may have implicitly in mind.

In the BC model, merchants are heterogeneous and receive benefits from consumers that vary from transaction to transaction, but they can only decide whether or not to accept cards on the basis of the average expected benefit of doing so. Heterogeneous cardholders, in contrast, can decide how to pay on a transaction-by-transaction basis. It turns out to be both privately profitable and socially efficient to charge merchants only a per-transaction fee but to charge consumers both a per-transaction fee, which could be positive or negative, and a fixed per-period fee for carrying the card. In our setting one can think of the fixed fee as subsumed in the various terms and conditions of a depository account relationship.

As shown in Professor Calvano's submission, the condition that must be satisfied by the socially optimal interchange fee has a relatively simple form under the assumptions that there are no fixed costs to cover, there is a single issuer operating a single network, total transaction volume is fixed, interchange fee changes are fully passed through by issuers and acquirers, and that consumers benefit only from using the card and not from carrying it.

$$\frac{f(i^*)}{m(i^*)} = \frac{\eta_B}{\eta_S} \div \frac{\upsilon_B}{\upsilon_S},$$

Here i^* is the socially optimal interchange fee, f and m, which depend on i^*, are the optimal per-transaction prices paid by issuers (and card-holders) and by acquirers (and merchants), respectively, η_B is the consumers' price elasticity of demand for card usage, η_S is the merchants' price elasticity of demand for card acceptance, and υ_B and υ_S are buyers' and sellers' average surplus per card transaction, respectively. It is important to note that the ratio on the left is independent of the costs of the two sides. If marginal costs change, the socially optimal interchange changes so as to maintain the optimal price ratio, which does not depend on the distribution of costs between issuers and acquirers.

---

[59] Bedre-Defolie and Calvano 2009. The BC analysis appeared too late to be discussed by the Fed Economists, but it clearly builds on and in some sense encompasses much of the literature they survey.
[60] See Board December 16, 2010 Open Meeting, at pp. 8-9 of 28.

The quantities on the right side of this equation depend on the demand curves of heterogeneous consumers and merchants, just as the Fed Economists stated in the quote above. These quantities are not constants and will generally depend on the fees charged to merchants and consumers.

Formulas like the one above, which makes it crystal clear that knowing only costs is not enough to estimate socially optimal interchange fees, also arise in other models in the interchange fee literature.[61] More realistic models that relax some of the assumptions noted above will generally not yield such an algebraically simple result, of course. But the Board's staff has considerable experience in obtaining numerical solutions to very complex economic models.

An experiment with the BC framework, discussed in more detail in the submission by Professor Calvano[62], has persuaded us that when the Board staff conducts the appropriate research and analysis, the Board staff will conclude that the socially efficient interchange fee is very close to the market-set fee. That strongly implies that the proposed regulations, which would lead to dramatic reductions in the market-set fee, would reduce social and consumer welfare. That prediction is, of course, consistent with the evidence we have reported that consumers would lose tens of billions of dollars if the proposed regulations were implemented.[63]

For the experiment, we assume that consumers' and merchants' demand functions are linear. This common modeling assumption dramatically simplifies the expressions for the difference between the market-set interchange fee, i^M, and the socially optimal fee, i^*:[64]

$$i^* = i^M - \frac{v_B + v_S}{12}.$$

If the market-set debit card interchange fee $i^M = 44$ cents,[65] then in order for the socially efficient interchange fee i^* to be equal to 12 cents, as the Board's proposed 12 cent cap proposal implies, the average total surplus per card transaction – the combined benefit to both merchant and consumer from using a card instead of cash or check – would have to be $3.84 (=12(.44-.12)). That is an absurdly high benefit of paying or being paid with a debit card relative to using cash or checks. It would amount to about 10 percent of the total value of the average debit card transaction of $38.50. Under the 7 cent safe harbor proposal the implied benefit would be $4.44, which would be almost 12 percent of the value of the average debit card transaction.

---

[61] See Rochet, Jean-Charles and Jean Tirole (2003), "Platform Competition in Two-sided Markets," *Journal of the European Economic Association*, 1:4, pp. 990-1029, (see equation 7); Rochet and Tirole 2006, (see equation 10); and E. Glen Weyl (2010), "A Price Theory of Multi-Sided Platforms," American Economic Review, 100:4, pp. 1642-72. It can be derived from equations presented in other papers as well.

[62] Calvano Report, at pp. 8-13.

[63] See generally, Consumer Impact Study, at pp 6-8.

[64] We retained the BC assumption that banks can perfectly capture consumer benefits from interchange fee changes. Relaxing that extreme simplifying assumption would lead to a higher value for the privately optimal interchange fee, so that the equation below arguably gives an upper bound on the difference.

[65] The Proposed Rules, at p. 81725.

In light of the ready availability and frequent use of cash, checks, and credit cards, the implied consumer benefit from being able to use a debit card is likely to be at most a small fraction of a dollar. Similarly, merchants' costs of processing transactions are generally measured in dimes, not dollars. This suggests that the Board's proposed cap and safe harbor are significantly below the socially optimal interchange fee.

In addition, we considered the impact of the facts that published interchange fees vary by type of merchant and that the fees for the largest merchants are individually negotiated. BC show (Proposition 5 in their paper) that if all merchants are identical, market-set interchange fees are socially optimal in their model. If interchange fees varied in reality so as to perfectly discriminate among merchants, an assumption that several authors consider plausible,[66] it follows that there would be no gap between market-set and socially efficient fees. Interchange fees in fact vary in a fairly fine-grained fashion by merchant category and merchant size.[67] While the current systems of interchange fees cannot, of course, perfectly discriminate, there would have to be quite substantial heterogeneity not captured by the existing interchange regime in order to support the Board's drastic proposed regulation.

To be sure, these two analyses do not prove that the Board's proposed cut in interchange fees goes far beyond what would be socially efficient, but they suggest that the Board has overshot the mark. Moreover, the Board has apparently not conducted any similar analysis suggesting that it has *not* gone too far and has in fact devised a regulation that will do good and do no harm. Policy makers cannot draw confident assertions about socially optimal interchange fees until the Board staff has done the serious empirical research and analysis necessary to support such assertions.

VII. REGULATING NOW, WITHOUT SOLID ESTIMATES OF SOCIALLY EFFICIENT INTERCHANGE FEES

We understand that the Board is required by Congress to promulgate standards for accessing debit card interchange fees by April 21, 2011 and that these must be implemented by July 21, 2011. We do not believe it will be possible for the Board staff to complete the empirical work necessary to estimate socially efficient interchange rates, starting from February 23, 2011, by April 21, 2011, though we would expect that the Board could complete such as analysis in a matter of months with sufficient resources. Given this situation, we have three basic recommendations for the Board.

---

[66] See Rochet, Jean-Charles and Jean Tirole (2002), "Cooperation among Competitors: Some Economics of Payment Card Associations," *The RAND Journal of Economics*, 33:4, pp. 549-570.; Rochet, Jean-Charles and Jean Tirole (2010), "Must-Take Cards: Merchant Discounts and Avoided Cost," *Journal of the European Economic Association*, forthcoming.; Chakravorti, Sujit and Ted To (2007), "A Theory of Credit Cards," *International Journal of Industrial Organization*, 25:3, pp. 583-595.; and Zhu Wang (2010), "Regulating Debit Cards: The Case of Ad Valorem Fees," Economic Review, 95:1, pp. 71-93.

[67] MasterCard's published debit card rate schedule, for instance, has 41 different categories; see http://www.mastercard.com/us/merchant/pdf/MasterCard_Interchange_Rates_and_Criteria.pdf, at pp. 74-89.

First, the Board should begin now to conduct the economic research necessary to identify the market failure or failures, if any, in the debit card market and to estimate socially efficient interchange fees. In this task, the Board staff should be guided by the extensive economic literature on two-sided markets in general and payments markets in particular.[68] This approach requires the Board to follow the guidance of the Fed Economists and the literature they survey and to abandon the indefensible premise that regulation based on cost alone, and variable cost in particular, can ever be anything but arbitrary.

As noted above, we do not claim that this task will be easy, but the Board is required by law to set standards for accessing reasonable interchange fees. Without a defensible estimate of how, if at all, market-set interchange fees depart from the efficient level, the Board cannot argue that *any* standards it promulgates will not harm consumers and worsen market performance. Moreover, the Board's economic expertise and data-gathering capability should be more than adequate to this task. Given the costs and unintended consequences of regulation, if the gap between market-set fees and the Board's ultimate estimates of socially optimal fees is small, then the Board may best serve the public interest by finding that the default interchange fees set by debit card networks are reasonable and appropriately proportional to cost.

Second, before this necessary research and analysis is completed and duly considered, the Board should not promulgate regulations that are likely to do significant net harm. The proposed drastic cuts in market-set interchange fees would be likely to harm consumers substantially, contrary to the stated intent of the Dodd-Frank Act to protect consumers. Drastic cuts would disrupt depository account relationships, raising fees and reducing services. It does not seem reasonable to impose significant costs of these sorts before conducting a sound and thorough economic analysis that might or might not support the proposed regulations and might, in fact, support a finding that market-set interchange fees are reasonable and thus call for another drastic change in the opposite direction in the future. We have seen no evidence that the socially efficient interchange fee is dramatically lower than the market interchange fee and, as noted above, the evidence suggests that it is not. The greater the cut in interchange fees the Board orders this year, the greater the likelihood of substantial harm to consumers and the greater the disruption to their depository account relationships. These considerations, and the guiding principle that government regulation should first of all do no harm, argue that at most modest reductions in interchanges fees are appropriate at this stage.

Third, the Board, in fact, should seriously consider finding that market-set interchange fees are reasonable and proportional to cost until serious research and analysis proves otherwise. It is quite possible that such a finding would ultimately be supported by the Board's careful empirical analysis. If so, any regulatory apparatus put in place now would need to be dismantled. Moreover, regulation in the absence of any supporting analysis is a throw of the dice with potentially significant risks to consumers. As the Fed Economists concluded, appropriately, "… the possible effects

---

[68] See, for instance, Rysman 2009 and Wright 2004.

of any intervention are highly uncertain."[69] Besides the adverse impacts on consumers that we have discussed, price regulation almost always slows innovation and has a variety of unanticipated, adverse consequences.

We have seen no empirical analysis showing that the efficient interchange fee is substantially below the market-determined rate. Our work with the BC model, which reflects the features of the debit card market that the Board staff appears to find to be most important, suggests otherwise. The market-set interchange fee is presumptively more reasonable than the Board's proposed ceiling in the current state of knowledge given the lack of indicia that performance or output of debit cards has been in any way impaired, and, as costs vary widely among issuers, it seems as "proportional to cost" as the ceilings proposed by the Board. The Board should err on the side of caution and avoid imposing regulations that run the risk of harming consumers.

---

[69] The Fed Economists (2009), at p. 42.

chapter 3

THE EFFECT OF REGULATORY INTERVENTION IN TWO-SIDED MARKETS: AN ASSESSMENT OF INTERCHANGE-FEE CAPPING IN AUSTRALIA

By

Howard Chang, David S. Evans, and Daniel D. Garcia Swartz

I. INTRODUCTION

This article examines the effect of a significant regulatory-mandated alteration in pricing policy in a two-sided industry.[1] In doing so it provides empirical evidence that is helpful for understanding how two-sided industries work. It also sheds light on the interaction between the design of regulatory interventions and the pricing policies in two-sided industries.

In 2003, the Reserve Bank of Australia (RBA) mandated a reduction in the "interchange fee". In the context of a credit card transaction, this is the fee that the bank that acquires the receivable from the merchant pays to the bank that issued the card to the consumer. Three associations of banks in Australia had centrally set the interchange fee at around 0.95 percent of the transaction value. The RBA imposed cost-based regulation that resulted in a reduction of the interchange fee to around 0.55 percent. Absent any other adjustment, this 0.40 percentage-point reduction in interchange fees eliminated roughly AU$490 million in revenues that banks would have received from these fees in 2004.[2]

The credit-card industry is often cited as a classic two-sided product: it intermediates the transactions between merchants and cardholders.[3] This massive regulatory intervention therefore provides a natural experiment, almost, for assessing how an alteration in the price on one side of a two-sided industry affects the other interdependent parts of the system. In addition, more so than many interventions, the RBA's mandated reduction in interchange fees is so substantial that it provides the hope that one can determine empirically whether the intervention achieved its objectives.

After a number of studies, the RBA concluded that interchange fees that were "too high" helped sustain card transaction prices (to consumers) that were "too low" from a social perspective. This resulted in the overuse of cards relative to other, allegedly cheaper, payment instruments. The main objective of the regulation, therefore, was to raise the price of credit transactions to cardholders and thereby reduce the use of cards. Of course, at the time of this writing this experiment has only lasted for less than two years – it is possible at this time to assess only short-run effects.

In Section 2 we provide some background on the Australian credit-card industry. Then we turn in Section 3 to a summary of the RBA's theory for regulatory intervention. Section 4 provides a brief discussion of the possible effects of this intervention based on economic theory. Section 5 presents our empirical analysis and Section 6 lays out its implications for the RBA's intervention. We end with conclusions and suggestions for further research in Section 7.

---

[1] See Rochet and Tirole (2003) for the seminal work on two-sided markets, and Evans and Schmalensee (2005c) for a review of the industrial organization of two-sided markets.
[2] The reduction was 0.40 percent. According to the RBA, total nominal purchase volume on credit and charge cards was about $147 billion in 2004. Furthermore, Bankcard, Visa and MC accounted for about 83.8 percent of total volume in that year, that is they accounted for about $123 billion. See RBA (2005c).
[3] See Baxter (1983), Rochet and Tirole (2002, 2003) and Schmalensee (2002).

II. THE AUSTRALIAN CREDIT CARD INDUSTRY

The geography and demographics of Australia have shaped the card industry and retail sector that are the focus of this paper. Australia had a population of roughly 19 million people in 2001.[4] About 65 percent of its population lived in 8 coastal cities that year.[5] The distance between cities is great and much of the country has a very low population density.

Credit cards were first issued in Australia in 1974. Bankcard, a product that arose from the collaboration among Australian banks, was the first credit card issued in the country – by 1977 it was accepted nationally. As in the rest of the world, MasterCard and Visa marketed their products in Australia as associations of banks. Their cards started gaining traction in the mid-1980s. American Express and Diners Club came to Australia as proprietary systems, while MasterCard and Visa have had members that issue cards to consumers (issuers) and sign up and service merchants to take association cards (acquirers). American Express and Diners Club have acquired merchants on their own.[6]

Banking in Australia is relatively concentrated. There are 53 banking groups in total.[7] The four leading banks are National Australia Bank, Australia & N.Z. Banking Group, Westpac Banking Corp., and Commonwealth Bank Of Australia, which collectively account for 66 percent of total deposits.[8] Furthermore, credit card issuing and acquiring are highly concentrated. In 1999, the cards that the four major banks issued accounted for about 85 percent of all credit card transactions; these same banks accounted for about 93 percent of credit card transactions acquired.[9]

Consider the situation when a consumer presents her card for payment at a merchant. When the entity that serves the cardholder is the same as the entity that serves the merchant, the transaction is "on-us". While the entity may have transfer pricing and other matters to deal with between its issuing and acquiring "divisions", the transaction is internal to the firm. That is always the case for proprietary systems that integrate acquiring and issuing and sometimes the case for association-based systems. When the cardholder and merchant entities differ, they have to have some agreement as to who bears various risks and how the costs and benefits of the transaction get divided up. In principle that could happen through either bilateral negotiations between them, or a fee and

---

[4] See Australian Bureau of Statistics (2001).
[5] See Australian Bureau of Statistics (2003).
[6] See Reserve Bank of Australia (RBA) and Australian Competition and Consumer Commission (ACCC) (2000, p.15). For a general introduction to payment cards see Evans and Schmalensee (2005a). American Express reached an agreement with AMP in 1998 to issue cards in Australia. More prominently, as we discuss below, major Australian banks have signed up with American Express and Diners Club since the RBA's interchange fee regulation.
[7] Excluding subsidiaries. Source: RBA, at http://www.rba.gov.au/FinancialSystemStability/FinancialInstitutionsInAustralia/the_main_types_of_financial_institutions_in_aus.html
[8] See Australian Prudential Regulation Authority (2005). The APRA calculates total deposits as the sum of transaction deposit accounts, non-transaction deposit accounts, and certificates of deposit. It excludes intra-group deposits.
[9] See RBA and ACCC (2000, p.17).

TABLE 1: Shares of major credit and charge card brands, percent of cards on issue, 1999/2000

Brand	Percent of cards on issue
Visa	51.4
MasterCard	22.7
Bankcard	19.2
American Express charge	2.8
American Express credit	2.2
Diners Club	1.7

other contract terms that are set centrally by the association or regulators, or an industry standard that substitutes for an agreement.[10] In Australia, Bankcard, MasterCard, and Visa adopted a multilaterally set fee.[11] As mentioned, that fee was slightly less than one percent of the transaction amount before the regulatory intervention.[12]

The interchange fee is a cost to the acquirer and is passed on to the merchant in whole or in part. The merchant discount is the percent of the transaction that the merchant pays to the acquirer. The merchant service fees for the four card brands were the following just before regulation: for Amex, 2.57 percent; for Diners Club, 2.35 percent; and for Visa and MasterCard, 1.41 percent.[13]

As of 2001, the number of merchants accepting MasterCard, Bankcard, and Visa cards was about twice as large as the number of merchant accepting American Express. The merchant base for Diners Club was apparently smaller than for American Express.[14] At this time there were roughly 13 million credit cards in use by consumers in Australia.[15] Table 1 shows the shares of each brand.

---

[10] See Evans and Schmalensee (2005b) for further discussion on interchange fee setting.

[11] See, for example, RBA (2001, p.14).

[12] According to the Joint Study, the average interchange fee that issuers received in 1999 was 0.95 percent. Strictly speaking, interchange fees differed for Visa and MasterCard depending on whether the transaction was carried out with the "card present" or not. As of the end of 2001, the electronic (card-present) rate for Visa and MasterCard was 0.8 percent and the rate for all other transactions was 1.2 percent. The Bankcard banks charged 1.2 percent on all transactions, although apparently they had agreed to introduce an electronic rate of 0.8 percent toward the end of 2001. See RBA (2001, pp.14-15).

[13] See RBA, Merchant Fees for Credit and Charge Cards, available at http://www.rba.gov.au/Statistics/Bulletin/C03hist.xls

[14] See RBA (2001, p.119).

[15] See RBA and ACCC (2000, p.15).

III. REGULATION AND ITS RATIONALE

The RBA and the Australian Competition and Consumer Commission (ACCC) published a "Joint Study" of payment systems in October 2000.[16] The Joint Study found that credit card interchange fees encouraged the provision of credit card services at negative prices to consumers and this fostered the use of credit cards instead of PIN debit cards, which the Joint Study believed to be a less costly instrument.[17]

In December 2001, the RBA published a "Consultation Document", outlining the need for regulation of the payment system. According to the Consultation Document, the pricing of credit card services was sending "consumers a quite misleading signal about the cost to the community of different payment instruments".[18] The Consultation Document proposed regulating the credit card schemes using "an objective, transparent and cost-based methodology for determining interchange fees".[19]

The Joint Study and the Consultation Document identified three aspects of credit card scheme rules that allegedly impeded the efficiency of the overall payments system – the collective setting of interchange fees, the "no surcharge" rule, and certain restrictions on entry to the schemes. These were the key issues addressed in the regulations introduced in the years that followed.[20] After designating the credit-card schemes as payment systems under its regulation, the RBA undertook a process of consultation and analysis to determine whether the RBA's intervention would be in the public interest. The RBA published final standards regarding interchange fees and the no-surcharge rule in August 2002 and on the access regime in February 2004.[21]

It is outside the purview of this paper to discuss the reasoning and evidence that the RBA relied on in any detail. We provide a quick summary. When customers make a purchase with their credit cards at the point of sale, the acquirer passes the interchange fee costs on to the merchant. With the no-surcharge rule, the merchant cannot effectively charge cardholders for any additional costs it incurs in accepting credit-card payments. As a result the cardholder does not have the correct incentives to use the most efficient form of payment. Prices faced by consumers do not fully reflect social costs and there is a resulting distortion.

The RBA buttressed this argument with evidence suggesting that credit cards are more costly than debit cards. Furthermore, the merchant passes the cost of payment methods onto its customers just like it passes all costs on. Since it cannot charge cardholders specifically for their use of cards, it passes the interchange fee – part of the merchant discount – on to all

---

[16] See RBA and ACCC (2000).
[17] The debit cards the RBA views as less costly are the EFTPOS PIN debit cards, not the Visa debit cards that are also offered. MasterCard does not offer a debit card in Australia.
[18] See RBA (2001, p.vi).
[19] *ibid*, p.116.
[20] See RBA (2004, p.7).
[21] *ibid*, p.7.

TABLE 2:	Timeline of RBA investigation and regulation
Date	Event
October 2000	Publication of the Joint Study
April 2001	Designation of Visa, MC, and Bankcard as payment systems subject to regulation
December 2001	Publication of the Consultation Document
August 2002	Publication of final standards regarding no-surcharge and interchange fees
September 2002	Visa and MC challenge standards in court
January 2003	No-surcharge standard comes into effect
July 2003	Interchange standard comes into effect
September 2003	Court rejects the Visa-MC challenge of the standards
October 2003	New interchange fees are implemented
February 2004	Publication of final standard on entry

Source: RBA and ACCC (2000), RBA (2001), and RBA (2004).

customers. The issuer, in turn, receives interchange fees as revenues. To increase this source of revenue it has incentives to encourage consumers to use their cards and it does so by providing rewards and other inducements. As a result, cardholders face negative prices for using cards and the price of using cards at the point of sale is lower than their cost. This results in a misallocation of resources (the overuse of cards and under-use of allegedly more efficient forms of payment) and a perverse distributional effect (people who do not use cards at the point of sale subsidize cardholders).[22]

In September 2002, MasterCard International and Visa International challenged the RBA's decision in the Federal Court on procedural and jurisdictional grounds. The Court rejected the challenge in September 2003, finding against MasterCard and Visa. The no-surcharge standard came into effect on January 1, 2003. The standard on interchange fees came into effect on July 1, 2003. The Bank required the credit card schemes to publish and put in force the new interchange fees by October 31, 2003. For all practical purposes, in November 2003 interchange fees declined from an average of around 0.95 percent to around 0.55 percent.[23] The timeline is shown in Table 2.

---

[22] We do not dispute this analysis for the purpose of this article; see Evans and Schmalensee (2005b) and Rochet (2005) for some comments. Our focus here is only on whether the RBA intervention achieved its goals.
[23] See RBA (2004, pp.8-9).

IV. SOME THEORETICAL CONSIDERATIONS ON THE EFFECT OF THE INTERVENTION

The effect of this regulation depends on the manner in which prices are determined in this industry and the market structure of the participants. The theory of two-sided markets provides a framework for considering these issues. Businesses in two-sided markets determine price levels and price structures recognizing that the demands of their two customer groups are interdependent (Rochet and Tirole, 2003). Two-part tariffs are common in recognition of the fact that many two-sided bases involve membership and use (Evans and Schmalensee, 2005c). In the case of credit cards, card systems typically have a nominal or zero membership fee for merchants (although merchants do have to buy equipment), a membership fee for cardholders that is greater than or equal to zero (positive fees include an annual fee and various service fees), a usage fee for merchants which is usually a percent of the total transaction, and a usage fee for cardholders that is usually less than zero (float for several weeks, reward miles and other perquisites that are usually a function of volume). Credit cards bundle a transaction and finance feature; cardholders pay a finance fee on the amount they choose not to pay when their bill is due.

Average prices for reward cards with a grace period, as well as merchant fees, as of 2001, are shown in Table 3.

The regulatory intervention did not affect any of these prices directly. However, by reducing the interchange fee by almost half the intervention reduced significantly a major source of revenue to bankcard issuers. This naturally would be expected to lead them to re-equilibrate their prices. While that seems certain as a matter of economic theory, two issues remain open – the extent to which they will adjust fixed versus variable prices, and the extent to which the reduction in prices on one side will get passed on to the other side. There is, to our knowledge,

TABLE 3: Cardholder and merchant fees, 2001	
Nature of fee	**Fee**
I. CARDHOLDER FEES	
Annual fee – standard cards (AU$)	48
Annual fee – gold cards (AU$)	87
Late payment fee (AU$)	20
Over-limit fee (AU$)	6
II. MERCHANT FEES (*)	
Merchant service fee – Visa, MasterCard, and Bankcard	1.41 percent
Merchant service fee – American Express	2.55 percent

Sources: RBA (2005a). (*) The merchant service fees are from March 2003. The source is Merchant Fees for Credit and Charge Cards, available at http://www.rba.gov.au/Statistics/Bulletin/C03hist.xls

no off-the-shelf theoretical guidance on how a binding ceiling on one of the four possible prices will affect the other three prices in a two-sided market. As in other markets, the extent to which the loss in revenue from merchants will get passed on to cardholders depends on the degree of competition among card issuers. Given that card issuing in Australia is relatively concentrated we would not expect full pass through, at least in the short run.[24]

It is well known that in perfectly competitive markets there is full pass through of cost changes. A $1 decrease in marginal costs will lead to a $1 decrease in price. With imperfectly competitive markets the extent of pass through depends as a theoretical matter on the shape of the demand curve.[25] With linear demand curves there is less than a 100 percent pass through of costs to final consumers. For the very small cost decreases involved here it is reasonable to assume linear demand (since the curvature of demand can be ignored for such small changes) and therefore to expect less than 100 percent pass-through as a matter of theory. Empirical studies tend to find less than 100 percent pass through more frequently than greater than 100 percent pass through; the greater-than-100-percent pass through rate appears to happen in the empirical tax incidence literature and the empirical effects are confounded with the sticky-price issue discussed below.[26] Thus, we would expect less than 100 percent pass-through as an empirical matter.

---

[24] See below for a discussion of the theoretical and empirical evidence on the degree of pass through.

[25] Cotterill (1998) provides a summary of the relationship between market structure and cost pass through. If the industry is perfectly competitive and firms maximize profits, then the rate of pass through is 100 percent, no matter what the value of the market elasticity of demand is. If the industry is a monopoly, demand for its product is linear, and the monopolist maximizes profits, the pass through rate is less than 100 percent. More specifically, for a monopolist that faces a linear demand curve, the pass through rate is 50 percent. See, for example, Bulow and Pfleiderer (1983). If, on the other hand, a monopolist faces a constant-elasticity demand curve over the relevant range it is possible that pass through could be greater than 100 percent. Assuming a linear demand curve is reasonable for small changes in costs but not necessarily for larger changes in cost.

[26] The empirical literature on pass through is fairly vast and covers a number of areas, including exchange rate and tax rate pass through to prices. The literature on pass through of exchange rate changes to domestic prices of traded goods finds that the median rate of pass through is roughly 50 percent for shipments to the US. See Goldberg and Knetter (1997). In the context of the proposed merger between Staples and Office Depot, Ashenfelter et al (1998) made a distinction between the firm-specific cost pass through rate and the industry-wide pass through rate – that is, the reaction of the firm's prices to changes in its own costs and to changes in costs common to all firms in the industry. They found that the firm-specific pass through rate for Staples was roughly 15 percent, whereas the industry wide pass through rate was around 57 percent. Furthermore, there is a literature focused on pass through of trade promotions to retail prices, which is a form of firm-specific pass through. There are a number of relevant studies in this area, including Chevalier and Curhan (1976), Walters (1989), Armstrong (1991), and Besanko, Dube, and Gupta (2005). Besanko et al (2005) analyze the degree of pass through of trade promotions using scanner data for eleven product categories at a Chicago supermarket chain. 8 out of 11 categories show pass through rates of less than 100 percent. At a more disaggregated level, only 165 products out of 1164 (about 14 percent) show pass through rates significantly larger than 100 percent. Besanko et al (2005) cite a study of trade promotions according to which retailers themselves said that they pass through roughly 62 percent of the promotion, use 24 percent to cover promotion costs, and keep the rest as profits. In the context of this literature, Blattberg et al (1985) suggest that, as an empirical matter, most products display pass through rates much smaller than 100 percent. Furthermore, Tyagi (1999) suggests that pass through rates of less than 100 percent should occur much more frequently than pass through rates of more than 100 percent, since the set of demand functional forms that imply less than 100 percent pass through is quite large. It seems to us that pass through rates of more than 100 percent are less frequent as an empirical matter than rates of less than 100 percent, and they tend to appear most often in the tax incidence literature. Poterba (1996), for example, is unable to reject the hypothesis of 100 percent pass through for the commodities he examines, but Besley and Rosen (1999) find greater than 100 percent pass through for several of the commodities in their sample. In line with our discussion of sticky prices below, note that empirical estimates of pass through mix pass through effects and sticky price effects.

There is a further consideration, from a theoretical perspective, on how the regulatory intervention would affect final good prices. It is well known that many prices are sticky in the short run (Stigler and Kindahl, 1970; and Carlton, 1986). Of particular interest in our case is the finding that prices tend to rise faster than they fall. A number of studies in the 1990s found that retail prices respond faster to input price increases than to input price decreases (Karrenbrock, 1991; Newmark and Sharpe, 1992; Borenstein, Cameron, and Gilbert, 1997; and Jackson, 1997). More recently, Peltzman (2000) confirmed this finding with a large sample of consumer and producer goods. This is especially important for considering short-run versus long-run effects of the intervention.

The credit-card acquiring business in Australia is highly concentrated. The four major banks accounted for 93 percent of credit card transactions acquired in 1999.[27] In contrast, the share of the four major acquirers in the United States is around 41 percent.[28] As we note below, the RBA has reported that the reductions in the interchange fee appear to have been fully passed through to merchants. This is not surprising because, despite the relative concentration of acquirers, many merchants are large customers and can bargain effectively with acquirers. In addition, the acquirers are aware that their actions have been monitored closely by the RBA. As noted above, credit-issuing is also highly concentrated. We would therefore not anticipate full pass-through and, at least for the short-run, that is what we find.

Comprehensive government statistics on merchant concentration are not available for Australia. We have identified what data we could find from a range of sources. Many merchant categories appear to have significant levels of concentration. For example, within their respective categories, the top department store had a 71 percent share (and the top two had an 83 percent share) in 2003;[29] the top three supermarket and grocery stores had a 75.4 percent share in the late 1990s;[30] the top two mobile telephone operators had a 78 percent share in 2005; the top land-line telephone operator had a 75 percent share in 2005;[31] and the top two airlines had an 83 percent share in 2005.[32]

There are significant differences between the cardholder and merchant sides of the business that likely affect relative pass through rates to consumers on each side. The regulatory intervention caused issuers to experience a significant reduction in revenue (which could also be viewed as an increase in costs). That makes menu costs and other sources of sticky prices less binding. Moreover,

---

[27] See RBA and ACCC (2000, pp.16-17).
[28] These calculations are based on data from HSN Consultants Inc. (2003).
[29] See Euromonitor International (2005a).
[30] See http://www.aph.gov.au/senate/committee/retail_ctte/report/c04.htm. The Australian Bureau of Statistics reported the 75.4-percent figure, which was based on sales of all supermarkets and grocery stores, including the non-petrol sales of convenience stores at petrol stations. Furthermore, Euromonitor International (2005b) estimated that, in 2003, the size of the total grocery stores/food retailers/supermarkets sector was AU$ 72.5 billion and the supermarket sub-sector represented 60.5 percent of that. The top two supermarkets had a combined market share (in the total sector) of 37.9 percent. Therefore, they had a combined market share in the supermarket sub-sector of 62.6 percent.
[31] See Maxwell (2005).
[32] See Bureau of Transportation Statistics (2000).

it appears that it is quite easy for issuers to adjust prices by varying service and other card fees. For example, it seems that average annual fees on standard and gold cards changed (in a non-trivial manner) every year between 2000 and 2004.[33] Lastly, linear demand is a more reasonable assumption for the merchants who experience a small relative cost decrease than for issuers who experience a relatively large cost increase (decreased interchange fees).

The main source of friction for issuers concerns the annual fee and other prices that issuers commit to in trying to persuade people to take their cards or to switch from another card. Cards are replaced about every three years; consequently that is the opportunity to institute or increase annual fees for current cardholders. For new solicitations it is easy to change fees whenever the solicitation goes out.

Merchants on the other hand experienced a relatively small reduction in cost. If fully passed through by acquirers, the interchange fee reduction amounts to less than half a percent of their selling price (and only on those transactions that take place on credit cards). The evidence on price rigidities, and particularly the one on asymmetric price responses cited above, makes one doubt that such a small cost reduction would affect final goods prices very quickly, even if there were extensive retail competition. We return to this point below.

V. EMPIRICAL ANALYSIS: PRICES AND QUANTITIES

Although there was a sharp reduction in interchange fees on a particular date as a result of the RBA intervention, we cannot simply compare markets before and after this intervention. The credit-card industry learned over the course of several years that an intervention was increasingly likely. Furthermore, over time it developed a sense of the impact that the intervention would have. We thus begin by examining the time line a bit more carefully.

Although regulated interchange fees did not come into effect until the end of October 2003, there was anticipation that regulation was coming. That is not to say, however, that even if a bank in say January 2002 was certain that regulation would be implemented in October 2003, it would necessarily have changed its pricing or strategy in January 2002, since interchange fee levels for itself and its competitors were still at prior levels. Nor does it mean that a bank would necessarily wait until the actual date of the regulation to change its behavior. A bank would not offer a cardholder annual fees in, say, September 2003 based on pre-regulation interchange fee levels if it knew that the post-regulation levels would be in place two months later.

Our best estimate on timing is that there were at least some changes in bank behavior in early 2003 in anticipation of the regulatory intervention.[34] The annual report for one of the major banks, ANZ, noted that in 2003 it had reshaped its "product set across the Australian Cards

---

[33] See RBA (2005a).
[34] Some changes in fees may have been happened already in 2002.

Issuing portfolio to address the impact of the Reserve Bank interchange reforms".[35] There are a number of newspaper articles along the same lines in the period prior to October 2003.[36] The *Sunday Telegraph* (Sydney), for example, reported in its September 21, 2003 edition that the five major banks had increased credit card fees by up to 50 percent in the previous 12 months. The article goes on to quote a bank executive who expressed that the rise in fees had the goal of making up for the loss in interchange income that would happen after the implementation of the regulatory scheme.[37] In our analyses below, we consider whether we see any effect of regulation starting in 2003 and, alternatively, starting in 2004.

We analyse two questions: (1) How did the intervention affect prices to issuers, cardholders, merchants, and consumers? (2) What was the effect of the intervention on card use? Appendix A provides information on our data sources and detailed statistical results for interested readers.

A. Effect on prices

1. Issuers and cardholders

Visa Australia provided the data used in the calculations in this section. The dataset was constructed with information from the operating certificates that banks submit to the Visa organization. The dataset provides quarterly information on the number of Visa credit cards, credit card purchase volume, other service charges (that is, fees that issuers charge cardholders, primarily annual fees and service fees), finance charges, and outstanding balances on credit cards in Australia between the third quarter of 1992 and the first quarter of 2005.[38]

Between the last quarter of 1992 and the fourth quarter of 1999, real interchange income per Visa card grew at an average quarterly compound rate of about 4.2 percent, from around AU$5.79 to around AU$18.34, driven by the rise in purchase volume per card.[39] Between the first quarter of 2000 and the third quarter of 2003, the quarter prior to the introduction of the new interchange rates, real interchange income per card grew at an average quarterly compound rate of about 3.12 percent, from around AU$17.26 to around AU$26.55.

Interchange-fee regulation was implemented in the fourth quarter of 2003. If we compare the first two quarters of 2003 with the first two of 2004, we find that issuers lost, on average and in real terms, about AU$9.35 per card in interchange income per quarter, a loss of about 40 percent on total interchange income per card of about AU$23.52 per quarter in the first two quarters of 2003.

---

[35] See ANZ (2003, p.31).
[36] See, for example, McKinnon (2001), Hanna (2002), Brammall (2002, 2003), Horan (2003), and Graeme (2003).
[37] See Horan (2003).
[38] At the time of this writing the information on other service charges and finance charges was available only through the second quarter of 2004.
[39] As noted above, all figures are reported in real 2004 Australian dollars.

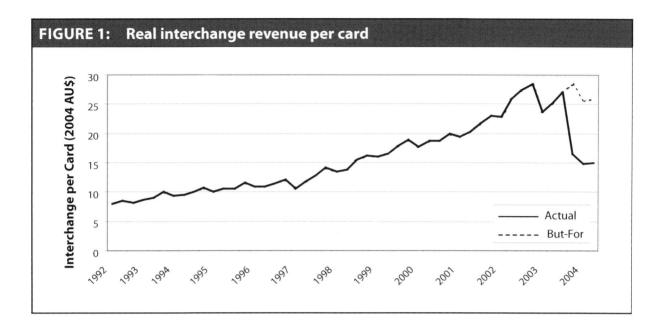

FIGURE 1: Real interchange revenue per card

A more interesting way to look at this loss is to ask how much the issuers would have made in interchange income in the absence of regulation. From this perspective, we calculate a "but for" interchange income per card under the assumption that the regulatory scheme was not implemented and the interchange rate remained at an average of 0.95 percent. We then subtract the actual interchange income per card from the "but for" interchange income per card and we find that, on average, in the first two quarters of 2004 issuers lost about AU$10.31 per quarter per card. This represents a loss of about 42 percent with respect to the interchange income they would have obtained in the "but for" world. Figure 1 shows these facts.

The evidence thus suggests that issuers started losing, in real terms, roughly between AU$9.30 and AU$10.30 per card per quarter in interchange income as a consequence of the RBA intervention. In the months that followed the introduction of the regulation (and likely in the months that preceded the regulation as well) they recovered between 30 and 40 percent of that loss through the imposition of higher fees.

Appendix A provides the support for this conclusion. A regression model that compares the level of real other service charges per card after regulation with the level before, controlling for seasonal effects, changes in the real purchase volume per card, and changes in unobserved factors over time, suggests that the regulation (or its anticipation) was accompanied by a rise in real other service charges of roughly 30 to 40 percent of the interchange loss amount. (As we discuss further in the appendix, the quarterly Visa data we used track closely with annual RBA data on fees. The increase in issuer annual and service fee revenue per card from 2001 to 2003 was AU$20.84 from the RBA data and AU$22.78 from the Visa data.) A similar model for real finance charges per card produces positive coefficients for the post-regulation period. The coefficients, however, are for the most part not statistically significant. Furthermore, we found no evidence of a structural break (associated with the RBA regulation) in the interest rate that issuers charge on outstanding balances.

The components of the "other service fees" variable from the Visa data are annual fees and service fees. Annual fees are fixed with respect to transaction volume. Service fees (such as late payment fees and over-limit fees) are also primarily fixed fees. A late payment fee, for example, is independent of the amount charged.[40]

In addition to the increases estimated above for these fixed fees, there has also been an impact on the level of rewards offered by issuers. The RBA has reported that the average reward decreased from 0.8 to 0.6 percent for most of the bank schemes.[41] While rewards (miles or points accumulated as a function of purchase volume) affect marginal incentives to use cards, the way in which issuers have implemented changes has likely limited the impact on purchase volume. First, some of the changes have been in the form of caps on the number of reward points accumulated. For example, National Australia Bank (NAB) capped rewards on its Visa rewards card. It offers 1 point for each dollar spent up to AU$3,000 per month. Above the $3,000 a month spending threshold, cardholders receive 1 point for every two dollars spent, up to a maximum of 13,000 points a month. For cardholders below the AU$3,000 threshold, the marginal incentive to use cards has not changed as a result of the imposition of the cap.[42]

For customers who are likely to exceed the monthly cap on a regular basis, the marginal incentives have changed on the NAB Visa rewards card. However, one of NAB's other responses to the regulation was to partner with American Express, in offering a rewards card without a cap (in fact offering 1.5 points for each dollar in the first year). Similarly, Westpac now offers an American Express rewards card and ANZ offers a Diners Club rewards card, both without rewards caps and both more generous than the MasterCard/Visa rewards cards from the respective banks.[43] As we note below, while the interchange fee regulation appears to have had relatively little effect to date

---

[40] The over-limit fee may be partially variable, in the sense that a consumer may be more likely to exceed the credit limit at higher purchase volumes. But it is not clear that higher over-limit fees would significantly affect consumer purchase volume on credit cards. Among other things, over-limit fees would appear to be more directly related to accumulated revolving balances as opposed to purchase volume (although the two are related).

[41] See Testimony of Dr. Philip Lowe, House of Representatives Standing Committee on Economics, Finance and Public Administration (EFPA) (2005), at pp.26-27. There is insufficient detail on this data point for us to conduct a detailed analysis. The RBA does not report, for example, how this estimate is constructed, nor does it provide a data series over time (or even which years are the beginning and end points). It is also unclear whether this includes rewards for cards issued on the American Express and Diners Club systems.

[42] The cost of having rewards cards has increased, which may result in fewer consumers deciding to hold them, but contingent on having a card, the marginal incentive to use a card has not changed for consumers below the threshold.

[43] See, Westpac Bank, at http://www.westpac.com.au/internet/publish.nsf/Content/PBCCCSCR+Altitude; ANZ Bank, at http://www.anz.com/australia/support/library/MediaRelease/MR20030912.pdf

on overall card volume, it does appear to have switched cards from MasterCard and Visa to the American Express and Diners Club systems.[44]

What we have estimated is the short-run impact. Since cardholders are valuable assets – issuers spend considerable resources to acquire new cardholders and pay a premium on portfolio purchases – one would expect issuers to be cautious in raising prices quickly to their existing mature cardholder portfolio. Over the longer run, as cardholders switch from one issuer to another, one would expect price effects to be more fully realized.

2. *Acquirers, merchants, and consumers*

According to the RBA, the reduction in interchange fees imposed by regulation led to a reduction in merchant service fees (that is, the merchant discount). The average merchant service fee that the now regulated systems charge fell from 1.41 percent immediately before regulation to 0.99 percent in the quarter ending June 2004.[45] The RBA estimates that the fall in the merchant discount represents savings to merchants of over $500 million per annum.[46]

We consider the extent to which this decrease in costs to merchants was passed on to consumers.[47] To begin with, the reduction in cost was quite small for retailers. The cost of a credit-card transaction made with a BankCard, MasterCard or Visa card fell by 0.42 percent. However, these transactions comprise only about a quarter of retail transactions.

According to the RBA, total purchase volume on credit and charge cards in 2004 was roughly AU$147 billion, and the regulated systems accounted for 83.8 percent of that (that is, roughly 123 billion). Total household consumption in 2004 was roughly AU$500 billion, so that purchase volume on regulated credit cards represented roughly 25 percent of total consumption. To be conservative, we take the card share of retail transactions to be 50 percent, which will likely overstate the card share for many merchants, especially those in the service sector.[48] Taking this 50 percent

---

[44] See EFPA (2005, p.25). See also, Diners Club of Australia website, at http://www.dinersclub.com.au/s06_media/p62_view.asp?id=144

[45] See RBA (2004, p.9).

[46] We have not made any attempts to verify this independently. In any case, according to the RBA, total nominal purchase volume on credit and charge cards was about $147 billion in 2004. According to the RBA, Bankcard, Visa and MC accounted for about 83.8 percent of total volume in that year, that is they accounted for about $123 billion. The reduction in the merchant discount was 0.0042 percentage points, which gives savings to merchants of roughly $517 million.

[47] The RBA claimed in testimony before the Australian House of Representatives in 2005 that these cost savings would be passed on almost entirely to final consumers. It reasoned that the retail sector overall was not concentrated even though particular segments such as supermarkets were. This analysis ignores the point, of course, that the extent of pass through depends on the structure of the relevant market, which is not overall retail but the individual markets that comprise it. Testimony of Mr. Ian MacFarlane, House of Representatives Standing Committee on Economics, Finance and Public Administration (EFPA) (2005), at pp.23-24.

[48] The 25 percent figure of share of cards of total consumption may be an underestimate of the percent of retail transaction dollars on cards since the consumption figure includes some non-retail merchants where cards are not commonly used. Unfortunately, more precise data are not available for Australia. In the United States, where the card share of total consumption is only slightly higher than Australia, the portion of transactions at merchants paid for with cards is slightly under 50 percent for retail and travel and entertainment merchants, and less than 10 percent for service merchants.

estimate, then the average reduction in overall merchant costs as a result of the interchange fee reduction was 50 percent of 0.42 percent or 0.21 percent.

There are three reasons, mentioned earlier, why we would expect that prices to consumers would have fallen by less than 0.21 percent. First, this decrease in costs amounts to roughly 8 cents on an AU$40 transaction. The empirical literature on price rigidities makes it doubtful that a decrease in cost of this small magnitude would be passed on to consumers quickly. Second, many of the significant retail markets in Australia are highly concentrated. Given the small decrease in cost it is reasonable to approximate the demand curve facing these merchants with a linear demand curve. In this case, pass through rates will be less than 100 percent. Third, it seems that the empirical evidence on pass through – while not specific to Australia – finds rates of less than 100 percent more often than rates of more than 100 percent.[49] With a 50 percent pass through rate, the reduction in prices to consumers from the RBA's interchange fee reduction would be 0.105 percent. That amounts to roughly 4 cents on a AU$40 transaction. It would not require much in the way of price rigidities for merchants to decide not to adjust prices in the short run.

The very little empirical evidence there is suggests that, in fact, merchants have tended not to pass through the reduction in the merchant discount to consumers in the form of lower prices. Cannex, an independent research group, surveyed merchants in Australia regarding the impact of the interchange fee regulation on their regular business practices.[50] Among merchants who reported a change in the merchant discount during the previous year, less than 5 percent declared that they had reduced prices to consumers. On the other hand, more than 20 percent reported that their profits had increased and almost 60 percent reported that they had not experienced any changes in their regular operations.

Surcharging for credit card transactions, following the repeal of non-surcharge rules, is still the exception in Australia, as it has been in other countries.[51] One survey of Australian merchants in November 2004 found that only 2.3 percent of all merchants surcharged, with larger merchants slightly more likely to surcharge, at slightly over 5 percent.[52] A different survey found that 7 percent of all merchants surcharged regularly.[53] It is also worth noting that the average surcharge was 1.8 percent, which is higher than the merchant discount fee on credit card transactions, and also almost surely higher than any differential between the costs to merchants of processing credit cards versus other forms of

---

[49] See *supra* notes 25-26.
[50] See Cannex Australia (2004).
[51] Only about 10 percent of merchants imposed surcharges in the Netherlands, and only about 5 percent of merchants imposed surcharges in Sweden. Surcharging is also uncommon in the United Kingdom. See Evans & Schmalensee (2005b, p.27).
[52] See Network Economics Consulting Group (NECG) (2005, p.46), citing East & Partners 2004, "Australian merchant acquiring and cards markets: Multiclient market analysis report," December.
[53] The survey reported that 19 percent of merchants "sometimes" surcharged, but it is unclear how commonly and on what criteria they did so. Two other surveys that asked incidental questions on surcharging reported that 12 percent and 2.9 percent, respectively, of respondents surcharged (although the frequency of surcharging was unknown). See NECG (2005, p.44).

payment. This suggests that at least some of the surcharging that takes place may be opportunistic and does not increase the efficiency of relative prices for payment instruments facing consumers.

B. Effect on transaction volume

If the preceding estimates are correct we can make some surmises about the effect of the regulatory intervention on transaction volumes. It appears that cardholders are not facing substantially different prices at the point of sale for using credit cards. The usage prices assessed by the issuers do not appear to have risen generally and remain negative in many cases. At the same time the preponderance of merchants are not availing themselves of surcharging. Therefore, holding the number of cards constant we have no reason to expect more than a modest change in the volume of transactions in the short run.

However, the increase in fixed fees means that we would expect that fewer individuals have cards. The elasticity of demand of card membership with respect to membership and usage fees determines the relative decline in cardholders. We would expect that any decline in usage of MasterCard and Visa cards as a result of a decline in membership would take place gradually as people adjust the number of cards they have. A further complication is that the RBA did not impose any price regulation on American Express and Diners Club. Some banks have started issuing American Express cards, in particular, in response to the higher effective price they receive for those cards relative to the regulated MasterCard and Visa cards. Therefore, from the standpoint of a regulatory desire to reduce the use of cards, we need to consider total credit-card transactions and not just those of the regulated systems.

Despite a rather massive regulatory intervention that eliminated about 30 percent of issuer revenue in the stroke of a pen,[54] there is little evidence to date that the intervention has significantly affected the use of credit cards in Australia. At the same time it appears that some proportion of transaction volume has moved from association cards to proprietary cards.[55]

Figure 2 shows the level and growth rate of real purchase volume on credit cards along with key points in the timeline for the regulatory intervention. Despite the massive degree of the RBA's intervention, there appears to be no evidence of any effect of the intervention on the use of cards. Table 4 goes into more detail by showing the trends over time in several measures of card use.

Other than the number of accounts, the indicators of credit-card use grew at an increasing rate through 1999 and then grew at a declining rate through 2002. Assessing the impact of the RBA's regulation depends on our assumptions about card industry performance in the absence of regulation. For example, if the question is whether the regulations stopped the growth of card ownership and usage, then the answer is "no" – all card metrics continued to grow post-regulation. Our main focus is on two different questions, namely (1) whether growth rates were lower post-regulation

---

[54] In this calculation we are excluding revenues derived from the so-called "interest margin".
[55] According to the RBA data, the regulated systems accounted for 86.3 percent of the total value of credit card purchases in September 2003. In June 2005 they accounted for 83 percent. See the market-share data available at http://www.rba.gov.au/Statistics/Bulletin/C02hist.xls

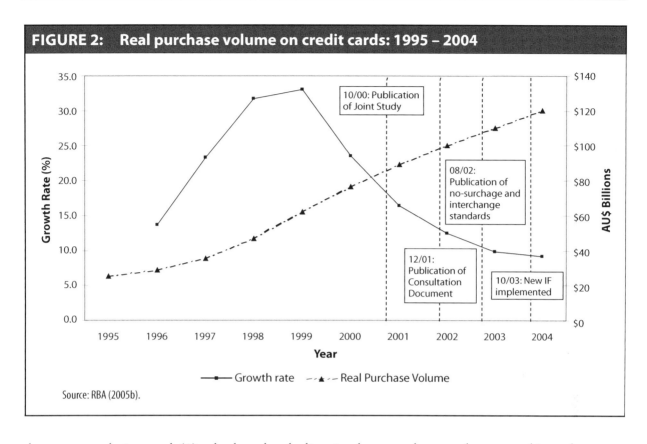

FIGURE 2: Real purchase volume on credit cards: 1995 – 2004

Source: RBA (2005b).

than pre-regulation and (2) whether the decline in the growth rates that was taking place pre-regulation accelerated or decelerated.

The aggregate data suggest that (1) industry growth was lower after regulation than before, with the exception of the number of accounts, and (2) the decline in the rates of growth that started around 1999 has continued, again with the exception of the number of accounts, but has not accelerated. These basic empirical regularities are confirmed by our detailed analysis discussed below. The first comparison would say that regulation has lowered the growth rates, while the second would say that the decline in the growth rates was already taking place and the regulation had relatively little impact. Our prior is that the second comparison is more appropriate, as we observe a significant slowdown in the rate of growth in the pre-regulation period. We acknowledge, however, that our analysis does not come close to explaining the dramatic shifts in industry output that have taken place – either the accelerating growth leading up to 1999 or the decelerating growth following 1999. Therefore, we believe it is at least possible that absent regulation, growth rates of the different card metrics might have levelled off, or even increased.[56]

---

[56] For example, the entry of Virgin as an issuer in 2004 could have increased output, all else equal. To the extent that is true, our comparisons would underestimate the impact of the RBA's regulation. We do not have detailed and systematic data on industry concentration, or on entry and exit, to attempt to control for these factors.

TABLE 4:	Annual growth rates of indicators of credit card use, all credit cards, 1996–2004				
	Accounts	Purchase Transactions	Purchase Transactions per Account	Real Purchase Volume	Real Purchase Volume per Account
1996	7.7	14.2	6.1	13.7	5.6
1997	5.6	19.7	13.3	23.3	16.7
1998	6.1	30.8	23.2	31.7	24.2
1999	5.9	32.5	25.1	33.0	25.6
2000	7.0	24.0	15.9	23.5	15.5
2001	2.5	16.9	14.0	16.4	13.5
2002	1.5	13.9	12.2	12.4	10.7
2003	4.7	8.9	4.0	9.9	4.9
2004	6.0	8.7	2.5	9.2	3.0

Source: all the growth rates have been calculated on the basis of RBA (2005c).

In order to address the first question – that is, whether growth rates were lower post-regulation – we estimated a number of simple regression models of the quarterly growth rates of the credit card use variables on a set of quarterly binary variables, a binary variable that takes on the value 1 between 2000 and 2002 and 0 otherwise,[57] and a binary variable that takes on the value 1 starting in 2003. The results are reported in Table 4a.[58]

The interpretation of these results is straightforward. In the case of the number of accounts, growth rates in the regulated period have been no different from what they were through 2000 and higher than they were in 2001-2002. In the case of all other variables, however, growth rates in the regulated period have been lower than they were through 1999 and also lower than they were in 2000-2002. From this perspective, the regulated period has been associated mostly with lower growth rates in the indicators of credit card use.

We then addressed the second question – that is, has the decline in the growth rates that started in the late 1990s accelerated or decelerated with regulation? We used regression methods to examine more carefully whether credit card activity grew more slowly than it would have in a

---

[57] In the accounts model this binary variable takes on the value 1 in 2001-2002 rather than in 2000-2002.
[58] All the regressions include binary variables for the second, third, and fourth quarters on the right hand side. When the growth rate in the number of accounts is the dependent variable, we control for changes in population and income per capita. In the case of the number of purchases and real purchase volume, we control for changes in real consumption. In the case of the number of purchases per account and real purchase volume per account, we control for changes in consumption per capita.

TABLE 4a: Regression of the quarterly growth rates of the credit-card-use variables on a binary variable for 2000-2002 and a binary variable for the regulated period (P-values calculated on the basis of Newey-West standard errors)

Growth in Number of Accounts		
2001-2002	-0.0096	0.000
2003-2005	-0.0013	0.682
P-value for F test of equality between binary-variable coefficients = 0.0116		
Growth in Number of Purchases		
2000-2002	-0.013	0.214
2003-2005	-0.033	0.001
P-value for F test of equality of binary-variable coefficients = 0.0184		
Growth in Number of Purchases per Account		
2000-2002	-0.007	0.362
2003-2005	-0.032	0.002
P-value for F test of equality of binary-variable coefficients = 0.0026		
Growth in Real Purchase Volume		
2000-2002	-0.012	0.278
2003-2005	-0.033	0.001
P-value for F test of equality of binary-variable coefficients = 0.0259		
Growth in Real Purchase Volume per Account		
2000-2002	-0.007	0.445
2003-2005	-0.032	0.002
P-value for F test of equality of binary-variable coefficients = 0.0021		

world without the RBA regulation. We studied the growth patterns in greater detail by regressing the growth rates of the relevant variables on a linear spline function.[59] We performed the analysis with annual data and quarterly data. With quarterly data, we calculated proportional growth rates between quarter q and quarter $(q-1)$.[60]

---

[59] On linear spline functions see, for example, Poirier (1976, ch. 2); Poirier and Garber (1974); Johnston (1983, p.392ff); and Greene (1993, p.235ff). For a study that uses linear splines in the context of testing for the existence of unit roots in economic time series, see Perron (1989). For a discussion of the various Perron models, see, for example, Enders (2004, pp. 200-207).

[60] We also performed the analysis with the growth rates calculated between quarters q and $(q-4)$. Although the magnitude of the coefficients was, of course, different, the substance of the conclusions we draw did not change much.

We describe the model on the basis of quarterly data. We first created a linear trend t that starts at 1 in the first quarter for which growth rates can be calculated and grows by 1 every quarter through the first quarter of 2005. We then defined the spline time dimension variables as follows:

$$X(t) = t, t = 1, 2, \ldots, T;$$
$$Y(t) = \max(0, t - a);$$
$$Y(t)' = \max(0, t - b); \text{ and}$$
$$Z(t) = \max(0, t - c).$$

In this model, a is the number that corresponds to the last quarter of 1999 in the trend sequence, b is the number that corresponds to the last quarter of 2000, and c is the number that corresponds to the last quarter of 2002.

Think of a world where the number of credit card accounts, the number of credit card purchases, and the real purchase volume on credit cards are functions of a set of demand shifters. For example, the number of credit card accounts is a function of population and income per capita, and the number of credit card purchases is a function of real consumption. Then in order to assess whether there have been significant changes in the trend of the growth rates of the credit card use variables, we can estimate models of the following form:

$$G_{CC}(t) = \alpha_1 + \delta_{11} X(t) + \delta_{12} Y(t) + \delta_{13} Z(t) + \gamma_1 C(t) + u_1(t), \text{ or}$$
$$G_{CC}(t) = \alpha_2 + \delta_{21} X(t) + \delta_{22} Y(t)' + \delta_{23} Z(t) + \gamma_2 C(t) + u_2(t).$$

In these models, $G_{CC}(t)$ stands for the growth rate of the credit-card-use variable in question and $C(t)$ stands for the growth rate of the relevant demand shifter. These models focus on the percentage-point change in growth rates over time.[61]

The δ_{i1} parameters (for i = 1, 2) capture the trend in the growth rate between the starting point and 1999 (or between the starting point and 2000). The δ_{i2} parameters capture the change in the trend of the growth rate over 1999-2002 relative to the previous period (or 2000-2002 relative to the previous period). The δ_{i3} parameters, finally, capture the change in the trend of the growth rate over 2003-2004 (the regulatory period) relative to 1999- 2002 (or 2000-2002).

The estimated parameters with the p-values calculated on the basis of the Newey-West standard errors are reported below in **Table 5**.[62]

---

[61] The results we obtain do not change in any substantive manner if we exclude the demand shifters from the estimated regressions.

[62] All the regressions include binary variables for the second, third, and fourth quarters on the right hand side. When the growth rate in the number of accounts is the dependent variable, we control for changes in population and income per capita. In the case of the number of purchases and real purchase volume, we control for changes in real consumption. In the case of the number of purchases per account and real purchase volume per account, we control for changes in consumption per capita. We also tried estimating the models via instrumental variables – we instrumented the growth in real consumption and the growth in real consumption per capita. We calculated the Newey-West standard errors for the IV-estimated coefficients. Overall, as far as the trend coefficients are concerned, the results were not substantially different from the ones obtained via OLS with Newey-West standard errors. We also calculated feasible-generalized-least-squares (Prais-Winsten) estimates. The conclusions we draw did not change under the FGLS approach.

TABLE 5:	Regression of the growth rate of the credit-card-use variables on a linear spline function on the basis of quarterly data, 1994-2005 (P-values calculated on the basis of Newey-West standard errors)	
Growth in Number of Accounts		
d(1)	0.0001	0.592
d(2)	-0.0018	0.001
d(3)	0.0039	0.000
Growth in Number of Purchases		
d(1)	0.0021	0.000
d(2)	-0.0066	0.000
d(3)	0.0044	0.003
Growth in Number of Purchases per Account		
d(1)	0.0018	0.001
d(2)	-0.0049	0.000
d(3)	0.0010	0.499
Growth in Real Purchase Volume		
d(1)	0.0020	0.002
d(2)	-0.0063	0.000
d(3)	0.0044	0.005
Growth in Real Purchase Volume per Account		
d(1)	0.0016	0.014
d(2)	-0.0047	0.001
d(3)	0.0010	0.509

The results, based on quarterly growth rates, show the following. All of the models estimated show a positive point estimate for the trend that starts in 2003. In three of the models, the relevant coefficients are statistically significant – the exceptions are purchases per account and real purchase volume per account. These models convey the idea either that the trend of growth of the relevant card-use variable accelerated during the regulated period (for example, number of accounts) or that the decline in the trend of growth that had started in the late 1990s decelerated during the regulated period (for example, number of purchases).

The two models that raise some questions are the ones estimated in the growth rate for the number of purchases per account and real purchase volume per account. They both show a positive coefficient for the trend that starts in 2003 but the coefficients are not statistically

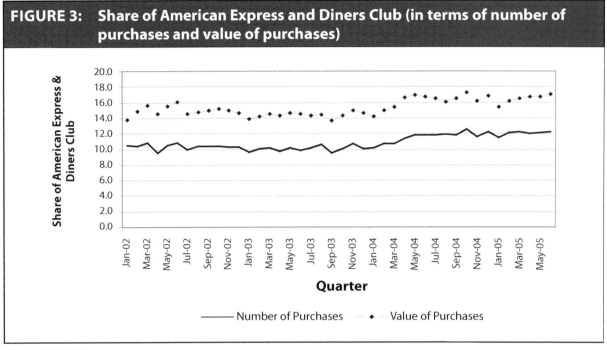

FIGURE 3: Share of American Express and Diners Club (in terms of number of purchases and value of purchases)

Source: RBA (2005d)

significant. (A simple examination of Table 4, furthermore, shows that these two series seem to have exhibited considerably lower rates of growth in the post-regulation period than in the pre-regulation period as compared to other indicators of credit card use.) Whether the regulation had any impact in terms of curtailing purchases per account and purchase volume per account is thus an open issue.

Overall, taking into account existing trends in the growth rates of card variables, there is little evidence that the regulatory intervention has affected overall card use in the admittedly short period of time examined here. Figure 3 above, however, reveals that there have been important compositional changes – volume has shifted from the regulated systems to the unregulated ones.[63] More specifically, between October 2003 and June 2005 the share of American Express and Diners Club increased by roughly 21 percent in terms of the number of purchases and by roughly 19 percent in terms of the value of purchases. This has happened because, as a consequence of regulation, relative prices seem to have changed. First, the relative price that issuers receive from a Visa or MasterCard transaction has declined relative to, say, an American Express transaction, since interchange has been capped for Visa and Master Card but American Express

---

[63] Analysis of Visa data on card and volume also indicates that Visa output declined relative to total industry output following regulation.

is allowed to sign issuing deals with banks under no interchange ceiling. Therefore, issuers have an incentive to shift volume to American Express, and they have. Secondly, the price of a card (or account) that cardholders face may have increased for the Visa and MasterCard cards relative to the proprietary ones, since Visa and MC issuers have attempted to recover some of the lost interchange income via an increase in other service charges, most of which are fixed fees. (Of course, in light of the fact that Visa and MasterCard issuers have raised other service charges, American Express and Diners Club may have done the same, so it is not altogether clear whether this relative price has changed much or not.)

Note, by the way, that the shift in volume from the regulated systems to the unregulated ones has a "perverse" effect on prices. In other words, the merchant discount on the regulated systems has come down significantly and the merchant discount on the unregulated systems has declined slightly, but it is considerably higher than the associations' pre-regulation merchant discount. Although the pure price effect leads to a lower average merchant discount, the compositional-change effect leads to a higher average merchant discount. (Of course, it will take an extremely large compositional change effect to produce an average merchant discount rate that is higher than the average pre-regulation rate.)

VI. ANALYSIS OF THE RBA INTERVENTION

The RBA's regulation of interchange fees has had some economic consequences that were entirely predictable and hardly surprising and others that raise some interesting questions both for regulators and students of two-sided markets.

One predictable result is that a massive reduction in revenue from one side of a two-sided market had consequences on the other side. Banks lost roughly $490 million in interchange fee revenue but appear to have regained between 30 and 40 percent of that through increased membership fees for cardholders. We believe this is a lower bound on the portion passed on to cardholders because of the cycle of replacing cards.

Another predictable result is the absence of evidence that consumer prices have fallen as a result of lower merchant discounts. This is not surprising because the cost savings are too small to be measurable with any degree of confidence. However, based on the economics literature on pass-through effects, we believe that it is highly unlikely that consumers have received any significant benefit over the period of time considered given the likely sticky prices and high concentration in the Australian retail sector.

Two results are, viewed prospectively, surprising. It appears that issuers have chosen thus far to adjust their pricing structures mainly through fixed fees – that is, fees that are independent of transaction volume. That is so despite a reduction in the variable revenue they received from the merchant side that had translated into negative variable prices on the cardholder side. Related to this is the finding that the near halving of interchange fees has not thus far led to a substantial reduction in card use.[64] That is to be expected for now given that marginal prices for completing transactions with cards have not changed significantly as a result of the regulation.

Over time we would expect a reduction in total credit-card use on the regulated side as a result of the decrease in the number of cardholders. However, it is difficult to predict the magnitude of that reduction without knowing the responsiveness of cardholders to increased membership fees. As noted, offsetting this decrease will be the increased use of cards from the unregulated proprietary systems. It appears that especially for high-spenders on rewards cards, issuers have made a serious, and predictable, effort to move them from the regulated associations to the unregulated proprietary systems. The RBA's hope that regulating the associations' interchange fees would exert substantial downward pressure on the American Express and the Diners Club merchant discount rates is particularly unlikely to be realized as high-spend rewards cardholders move to the unregulated systems.

VII. CONCLUSIONS

Did the RBA regulatory intervention achieve its goals? One answer is that it is too soon to tell. It takes time for markets to adjust and it may be that banks and merchants will make further adjustment over time. But to the extent that the first couple of years provide information, the evidence indicates that the intervention has not achieved its goals for a reason that was not apparent to either the RBA or the card associations at the time the intervention was being debated.

The purpose of the intervention was to raise the cost of transacting with credit cards, to bring social costs and benefits in alignment, and thereby to reduce the use of what was thought to be an inefficient instrument. The RBA saw the interchange fee as the source of the problem because banks subsidized card use to get this revenue source and merchants could not make cardholders bear the differential costs of card use. If the intervention had resulted in banks raising usage fees in lockstep with the reduction in interchange fees or if merchants had raised surcharges to account for the interchange fees, the RBA would have achieved its objectives.

Neither expectation was fulfilled. For the most part, it seems that banks raised fixed fees and left the per-transaction incentives alone. In addition, the banks started to switch volume from the regulated to the unregulated systems. By and large, merchants have not chosen to impose surcharges. Thus far the incentives that cardholders face to use cards at the point of sale do not seem to have changed radically. If these patterns persist, the effects of the RBA regulation, if any, will likely take place through a reduction in total cards on the regulated systems.

This result does not just provide further support for the law of unintended consequences. It

---

[64] As we note above, growth rates of card output are lower post-regulation than pre-regulation. Although our prior is that this is a continuation of pre-existing declines in the growth rate, we do not rule out the possibility that growth rates might have levelled off absent regulation, and that the regulation has therefore lowered card growth.

also raises interesting research questions. For the study of two-sided markets, it emphasizes that further work is needed to understand the role of two-part tariffs in guiding membership and usage decisions. This is an important topic for many two-sided industries since these two-part tariffs are quite common. For the study of regulatory interventions, it emphasizes that we need to know more about how two-sided businesses set prices to design interventions in those industries that can accomplish specified goals.

APPENDIX A

In order to determine whether issuers have made an attempt at recovering from cardholders some of the income lost due to the RBA regulation, we posed the question: In the period associated with the RBA regulation, is there evidence of a jump in the level of the card fees that issuers charge cardholders?

An examination of the Visa Australia series for other service charges per card and finance charges per card revealed that a few data points dramatically break the series trends. In the case of other service charges per card, the outliers are located in the second and third quarters of 1999 and the second quarter of 2000. In the case of finance charges per card, the outlier is located in the first quarter of 2004. To our knowledge, these are data problems rather than reflections of true change in the economic time series.

We took two different approaches in order to preclude our estimation from being driven by a few "influential" observations. First, we replaced the outliers with observations obtained via linear interpolation (Newton method). The results we report below were obtained on the basis of the interpolated data. Second, we kept the outliers in the dataset but ran robust regressions *a la* Huber (1964). In this iterative approach, observations receive weights that are a function of the magnitude of the associated residuals. For any given specification of the relevant model, the results obtained via robust regression were not substantially different from the ones obtained on the basis of the interpolated data.

A. Fee levels

In order to explore the question regarding the jump in fee levels in the regulatory period, we estimated a model of the following form:

$$Y(t) = \alpha + \beta\, t + \gamma\, D(t) + \delta\, X(t) + \varepsilon(t) \tag{A1}$$

In equation (A1), $Y(t)$ is the level of the fees that issuers charge cardholders in each quarter, t is a trend variable that takes on the value 1 at the starting point and grows by 1 each quarter, $D(t)$ is a binary variable associated with the regulated period, and $X(t)$ is a vector of other variables that may have had an impact on the level of $Y(t)$.

More specifically, we want to isolate the behaviour of issuers – therefore, we have to control for those elements of the behaviour of cardholders that could have had an impact on Y(t). For example, in a model where Y(t) is real other service charges per card (including annual fees and other usage fees) we may want to control for real purchase volume per card (in case there are elements of Y(t) that vary with the level of purchase activity). In a model where Y(t) is real finance charges per card we will certainly want to control for the level of real outstanding balances per card. The trend variable picks up the effect of unobservable factors that may have changed over time and may have exerted an influence upon Y(t). We also include binary variables for the second, third, and fourth quarters in order to control for potential seasonality in Y(t).

We estimated a number of different models to probe how robust our results were to various specifications. In some of these models we took into account the fact that real purchase volume per card and real outstanding balances per card may be endogenous – in other words, cardholders may choose the optimal level of these variables by taking into account the issuers' choice of fees and interest rates. In other words, we checked whether we obtained considerably different results with OLS vis-à-vis an instrumental-variable approach. For space reasons, we do not report the results of all the estimated models here. The results not reported were not substantially different from the ones reported and they are available from the authors upon request.

In estimating models like (A1), researchers usually take two potential issues into account – the presence of serial correlation and the presence of stochastic trends. The results we report here were obtained by estimating the models with robust standard errors – more specifically, Newey-West standard errors with four lags. We checked for the presence of stochastic trends by running Dickey-Fuller tests and co-integration tests on the relevant variables.

1. Real other service charges per card

We first estimated models where Y(t) is real other service charges per card per quarter. Other service charges include annual fees and other service fees, like over-limit and late-payment fees. A regression of Y(t) on a trend variable, binary quarterly variables, and a binary variable for the regulated period that takes on the value 1 starting in the first quarter of 2003 produced a coefficient on the regulation binary variable of 3.99 (p-value = 0.000).[65] Augmented Dickey-Fuller tests on the residuals rejected the null of a unit root with up to one lag. It is unclear whether the failure to reject the null with more than one lag was due to the lack of power of the test (due to the small sample size) or not.

We added the real sale volume per card on the right hand side and the coefficient on the binary variable dropped to 3.50 (p-value = 0.000).[66] Augmented Dickey-Fuller tests on the residuals

---

[65] For this model, the 4-lag Breusch-Godfrey test (that is, null hypothesis of no serial correlation) produced a p-value of 0.035. Furthermore, a Prais-Winsten AR(1) regression produced a coefficient on the reform binary variable of 3.57 (p-value = 0.003).

[66] The Breusch-Godfrey test for this model produced a p-value of 0.114. Furthermore, a Prais-Winsten AR(1) regression produced a coefficient on the reform binary variable of 3.56 (p-value = 0.002).

rejected the null (of no co-integration) with up to two lags. We then estimated a dynamic OLS (DOLS) model including the first difference of real sale volume per card on the right hand side, as well as one lag and one lead of the first difference. The coefficient on the binary variable dropped to 3.08 (p-value = 0.000).[67]

We followed a similar procedure starting with a regression of Y(t) (other service charges per card) on the trend variable, quarterly binary variables, and a binary variable that takes on the value one for the first time in the first quarter of 2004. The coefficient on the binary variable was 3.72 (p-value = 0.001).[68] We added real sale volume per card on the right hand side and the coefficient on the reform binary variable rose to 3.99 (p-value = 0.000).[69] We incorporated the first difference of real sale volume per card, and a lag and a lead of the first difference, and obtained a coefficient on the binary variable of 4.11 (p-value = 0.001).[70]

2. Consistency with RBA data

Our analysis based on quarterly Visa data is also broadly consistent with two separate sources of data on fees reported on an annual basis by the RBA.[71] The first source is total fee income (not including finance charges) received by banks on all credit cards. This series tracks closely to the Visa data. For example, average fee income per card in 2001 was AU$31.19 from the RBA data and AU$29.67 from the Visa data, and was AU$52.03 in 2003 from the RBA data and AU$52.45 from the Visa data. The increase from 2001 to 2003 was AU$20.84 from the RBA data and AU$22.78 from the Visa data.

---

[67] The Breusch-Godfrey test for this model produced a p-value of 0.030. A Prais-Winsten AR(1) regression produced a coefficient on the binary variable of 2.74 (p-value = 0.02). After incorporating only the 3rd lag of real sale volume per card on the right hand side, the model produced a coefficient on the reform binary variable of 2.83 (p-value = 0.008), and the Breusch-Godfrey test yielded a p-value of 0.114. After incorporating only the 4th lag we obtained a coefficient on the reform binary variable of 3.09 (p-value = 0.001) and a Breusch-Godfrey p-value of 0.341. With the 3rd and the 4th lags in the model we obtained a coefficient on the reform binary variable of 2.89 (p-value = 0.005) and a Breusch-Godfrey p-value of 0.209. Incorporating the real 30-day interest rate on the right hand side (in the model without the lagged real-sale-volume-per-card variables) generated an estimated coefficient of 3.18 (p-value = 0.002) for the reform binary variable.

[68] The Breusch-Godfrey test produced a p-value of 0.0003. A Prais-Winsten AR(1) regression produced a coefficient on the reform binary variable of 3.15 (p-value = 0.036).

[69] The Breusch-Godfrey test produced a p-value of 0.003. A Prais-Winsten AR(1) regression produced a coefficient on the reform binary variable of 3.62 (p-value = 0.016).

[70] The Breusch-Godfrey test for this model produced a p-value of 0.0001. A Prais-Winsten AR(1) regression produced a coefficient on the binary variable of 3.94 (p-value = 0.012). After incorporating only the 3rd lag of real sale volume per card on the right hand side, we obtained a coefficient on the reform binary variable of 4.75 (p-value = 0.001) and a Breusch-Godfrey p-value of 0.0004. After incorporating only the 4th lag, we obtained a coefficient on the reform binary variable of 5.40 (p-value = 0.001) and a Breusch-Godfrey p-value of 0.005. After incorporating both the 3rd and 4th lags, we obtained a coefficient on the reform variable of 5.19 (p-value = 0.001) and a Breusch-Godfrey p-value of 0.003. On the other hand, a model that incorporated four lags of real other service charges per card on the right hand side produced a coefficient on the reform binary variable of 3.78 (p-value = 0.000) and a Breusch-Godfrey p-value of 0.243. Incorporating the real 30-day interest rate on the right hand side (in the model without the lagged variables) generated an estimated coefficient of 3.90 (p-value = 0.001) for the reform binary variable.

[71] See RBA (2005a).

The RBA also reports survey data on average fees for cards with interest-free periods and rewards programs issued by major banks. From 2002 to 2004, fees increased significantly: from $61 to $85 for annual fees on standard cards; from $98 to $128 for annual fees on gold cards; from $21 to $29 for late payment fees; and from $13 to $29 for over-limit fees. Thus, taking annual fees alone, for cards in this survey, fees increased by $24 a year for standard cards and $30 for gold cards. If we include one late fee and one over-limit fee penalty per year, total fees increased by $48 a year for standard cards and $54 a year for gold cards.

There are at least two reasons why these survey data on rewards cards indicate higher fee increases than the calculations we have reported based on the aggregate data (leaving aside the fact that the limited annual data series do no allow for full controls). First, cardholder spending is higher on rewards cards, so the loss in interchange fee income is greater. Second, replacing existing cardholders with new ones is costly and banks may be reluctant to raise fees as much to existing cardholders as to new cardholders.

3. Real finance charges per card

We followed the same approach with Y(t) defined as real finance charges per card. So, for example, a regression of real finance charges per card on a trend variable, a binary variable for the regulated period starting in 2003, and quarterly binary variables, produced a coefficient for the regulated period of 7.72 (p-value = 0.002).[72] Dickey-Fuller tests did not reject the null of a unit root. After adding real outstanding balances per card on the right hand side, the coefficient for the regulated period dropped to 2.16 (p-value = 0.167).[73]

Augmented Dickey-Fuller tests rejected the null of no co-integration with two, three, and four lags. We estimated a DOLS model adding the first difference of real outstanding balances per card, and a lag and a lead of the first difference, and obtained a coefficient on the regulated period of 1.88 (p-value = 0.242).[74]

We followed the same approach starting with a regression of real finance charges per card on a trend variable, a binary variable for the regulated period starting in 2004, and quarterly binary variables. We obtained a coefficient on the regulation variable of 6.65 (p-value = 0.05).[75] The reform variable coefficient dropped to 1.89 (p-value = 0.047) after controlling for changes in real

---

[72] The Breusch-Godfrey test produced a p-value of 0.000. A Prais-Winsten AR(1) regression produced a coefficient on the reform binary variable of −0.098 (p-value = 0.940).

[73] The Breusch-Godfrey p-value for this model was 0.000. A Prais-Winsten AR(1) regression produced a coefficient on the reform binary variable of 1.01 (p-value = 0.389).

[74] The Breusch-Godfrey p-value for this model was 0.000. A Prais-Winsten AR(1) regression produced a coefficient on the reform binary variable of 0.23 (p-value = 0.868). The Breusch-Godfrey test continued to reject the null of no serial correlation even after adding lags of real outstanding balances per card and real finance charges per card on the right hand side. Incorporating a measure of the opportunity cost of funds on the right hand side (in the model without the lagged variables) generated an estimated coefficient of 1.78 (p-value = 0.287) for the reform binary variable.

[75] The Breusch-Godfrey p-value for this model was 0.000. Furthermore, a Prais-Winsten AR(1) regression produced a coefficient on the reform binary variable of 0.798 (p-value =0.542).

outstanding balances per card.[76] After adding the first difference of real outstanding balances per card, and a lag and a lead of the first difference, we obtained a coefficient on the regulated period of 1.14 (p-value = 0.316).[77]

4. Summary on fee levels

In summary, the evidence suggests that there was a jump in real other service charges per card associated with the RBA regulation. Depending on when we believe the structural break happened, the magnitude of the jump may have been roughly between AU$3 and AU$4 per quarter. The evidence of a jump in real finance charges per card is not as strong – the coefficients are much more sensitive to model specification and are, for the most part, not significant at standard confidence levels after controlling for changes in real outstanding balances per card.

---

[76] The Breusch-Godfrey p-value for this model was 0.000. A Prais-Winsten AR(1) regression produced a coefficient on the reform binary variable of 2.50 (p-value = 0.033).

[77] The Breusch-Godfrey p-value for this model was 0.000. A Prais-Winsten AR(1) regression produced a coefficient on the reform binary variable of 2.15 (p-value = 0.131). The Breusch-Godfrey test continued to reject the null of no serial correlation even after incorporating lags of real outstanding balances per card and real finance charges per card. Incorporating a measure of the opportunity cost of funds on the right hand side (in the model without the lagged variables) generated an estimated coefficient of 1.25 (p-value = 0.257) for the reform binary variable.

chapter 4

ECONOMIC ANALYSIS OF THE EFFECTS OF THE FEDERAL RESERVE BOARD'S PROPOSED DEBIT CARD INTERCHANGE FEE REGULATIONS ON CONSUMERS AND SMALL BUSINESSES

By

David S. Evans, Robert E. Litan, Richard Schmalensee

I. INTRODUCTION AND OVERVIEW

We have examined the economic impact of the Board's proposed regulations of debit card[1] interchange fees on consumers and small businesses.[2] Based on our research and analysis we have concluded that the Board's proposal, if implemented, will impose direct, immediate and certain harm on consumers, especially lower-income consumers,[3] and small businesses[4] that use checking accounts.[5]

We estimate that the proposed rules will eliminate $33.4-$38.6 billion of debit card interchange fee revenues for banks and credit unions during the first two years the rules are in effect.[6]

The proposed reductions of the fees that merchants pay for debit card transactions will dramatically reduce the profitability of checking accounts that banks and credit unions provide to consumers and small businessesBased on 2009 debit interchange fees, the average consumer checking account will lose between approximately $56 and $64 in annual revenue and the average small business checking account will lose between $79 and $92, if the Board's proposals were implemented.

To offset these lost revenues, banks and credit unions will increase fees to their retail customers for checking accounts, for the debit cards that are usually provided with their accounts, and for other retail banking services. Our analysis indicates that these changes will take place quickly after the implementation of the proposed rules. Some banks have already implemented changes in anticipation of the regulation, others have announced plans, and still others are reviewing changes in prices.

Banks and credit unions will likely modify some features of the debit cards for which they cannot recoup their costs and earn a fair rate of return under the proposed price caps, and the networks may be forced to do so as well. These changes could include limiting the use of debit cards for payment in situations such as high-value transactions that impose high levels of fraud and other risks on the banks and credit unions, or charging for cash back at the point of sale.

---

[1] The proposed regulations also apply to debit transactions that occur without a card such as mobile payment products that enable consumers to pay with funds from their checking accounts. For simplicity we refer to debit cards throughout this paper but the reader should understand that this includes all non-card based payment methods that are tied to the checking account.
[2] The Proposed Rules.
[3] Consumer checking accounts can be set up as individual accounts or as joint accounts often used by households.
[4] Most small businesses use the same checking account products and services as individuals.
[5] Checking accounts are often called "demand depository accounts" or DDAs.
[6] These figures are based on the estimated debit card interchange fee revenues that banks and credit unions would have received between July 21, 2011 and July 20, 2013 'but-for' the two proposals the Board has put forward. The interchange reduction calculations are based on the assumptions that exempt banks and credit unions face the same reduction in interchange fee revenues as non-exempt institutions and the debit card transaction growth beyond 2009 is equal to the average annual growth rate from 2005 to 2009. The calculations exclude interchange fees from all prepaid cards and are underestimates to the extent that some of these prepaid cards are covered by the regulations. We present the details of the calculation and further assumptions in Section II.

According to our analysis and research, banks and credit unions will pass on much of the $33.4-$38.6 billion reduction in interchange fees to consumers and small businesses in the form of higher fees or reduced services during the 24 month period following the implementation of the regulations.

Based on our research, these harms to consumers and small businesses will not be offset significantly by merchants charging lower prices for goods and services as a result of lower interchange fees. In fact, if implemented, the effects of the Board's proposal on merchant prices will occur slowly, and the amount of future reductions in retail prices is uncertain.

Merchants will save roughly 10 cents for a typical $59.89 purchase of a basket of goods from the proposed debit card interchange fee reductions if their merchant processors pass on all of the interchange fee savings to them.[7] Merchants in this case will save less than 2 cents for a $10 item. It is unlikely that most merchants will pass along such small reductions quickly. In fact, economic research has shown that retail prices are sticky and do not change often in response to small changes in costs and demand conditions.

Approximately three quarters of the merchants that accept debit cards, and virtually all small businesses, have contracts with their merchant processors under which the merchant pays a blended price covering all card transactions and is inclusive of all fees including interchange fees. Merchant processors are unlikely to pass on all of the debit card interchange fee reductions to these smaller merchants and may not pass on much, if any, of the reductions in the near term.

The Board staff has observed that merchants that operate in highly competitive industries will pass on most of debit card interchange fee savings to consumers. While we agree with that observation as a matter of theory, there is no basis in fact for assuming that there is intense competition in the merchant categories that account for most debit card transactions. In fact, for several key categories, such as big box retail and supermarkets, the antitrust authorities have defined product and geographic markets that indicate that there is not a high degree of competition in local markets in most parts of the country. Certain large retailers also are likely to have sufficient market power that they will not be compelled to pass on the entirety of the cost savings to consumers.

This paper focuses on the overall impact of the Board's proposed regulations of debit card interchange fees on consumers and small businesses. However, we note that the proposed regulations will have several distributional impacts across different segments of the economy that the Board may wish to take into consideration under its obligations under the Electronic Fund Transfer Act ("EFTA") and the Regulatory Flexibility Act ("RFA").

Lower income individuals have obtained significantly greater access to affordable retail banking services in the last decade, partly as a result of the debit card interchange fee revenues that have helped banks and credit unions defray the fixed costs of providing checking account services to accounts that maintain low average balances. It is likely that the reduction in debit card

---

[7] As discussed below these calculations are based on the average transaction amount at merchants and the proportion of those transaction dollars that are paid for with debit cards.

interchange fee revenues will result in a reduction in the number of lower income individuals with checking accounts and an increase in the number using alternative financial services, such as check-cashing services.

Small businesses that have checking accounts will face higher fees and reduced services as a result of banks and credit unions losing much of the debit card interchange fee income from their accounts.[8] Most of these small businesses do not accept debit cards and will, therefore, definitely lose from the proposed regulations. The small merchants that do accept debit cards will not receive much of a reduction in their merchant processing fees in the near term as a result of the debit card interchange fee reductions and will not receive the full benefit of those reductions over the longer term; merchant processors would not have strong incentives to pass on interchange fee reductions to these small merchants, most of whom face blended pricing for all payment methods, quickly or fully. Overall, small businesses will likely lose, at least in the first two years, if the proposed regulations are put into place.

We conclude from this economic analysis that the overall impact of the proposed interchange fee reductions will be to harm consumers, lower-income individuals, and small businesses. Large retailers will benefit, at least in the first 24 months, from a significant windfall at the expense of these other groups.

Section II provides background for the analysis conducted in this paper. It reports the estimated impact of the Board's proposals on debit card interchange fees received by debit card issuers and paid by debit card acquirers, describes the economics of retail banking, and provides an overview of the debit card product.

Section III examines how banks and credit unions will likely respond to the elimination of these fees. It shows that that the banking industry is intensely competitive and that, as a matter of economic theory, we expect that banks and credit unions will pass most of the revenue reductions on to consumers. It shows that banks and credit unions tend to quickly alter fees and services in response to significant changes in costs and revenues and that banks and credit unions will be likely to increase a number of fees, and reduce a number of services, in response to the proposed interchange fee reductions.

Section IV examines the extent to which the debit card interchange fee savings received by merchant processors will result in lower prices to consumers. It shows that the cost savings are very small as a percentage of retail prices. It also shows there is no presumption that the retail categories that will receive much of the reductions in interchange fees are intensely competitive and that, in fact, several are not. It concludes that merchants will lower prices slowly in response to the Board's proposed reductions and will not pass on most of the savings to consumers.

Section V considers the distributional impact of the Board's proposals on low-income individuals and small businesses. Section VI briefly summarizes our key quantitative findings.

---

[8] Based on data we have received from knowledgeable industry observers, roughly 9.1 percent of checking accounts (18 million) are held by smaller businesses.

II. BACKGROUND

This section reviews the Board's proposal, describes the economics of retail banking, and examines the debit cards that are the subject of the proposed regulations.

A. The Board's Interchange Fee Proposals and Their Effect on Interchange Fee Revenues

Signature and PIN networks have established "interchange fees" that acquirers, which provide debit card services to merchants, have to pay issuers, which provide debit card services to debit cardholders.[9] These fees generally involve a percentage of the transaction amount, with these percentages varying considerably across merchant categories and across merchants. In many cases there is also a fixed fee, although especially for signature cards the variable fee generally accounts for the bulk of the total.[10] Based on the Board's survey of payment card networks the average debit card interchange fee debit transactions was 44 cents in 2009.[11] The Board reported that the average retail transaction that was paid for with a debit card was $38.58.[12] The average effective interchange fee was thus 1.14 percent.

The Board has asked for comments on two proposals for regulating debit-card interchange fees received by banks and credit unions with assets of $10 billion or more on non-exempt products. Under the "12 cent cap" proposal banks and credit unions would be able to receive up to 12 cents of interchange fee revenues per transaction. Banks and credit unions would therefore face a reduction in interchange fee revenues per transaction of 73 percent ((44-12)/44).

Under the "7 cent safe harbor" proposal banks and credit unions would be able to receive at least 7 cents of interchange fee revenues per transaction (the safe harbor) and could receive up to 12 cents of interchange fee revenues per transaction (the cap) based on showing that their average variable cost of authorization, clearing and settlement was more than 7 cents. According to the Board, approximately half of the banks and credit unions in its survey of 89 financial institutions had average variable costs of authorization, clearing, and settlement of approximately 7 cents or less.[13] These banks and credit unions would therefore face an 84 percent reduction in interchange fee revenues per transaction ((44-7)/44). The other half of the banks and credit unions that had costs higher than 7 cents, and who obtain the ability to receive a higher interchange fee, would therefore face a reduction in interchange fee revenues per transaction of between 73 and 84

---

[9] As a practical matter most merchants receive most of their services from companies that are merchant processors (First Data Corporation for example) or, especially in the case of smaller firms, Independent Service Organizations (ISOs) that work on behalf of either merchant processors or acquirers. In much of this paper we refer to merchant processors rather than acquirers.
[10] PIN debit cards often have fixed transaction fees plus a variable fee based on the size of the transaction. See The Proposed Rules, at p. 81724.
[11] The Proposed Rules, at p. 81725.
[12] Ibid., at p. 81725.
[13] Ibid., at p. 81737.

percent. It is unclear how many banks and credit unions would apply for and obtain the ability to charge more than 7 cents under the second proposal or would risk charging more and then having to defend their rates to the Board. The legal cost and uncertainty of obtaining a waiver, or the risk of a challenge, might deter some or many banks and credit unions. It is also likely that the half of the banks and credit unions with average variable costs higher than 7 cents account for significantly less than half of the transactions.[14] For the purposes of this paper we assume that the Board's 7 cent safe harbor would result in a reduction of debit card interchange fee revenues per transaction of 84 percent; the actual reduction would be slightly lower.[15]

Based on its survey of all relevant networks, the Board reports that interchange fees for debit cards totaled $15.7 billion in 2009.[16] This figure includes banks and credit unions with assets of less than $10 billion, which are exempt by law from the interchange fee limits. However, it appears likely that the "exempt" banks and credit unions would also realize a significant decrease in interchange fees.

The exempt banks themselves believe they would not get the benefit of the exemption in practice.[17] While the exact details of what will happen under the new regulatory regime are difficult to determine, the exempt banks, as well as industry experts we have talked to, believe that the exempt banks will lose out as networks attempt to attract larger issuers and merchants. These observers indicate that networks that adopt dual interchange fee schedules—one for small exempt institutions and the other for large covered institutions—would face severe pressure to reduce the small institution fee to the same level as the large institution fee.[18]

---

[14] The transaction-weighted average of the average variable costs is 4 cents, which indicates that the banks with more transactions have lower average variable costs. See The Proposed Rules, at p. 81737. That implies that banks with average variable costs of greater than 7 cents account for a disproportionately small share of overall transactions.

[15] Under the assumption that banks with average costs as defined by the Board greater than 7 cents were able to charge a higher fee and that the average fee they charge would be at the midpoint between 7 and 12 cents (9.5 cents), the average debit card interchange fee would be $.5 \times 7 + .5 \times 9.5 = 8.25$. In this case the safe harbor plus cap proposal would result in an 81.3 percent reduction in debit card interchange fee revenues. As noted above it is likely that the transaction-weighted average would result in a fee closer to 7 cents than to 8.25 cents.

[16] The Proposed Rules, at footnote 22. We have excluded prepaid cards which accounted for $500 million of these fees because many of these cards are exempt from the regulations.

[17] See "ICBA: Two-Tier Debit Card Interchange Plan Won't Work for Community Bank Customers," Independent Community Bankers of America, January 10, 2011; and Letter from Bill Cheney to House Financial Services Committee Chairman Spencer Bachus and Ranking Member Barney Frank urging them to hold hearings on the Board's proposed rules related to Section 1075 of the Dodd-Frank Act (Interchange Fees), January 3, 2011.

[18] The Board staff questioned whether the exempt banks would receive higher interchange fees than the covered banks and expressed doubt that the exempt banks would continue to receive the current market levels of interchange fees: "So with regard to the small issuers, we really don't know what the net effect of the rules will be, because it depends on actions to be taken by the networks and the merchants, and we can't predict those actions…. The networks may decide that it's simply too costly or too complicated to maintain two separate interchange fee schedules and, therefore, they may simply say that everybody is going to operate under the same interchange fee schedule which complies with our standards. In that case, obviously, the exempt issuers would face a similar reduction in their interchange fees as would the covered issuers. If the networks do decide to establish two separate interchange fee schedules and allow higher interchange fees for the small issuers, it's possible that merchants would discriminate against those issuers by declining to accept their cards, because there are higher fees associated with accepting those cards." See "Federal Reserve Board of Governors Holds an Open Meeting," CQ Financial Transcripts, December 16, 2010, at pp. 14-15.

Under the proposed routing provisions merchants would be able to switch transactions to the low-cost network carried on the card and discriminate against networks in various ways.[19] Networks that adopt a high debit card interchange fee schedule for small institutions would therefore tend to lose transactions at merchants. Networks compete for the 20 large debit-card issuers that account for over 60 percent of debit card volume.[20] These large issuers would likely avoid networks that have high interchange fees for small institutions because merchants would discriminate against those networks' cards and therefore these networks would lose transactions.[21] Large issuers would also likely avoid networks that have high interchange fees for small issuer competitors that account for about one-third of checking account deposits and debit card transactions. We expect that these competitive pressures would force interchange fees for exempt institutions to roughly the same level as interchange fees for covered institutions.[22]

For the purposes of this paper we assume that the exempt banks and credit unions would face the same reduction in interchange fees as the covered banks and credit unions. Therefore, we assume based on total debit card interchange fees for 2009, that banks and credit unions would lose interchange fee revenues of between $11.4 (12 cent cap) and $13.2 billion (7 cent safe harbor).[23]

---

[19] Industry dynamics under these rules may be very different from competition in the absence of these regulatory requirements.

[20] "The Nilson Report Issue #947," The Nilson Report, April 2010.

[21] The recent settlement between the Department of Justice and MasterCard and Visa prevents the networks from limiting merchants from offering discounts and rebates based on the payment card used, from expressing a preference for a particular brand or type of card, promoting a particular brand or type of card, and communicating the costs to the merchant of different brands of cards. See "Justice Department Sues American Express, Mastercard and Visa to Eliminate Rules Restricting Price Competition; Reaches Settlement with Visa and Mastercard," Department of Justice, October 4, 2010. There would also likely be considerable scrutiny on any efforts by any other debit card networks to limit the ability of merchants to dissuade consumers from using particular networks.

[22] Industry experts we have talked to believe that competition between the two signature networks, MasterCard and Visa, for large issuers and large merchants will result in a small spread between the two interchange fee schedules should they be adopted. Similarly, PIN debit networks would face significant pressure, from large issuers and large merchants, if they attempt to maintain a substantial spread between interchange fees for exempt and non-exempt institutions. While a PIN debit network could attempt to become the network of choice for exempt issuers, it is not obvious that would be a successful strategy. There is a good chance that large merchants would negotiate low rates by threatening not to accept cards from such a network, and given that large merchants account for the majority of transaction volume, this would limit the effective rate received by issuers on a PIN debit network catering to exempt issuers. If the Board implements the version of the network exclusivity rules that requires two PIN debit networks (in addition to two signature debit networks), then there would have to be two PIN debit networks catering to exempt issuers and there would be pressure from large and smaller merchants (with the likely assistance of their acquirers) to route transactions to the PIN debit network with lower interchange fees. Under the version of the network exclusivity rules that requires only two debit networks (so that there is no requirement to have two PIN debit networks on the same card), a PIN debit network that attempted to maintain significantly higher interchange fees for exempt issuers would still face pressure from merchants to prompt customers to authorize using signature (which are likely to have lower interchange fees) rather than PIN. The requirement for a debit network to have acceptance nationwide and not be limited to a small number of merchant locations or at limited types of merchants imposes further pressure on a PIN debit network attempting to maintain significantly higher interchange fees for exempt issuers.

[23] Based on issuer debit transaction volume from The Nilson Report and financial institution asset data available through the Federal Deposit Insurance Corporation ("FDIC") and the National Credit Union Administration ("NCUA") Call Report data, banks with assets of under $10 billion account for approximately 33 percent of debit card transaction volume. If these banks continued to receive the current levels of interchange fees the reductions of debit card interchange fees under the proposed regulations would be $7.6 billion and $8.8 billion, respectively.

The Board's proposals would go into effect on July 21, 2011. Our research and analysis has focused on the impact on consumers and small businesses during the first 24 months of the regulations.[24] In the absence of the Board's debit interchange fee caps we estimate that banks and credit unions would receive approximately $45.9 billion of interchange fee revenue during that two-year period of time ($9.0 billion for the remainder of 2011, $22.7 billion in 2012, and $14.1 billion in the first roughly 7 months of 2013).[25] Under these assumptions banks and credit unions would lose $33.4 billion in interchange fee revenues over these 24 months should the Board adopt the 12 cent cap proposal and $38.6 billion in interchange fee revenues over these 24 months should the Board adopt the 7 cent safe harbor proposal.[26] These figures would be lower if the Board increases the safe harbor or cap or otherwise provides a way for debit-card issuers to receive reimbursement from merchants for fraud prevention costs.

B. Checking Accounts and Retail Banking

Consumers and small businesses had roughly 198 million checking accounts in 2010.[27] Checking accounts provide consumers and small businesses safety and liquidity for their funds.

---

[24] The Board has proposed collecting cost information in two years time and we would expect the Board would use that as an opportunity to consider revising the interchange fee regulations. See, e.g., The Proposed Rules, at § 235.8. Moreover, it is difficult to forecast the total harm farther into the future because the debit card interchange fee reductions and routing restrictions would likely alter the extent to which banks issue debit cards and the extent to which possible fees banks could impose would affect the usage of debit cards. These structural changes in the payments industry could increase the harm to consumers to the extent consumers lose the use of products they value or decrease the harm to consumers if the financial services industry figures out ways to provide alternative unregulated products that meet consumer needs.

[25] These figures are based on the estimated debit card interchange fee revenues that banks would have received for July 21, 2011-July 20, 2013 less the estimated reductions in those fees under the two proposals the Board has put forward. To determine debit card interchange fee revenues during this period in the absence of the rules we used the Board's estimate of debit card interchange fee revenues in 2009 and assumed that in the absence of the rules these revenues would increase at the average annual compound growth rate of debit card transactions between 2005 and 2009. We have assumed that the Board's 7 cent safe harbor proposal with a 12 cent cap would result in the average interchange fee of approximately 7 cents for the reasons discussed below. To calculate the percent reductions in fees we used the Board's estimate that the average debit card interchange fee was 44 cents in 2009.

[26] These figures would be approximately $22.2 billion and $25.7 billion if the exempt banks continued to receive the current level of debit card interchange fees. The figure for the 7 cent safe harbor would be $24.8 billion if we assumed that the average debit card interchange fee fell to 8.25 cents (as discussed above) and if exempt banks continued to receive the current level of debit card interchange fees.

[27] Reliable estimates of the number of consumer and small business checking accounts are not available from public sources. We have prepared these are estimates based on the following information. The total number of checking accounts (180 million) is estimated using the percentage of US households with a checking account from the 2007 Survey of Consumer Finances (89.7 percent), the number of US households from the US Census Bureau (117.5 million as of the March 2010 Current Population Survey), and information from knowledgeable industry observers that the average household has roughly 1.7 checking accounts. Also, from discussions with industry observers, we estimate that approximately 9.1 percent (18 million) of checking accounts are held by small businesses. The consumer accounts include individual and joint checking accounts. Checking accounts are the most commonly used form of depository accounts which also including savings and money-market accounts. We focus our discussion on checking accounts. Small business owners may sometimes use their personal checking account for their businesses or may have separate account in the name of the business; the 9.1 percent figure above refers to accounts in the name of the business.

They also provide the basic tools for household and small business budgeting and money management. A checking account is usually the first step toward establishing a credit history and being able to borrow money.

Most households and small businesses use these accounts to keep liquid assets that they use to pay for goods and services. Households typically deposit their paychecks, as well as other funds, into these accounts and small businesses deposit sales receipts, and other funds, into these accounts. Those funds may earn some interest, depending on the type of account and the amount of balances maintained. Individuals and small businesses can withdraw these funds through a variety of means to pay for goods and services.

Banks and credit unions provide many services to checking and other depository account holders. Account holders can usually obtain various depository services through bank branches, ATMs, online banking, and phone banking. Account holders can pay merchants using a variety of services provided by the depository account including checks, debit cards, prepaid cards, online bill payment, mobile payment, money orders, ACH, and wire transfers. Account holders can also put funds into the account through services, such as direct deposit for payroll, income tax refunds, and other private/public assistance benefits. Many of these services have become standard elements of checking accounts.

Banks and credit unions recover the cost of providing these services and earn profits through a variety of fees as well as by using checking account balances to make loans of various sorts. As with many multidimensional products bundles, banks and credit unions do not specifically charge for all services and they use higher margins on some features to offset low or negative margins on other features.[28] Banks and credit unions typically provide more services at no charge to customers who keep higher deposit balances (as the banks earn profits from those balances) or are likely to buy other complementary products that the bank offers (such as mortgages or insurance). Table 1 shows the checking accounts offered by Bank of America, which is the country's largest holder of depository accounts. It shows the main account offerings as of January 2011 and the associated fees.

The checking account is only one element in the sets of products that banks and credit unions offer their retail and small business customers. They also offer mortgages, various other kinds of loans, insurance, brokerage services, and retirement accounts. All of these sources of revenues cover banks' fixed costs, including the costs of maintaining bank branches. Banks balance the revenues and costs of various retail banking services features to ensure that they are recovering their overall costs and make a return on their investments. They incur fixed costs of offering the bundle of products and services included in the checking account and have to recover these costs. Changes in the revenue available or costs incurred for one element of the retail banking relationship therefore have effects on the fees charged for other features and the willingness of a bank to offer various features.

---

[28] N.B. Murphy (1991), "The Impacts of the Use of Electronic Banking Services and Alternative Pricing of Services," *Financial Services Review*, 1:1, pp. 35-44, notes in particular that "...the pricing of checking services in many cases does not reflect the marginal costs of providing the service..."

TABLE 1: Bank of America Basic Checking Account Features and Fees, February 2011

Account Features, Rates, and Fees	eBanking	MyAccess® Checking	Small Business Checking Bundle
Opening deposit requirement	$25	$25	$100
Minimum balance requirement	$0	$0	$0
Monthly Service Charge	$8.95	$8.95	$16.00
Monthly Service Charge Waiver	Monthly service charge waived when: • Deposits and withdrawals are made electronically or at our ATMs • AND You choose online paperless statements through Online Banking	Monthly service charge waived when: • Make direct deposits each statement period • OR Maintain an average balance of $1,500	Monthly service charge waived if you do one of the following: 1) Enroll in Business Fundamentals and make a monthly qualifying purchase with your Business Debit Card, 2) keep a $4,000 min daily balance, 3) keep a $10,000 avg monthly balance, 4) keep a $7,500 combined min daily balance of linked accounts, or 5) have a $15,000 combined min daily balance of linked account
Direct Deposit	x	x	x
Online Banking	x	x	x
Debit Card	x	x	x
Online Bill Pay	x	x	x
Fraud Protection	x	x	x
Free ATMs	x	x	x
Overdraft Items and NSF	$35	$35	$35
Extended Overdrawn Balance Charge	$35, each time the account is overdrawn for 5 or more consecutive business days	$35, each time the account is overdrawn for 5 or more consecutive business days	$35, each time the account is overdrawn for 5 or more consecutive business days
Keep the Change®	x	x	
Business Economy Checking			
Trade stocks online	x	x	x
Check enclosure fee	N/A	$3/per statement	$3/per statement
Stop payment fee	$30 each request	$30 each request	$30 each request
Non-BofA ATM fee in the US	$2	$2	$2
Non-BofA ATM fee outside the US	$5	$5	$5

Source: www.bankofamerica.com

The decision by a bank to offer various checking account services and other retail banking services to retail customers depends on the cost of those features and the revenue obtained directly from the fees for those features or indirectly from the purchase of other products or services from the bank.[29]

C. Debit Cards

In the mid 1990s banks and credit unions started replacing at an increasingly rapid rate the ATM cards that they had issued their checking account holders to take cash from ATM machines with ATM/debit cards that enabled checking account holders also to use their cards to pay for goods and services. In increasing numbers, banks and credit unions issued cards that could be accepted by merchants that accepted the Visa or MasterCard brands; these latter cards are known as "signature" cards because they require signatures in roughly the same situations in which a credit card would require a signature. Visa and MasterCard had offered signature debit cards to issuers since the mid 1970s. However, these cards became popular among issuers primarily as a result of investments that the card networks made in popularizing debit cards among consumers and as a result of the revenues that the banks could realize from debit card interchange fees.[30] Banks and credit unions also increased their issuance of cards that could be accepted by merchants that had PIN pads and that accepted cards associated with one of the Electronic Funds Transfer (EFT) networks.

Consumers liked these cards and increasingly used them to make payments. Table 2 shows the growth of the number of transactions and the dollar volume of transactions on debit cards from 2000-2009.[31]

According to data from the Board's Survey of Consumer Finances, the proportion of U.S. households using debit cards increased from 17.6 percent in 1995, to 47.0 percent in 2001, and to 67.3 percent in 2007 (the most recent year available).[32] The Survey of Consumer Payment Choice conducted by the Federal Reserve Bank of Boston found that 77.6 percent of consumers had debit cards in 2009.[33]

Consumers were able to increase their use of debit cards because merchants also embraced this new form of payment. Between 2005 and 2010 the number of merchant locations accepting

---

[29] JPMorgan Chase CEO, Jamie Dimon, explained this concept following the passage of the Dodd–Frank Wall Street Reform and Consumer Protection Act, "If you're a restaurant and you can't charge for the soda, you're going to charge more for the burger…Over time, it will all be repriced into the business." See "Banks Seek to Keep Profits as New Oversight Rules Loom," *The New York Times*, July 15, 2010.

[30] David S. Evans and Richard Schmalensee, *Paying with Plastic: The Digital Revolution in Buying and Borrowing*. Cambridge, MA: MIT, 2005, ch. 8.

[31] We note that the 2009 transaction and transaction dollars figures reported by the Nilson Report are slightly different than the figures reported in The Proposed Rules (37.7 billion transactions and $1.45 trillion in value). We use figures reported by The Nilson Report for the purpose of calculating the growth of debit cards usage between 2000 and 2009 to maintain a consistent time series.

[32] Loretta J. Mester (2009), "Changes in the Use of Electronic Means of Payment: 1995-2007," *Business Review*, pp. 29-37.

[33] Schuh, Scott, "Basic Facts about U.S. Consumer Payment Choice," Presented at the MPD Payments Innovation Institute, Harvard Faculty Club, Cambridge, MA, November 5, 2010 ("Schuh November 2010 Presentation").

TABLE 2: Debit Transactions and Dollar Volume 2000–2009		
Year	Transactions	Transaction Dollars
2000	8.4	$311.0
2001	10.3	$388.1
2002	12.7	$480.6
2003	14.8	$588.7
2004	17.6	$729.4
2005	21.6	$869.0
2006	26.3	$1,024.5
2007	28.3	$1,184.0
2008	32.2	$1,330.0
2009	36.6	$1,421.0

Sources: ATM & Debit News EFT Data Book, The Nilson Report.

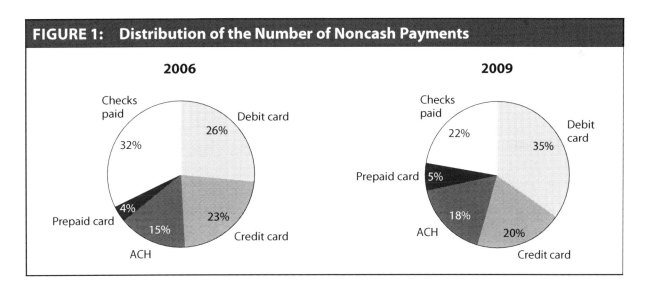

FIGURE 1: Distribution of the Number of Noncash Payments

Visa debit cards increased by 34 percent from 6.1 million to 8.2 million, and similarly, the number of merchant locations accepting MasterCard debit cards increased from 6.0 million to 8.2 million.[34]

---

[34] The Nilson Report. Prior to the Wal-Mart settlement in May 2003 merchants that agreed to accept MasterCard and Visa cards had to take both credit and debit cards. Since then, merchants could choose to accept credit cards without also accepting debit cards. It is our understanding from conversations with knowledgeable industry observers that very few merchants have done so.

Table 4: Comparison of Checking and Debit Cards

Feature/Function	Check	Debit Card
Payment Authorization	No real-time authorization capability. Use of third-party verification services[a] costs $0.35 - $0.50 per transaction plus monthly service fees of $12 - $20.[b]	Real-time account authorization of funds availability.
Payment Clearing & Settlement	Checks processed manually (deposited at a bank) take 1-3 business days to clear, after deposited. Checks converted to ACH transactions (BOC or POP) take 1-2 business days to clear.	0-1 business days to clear signature debit transaction. Same day clearing and settlement of PIN debit transactions.
Payment Guarantee	No built-in payment guarantee. Third party guarantee services cost +/- 1.85 percent[c]. Guarantee service provider determines what will be declined at the POS.	All authorized transactions are guaranteed in the sense that the "check won't bounce for nonpayment".
Payment Acceptance	Generally limited to face-to-face transactions.	Face-to-face transactions. Ability to make payments online, over the phone, and at unattended terminals such as gas stations and parking meters. Ability to pay for taxis and public transportation in many major cities.
"Bounced checks"	Merchant will be notified about insufficient funds 1-2 days after a check "bounces". Merchant has to handle collections if they haven't paid someone to do that.	All insufficient funds transactions are handled automatically, without need for merchant to do anything; under recent Reg E changes, both PIN and signature transactions will be declined at the POS if the consumer has not "opted-in" to NSF/OD protection. If the consumer has opted in, any NSF/OD situation will be resolved by the issuing bank, and the merchant will be paid regardless.
Chargebacks	No built-in process for disputing transactions. Both consumers and merchants have to handle disputes on their own.	Automated processes and rules for handling disputes, that minimize consumer and merchant effort and losses.
Fraud/Risk Management	No built-in capabilities for managing transaction risk. Fraud issues must be addressed individually by merchants and consumers.	Range of system-wide (Visa and MasterCard) and bank-specific tools for managing risk and fraud. Zero Liability for consumers who report fraud within specified time frame.
Cost of checks	Consumers (even with free accounts) typically pay $6 -$10 plus shipping and handling.[d]	No cost for initial debit card issuance. No cost for card reissuance.
Record keeping	Consumers must manage & reconcile all records for check writing. Carbon check "copies" in checkbooks typically increase cost of checks. Check number only on statements.	Receipt with every transaction. Merchant name and phone number on statements.

[a] Verification services do not provide real-time account authorization, but rather provide a review of negative file information and provide an algorithmic screen of likelihood of a check clearing successfully.

[b] First Data Independent Sales Website estimate of industry prices (http://www.instamerchant.com/checkguarantee.html). First Data owns the largest check verification and guarantee service, TeleCheck.

[c] Ibid.

[d] Cost of checks via Walmartchecks.com: $5.96 + shipping and handling. Bank websites cite check ordering costs of $8-$10.

TABLE 5: 2009 Trends in Consumer Payment Preferences		
Characteristic	Debit Card	Check
Very Easy to Use	48.4%	14.5%
Very Fast	34.6%	6.7%
Almost Always Accepted	47.9%	19.3%
Very Low Cost	33.2%	22.8%
Very High Control	23.0%	11.4%

Source: Kevin Foster, Erik Meijer, Scott Schuh, and Michael A. Zabek, "The 2008 Survey of Consumer Payment Choice," Federal Reserve Bank of Boston, April 2010.

Debit cards were heavily advertised as substitutes for writing checks. Many consumers in fact started using these cards instead of writing checks. Debit cards have become the most commonly used noncash method of payment according to Board data and appear to have driven the sharp decline of check use by consumers.[35]

Debit cards have been used more heavily in places such as supermarkets and drug stores where consumers had previously paid with cash or check rather than credit cards.[36]

Although debit cards were introduced as a substitute for writing checks, it was possible for the card networks and financial institutions to provide many other features and services for debit cards that were not available for checks. Table 4 presents a comparison between the features of checks and debit cards at typical financial institutions. From the standpoint of cardholders and merchants checks and debit cards are very different products.

As a result of these differences consumers have come to perceive checks and debit cards as different products. Table 5 summarizes the responses of consumers to various characteristics that consumers desire in a payment product. Almost half of consumers report that debit cards are very easy to use, while less than 15 percent of consumers report that for checks. More than one-third of consumers say that debit cards are very fast, while less than 7 percent say that for checks. Consumers also appear to value debit cards because they are accepted at more locations than checks. Almost half of consumers report that debit cards are almost always accepted, while less than one-fifth report that for checks.

Banks and credit unions would have several responses available to them in the event that the Board implemented the proposed reductions in interchange fees and thereby sharply reduced the profitability of debit cards. First, banks and credit unions could attempt to impose fees for debit

---

[35] "The 2010 Federal Reserve Payments Study: Noncash Payment Trends in the United States: 2006 – 2009," The Federal Reserve System, December 2010.

[36] Kevin Foster, Erik Meijer, Scott Schuh, and Michael A. Zabek (2010), "The 2008 Survey of Consumer Payment Choice," Federal Reserve Bank of Boston, Public Policy Discussion Papers, at table 23.

card transactions themselves. Debit card issuers may have some difficulty doing that because these consumers have cash, checks, and credit cards available as payment substitutes. Second, the debit card issuers and the networks that provide these products to the banks and credit unions could eliminate some features on debit cards such as covering fraud costs for consumers or providing payment guarantees to merchants. Banks and credit unions could also impose fees for some ancillary services provided by debit cards such as cash back at the point of sale. Third, banks and credit unions could attempt to impose fees for products and services that are complementary to debit cards. For example, it makes business sense to provide free checking to consumers when banks and credit unions obtain revenue from merchants when customers transfer payment to the merchant using their debit card; it would not likely make sense without the revenue stream from merchants. In the next section, we will discuss in more detail the likely impact of the proposed debit card fee reductions on the supply of debit card services to consumers and merchants.

D. "Pass-Through" and Its Determinants

The remainder of this paper examines the impact of the proposed interchange fee regulations on consumers and small businesses. To help answer this question we will be relying on what is known as the economics of "pass-through" which assesses the extent to which changes in costs lead firms and industries to change the prices they charge customers. There is a theoretical and empirical literature in economics that addresses this issue. It is useful to summarize some of the key findings here and provide an overview of the analysis in the next two sections.[37]

First, when firms in an industry face an increase in variable costs they will fully pass on that increase in variable costs to consumers in the form of higher prices if the industry is highly competitive. For example, if the government imposed a $1 tax per unit of output, then we would expect that firms in a highly competitive industry would increase prices by about $1.[38] Competitive firms have to pass on cost decreases because their competitors or new entrants will lower prices to increase sales, and firms have to pass on cost increases because they would not be able to earn a competitive return otherwise.

Second, when industries are not intensely competitive economic theory does not provide much guidance on the extent to which an increase in cost will be passed on consumers in the form of higher prices. Several empirical studies have found that in the particular situations examined firms eventually pass through between 40 and 70 percent of cost increases in the form of higher prices. The likely rate of pass through depends very much on the specifics of the business and the industry.

Third, changes in costs are often not passed on for some time because firms tend not to change prices very often for a variety of reasons including the fact that it is expensive and time consuming to change prices. Therefore, prices tend to be sticky over a period of about a year on average. Price changes are especially unlikely when the optimal changes in prices are small, so the gains from changing prices are small relative to the (menu) costs of implementing the changes.

---

[37] These findings are discussed and supported in more detail in Section V.
[38] In formal economic terms this will result if the industry is perfectly competitive and faces constant unit costs of production.

These principles are useful for analyzing the effect of interchange fees. In the next section we examine the effect of the reduction in interchange fee revenues on banks and credit unions. From the standpoint of economic theory the price caps on debit card interchange fee revenues have the same impact as an equivalent increase in cost to the depository account. We conclude that bank prices will not be sticky because the reductions in revenues incurred by the banks and credit unions would be large on a per account basis ($56-$64 per consumer account and $79-$92 per small business account per year) and as a percentage of profit and would therefore overwhelm the menu costs of changing prices. We show that most retail customers are served by a highly competitive retail banking industry and that there is therefore a presumption that banks and credit unions would pass on most of the revenue losses in the form of higher fees to their retail banking customers. We support this theoretical conclusion with evidence that during the 2000s banks appear to have reduced the prices of retail banking services to consumers (or increased the value of those services) at least in part as a result of increasing debit card revenues and net service fees. We demonstrate that banks have quickly raised rates in response to cost increases caused by Regulation E's limits on overdraft fees. We show that banks have already announced a number of increases in fees and reductions in service to recover the anticipated reduction in debit card interchange fee revenues.

Many merchants that accept debit cards for payment would have lower costs as a consequence of the proposed regulations. However, the reduction in costs for these retailers amounts to roughly 10 cents for a typical $59.89 transaction. The empirical literature on price stickiness strongly suggests that all else equal merchants would not reduce prices for many months and perhaps more than a year in response to such small cost decreases. Prices would be more likely to change in the longer term and then some pass through will occur. Moreover, several of the retail categories that account for a large portion of the debit card interchange fee reductions are not intensely competitive. A number of the very large retailers that would receive a significant portion of the savings also operate in categories that are not intensely competitive. We would therefore expect even after prices become flexible that retailers that account for a significant portion of debit card interchange fees would only pass on a portion of their savings in the form of lower prices.

III. ESTIMATED IMPACT OF THE BOARD'S DEBIT CARD INTERCHANGE FEE PROPOSALS ON BANK REVENUE AND PROFITS

As estimated above, the Board's proposals would reduce annual debit card interchange fee revenues earned by banks and credit unions by between $11.4 and $13.2 billion per year based on 2009 debit card interchange fees. Using our estimate of 198 million checking accounts in 2009,[39] the interchange fee reduction would decrease average revenue for each of those accounts, all else

---

[39] See footnote 29.

equal, by between $58 and $67. Debit card interchange fee revenues accounted for between one-quarter and one-third of bank DDA-specific revenues in 2008.[40] DDA-specific revenues accounted for about 30-40 percent of retail banking revenues in 2008.[41] Based on these data the proposed reductions in debit card interchange fees would, in the absence of efforts to mitigate the losses, reduce DDA-specific revenues by between 21 and 24 percent and would reduce the revenues from retail banking by between 7 and 9 percent.[42]

To get a rough idea of how these losses of revenue would affect bank profitability in the absence of efforts to mitigate them, we have calculated total income of banks and credit unions in 2007; we used 2007 since profits declined dramatically in 2008-2009 as a result of the financial crisis. The proposed reduction in debit card interchange fees amounts to approximately 9.4 percent-10.8 percent of the total net income of banks and credit unions in 2007.[43] Banks and credit unions do not report publicly the total income due to retail banking or depository accounts. The proposed debit card interchange fee reductions would be a much larger fraction of retail banking or depository banking profitability.

The Board's proposed reductions in debit card interchange fee revenues would therefore lead to significant financial consequences for banks and credit unions in the absence of efforts to mitigate their effects. To assess the impact of these reductions on the prices of retail banking services to individuals and small businesses we first examine the state of competition in this business.

A. Competition in Retail Banking[44]

There were 7,760 commercial banks and 7,402 credit unions in the United States as of September 30, 2010.[45] As a result of the end of interstate banking and branch banking laws, banks are now legally able to expand and compete anywhere in the country. When it comes to depository and other retail banking services, the day-to-day competition among banks and credit unions takes place in local areas. People still want to be able to go to a local branch sometimes and use the ATMs operated by their bank or credit union. A large number of banks and credit unions compete for customer business in local areas most parts of the country. To take one example, there are 83 banks and credit unions in

---

[40] These are rough estimates based on discussions with knowledgeable industry observers.
[41] These are rough estimates based on discussions with knowledgeable industry observers.
[42] The estimated revenue reductions are based on a 73 percent and 84 percent reduction of interchange fees and the assumption that interchange fee revenues are 29 percent of DDA revenues (29 percent is the midpoint between 25 percent and 33 percent—the range of estimates reported above) and DDA revenue is 35 percent of total retail banking revenues (35 percent is the midpoint between the range 30 percent and 40 percent reported above).
[43] Net income data is based on the FDIC and NCUA Call Reports. Estimate of 2007 interchange fees is based on the effective interchange fee rate of 1.14 percent for 2009 referenced in The Proposed Rules, at p. 81725 and the total debit transaction volume reported by The Nilson Report.
[44] We understand that the Board staff is very familiar with the material in this section but provide it for the sake of completeness and for readers who may not be familiar with it.
[45] FDIC "Statistics at a Glance", September 30, 2010. NCUA.

the Washington, D.C. metropolitan area.[46] In the Georgetown section of Washington, D.C. alone, people could walk into branches for 13 different banks and set up a checking account.[47]

The Board, U.S. Department of Justice, and the courts have found that for assessing the state of competition, retail banking is a relevant product market and that metropolitan areas are the relevant geographic markets for retail banking.[48] These market definitions are generally considered to understate the degree of competition. On the product side, government authorities recognize that customers can also use money-market funds and other nationally marketed services for managing liquid funds.[49] On the geographic side the government authorities recognize that entry into local geographic markets is often relatively easy and that the ability of national banks to set up branches locally increases competitive pressure.

A commonly used statistical measure of the intensity of competition is the Herfindahl-Hirschman Index ("HHI"), which is used by the Board to assess bank competition for merger analysis. The U.S. Department of Justice and the Federal Trade Commission also use the HHI for screening mergers. The HHI is calculated by, first, squaring the market share of each firm, and second, summing the squared shares together. It ranges from a low of 0 for a perfectly competitive market to a high of 10,000 for a monopoly market. Markets are more concentrated when a few businesses have a large share even if there are many competitors. Antitrust authorities consider markets with HHIs below 1,500 to be competitive and generally do not review mergers that do not raise HHI above that level. When the HHI is expected to be above 1,500 after the merger, mergers are reviewed if there is a significant change in concentration. For bank mergers, a higher threshold of 1,800 is used in recognition of competition from limited-purpose lenders and other non-depository financial institutions that are not included in the banking HHI calculations.[50]

---

[46] FDIC and NCUA.

[47] FDIC.

[48] "Statement by the Board of Governors of the Federal Reserve System Regarding the Application and Notices by Wells Fargo & Company to Acquire Wachovia Corporation and Wachovia's Subsidiary Banks and Nonbanking Companies," Federal Reserve System, October 12, 2008, at p. 10 ("The Board's Statement on Wells Fargo and Wachovia").

[49] The Board's Statement on Wells Fargo and Wachovia at footnote 30. Robert E. Litan, "Antitrust Assessment of Bank Mergers," Speech, April 6, 1994.

[50] The Board's Statement on Wells Fargo and Wachovia at footnote 30. The horizontal merger guidelines were revised in August 2010. Previously, the guidelines indicated that mergers were not generally challenged unless the post-merger HHI was between 1,000 and 1,800 with an increase in the HHI of more than 100 or if the post-merger HHI was above 1,800 with an increase in the HHI of more than 50. See "Horizontal Merger Guidelines," U.S. Department of Justice and the Federal Trade Commission, issued April 2, 1992 and revised April 8, 1997. Available at http://www.justice.gov/atr/public/guidelines/horiz_book/ hmg1.html. Bank mergers are reviewed under a set of guidelines specific to the industry. Bank mergers are not generally challenged unless the post-merger HHI would be above 1,800 and the HHI would increase by more than 200. That is, there are higher safe harbor thresholds for the post-merger level of, and increase in, the HHI. "Bank Merger Competitive Review -- Introduction and Overview," Department of Justice, 1995. Available at http://www.justice.gov/atr/public/guidelines/6472.htm. With the August 2010 revisions to the general (non-bank) merger guidelines, the thresholds were raised for non-bank mergers. Mergers are not generally challenged unless the post-merger HHI is above 1,500 with an increase in the HHI of more than 100. The thresholds under the existing bank merger guidelines remain in effect and are still more lenient than the revised general guidelines. See "Federal Trade Commission and U.S. Department of Justice Issue Revised Horizontal Merger Guidelines," Federal Trade Commission, August 19, 2010. Available at http://www.ftc.gov/opa/2010/08/hmg.shtm.

TABLE 6: HHI Measurement for the Top 25 Metropolitan Statistical Areas		
Metropolitan Statistical Area	**HHI**	**Population**
Pittsburgh, PA	2,466	2.4
San Francisco-Oakland-Fremont, CA	2,323	4.4
Minneapolis-St. Paul-Bloomington, MN-WI	2,259	3.3
Cincinnati-Middletown, OH-KY-IN	2,028	2.2
Phoenix-Mesa-Scottsdale, AZ	1,674	4.4
Houston-Sugar Land-Baytown, TX	1,551	6.0
Dallas-Fort Worth-Arlington, TX	1,513	6.6
Sacramento--Arden-Arcade--Roseville, CA	1,306	2.2
Portland-Vancouver-Beaverton, OR-WA	1,293	2.3
Baltimore-Towson, MD	1,281	2.7
Detroit-Warren-Livonia, MI	1,281	4.4
New York-Northern New Jersey-Long Island, NY-NJ-PA	1,276	19.2
San Diego-Carlsbad-San Marcos, CA	1,270	3.1
Atlanta-Sandy Springs-Marietta, GA	1,248	5.6
Philadelphia-Camden-Wilmington, PA-NJ-DE-MD	1,224	6.0
Seattle-Tacoma-Bellevue, WA	1,151	3.5
Riverside-San Bernardino-Ontario, CA	1,116	4.2
Boston-Cambridge-Quincy, MA-NH	1,071	4.6
Denver-Aurora, CO	1,016	2.6
Los Angeles-Long Beach-Santa Ana, CA	962	13.0
Washington-Arlington-Alexandria, DC-VA-MD-WV	959	5.5
Tampa-St. Petersburg-Clearwater, FL	958	2.8
Miami-Fort Lauderdale-Pompano Beach, FL	719	5.5
Chicago-Naperville-Joliet, IL-IN-WI	635	9.7
St. Louis, MO-IL	632	2.9

Source: FDIC Quarterly 2010-4, at p. 46.

Table 6 reports the HHIs for retail banking in 2009 for the 25 largest metropolitan areas in terms of population.[51] Six of the 25 largest metropolitan areas including Los Angeles, Chicago, and Washington DC had HHIs below 1,000 in 2010; two other metropolitan including Boston and Denver had HHIs slightly above 1,000 (below 1,100). Eighteen of the 25 largest metropolitan

---

[51] "FDIC Quarterly," FDIC, 2010, 4:4, at p. 46 ("FDIC Quarterly 2010-4").

areas including New York City had HHIs below 1,500. Twenty-one of the 25 largest metropolitan areas had HHIs below 1,800.[52] The median HHI for the 25 was 1,270.

Despite the mergers and acquisitions that have led to significant national consolidation of the banking industry "urban market concentration has remained virtually unchanged."[53] Concentration has remained low in banking markets in part because Federal deposit cap limitations prohibit any national bank from obtaining more than 10 percent of total deposits via acquisition[54] and because the Board has required divestitures to ensure continuing competition in retail banking in local markets.[55]

The retail banking industry is even more competitive than these concentration metrics suggest. As we noted earlier, it has become easier over the last two decades for banks to enter local markets.[56] A 2007 study by economists Berger, Dick, Goldberg and White found evidence that technological progress enabled large multi-geography banks to compete more effectively in local markets by leveraging scale from larger operations, while also creating greater utility for consumers through extensive branch and ATM networks.[57] This competition is seen in the growth in the number of branches of banks. Between June 2004 and June 2009 the number of branches for 113 banks with more than $10 billion in assets increased by more than 7,000 (a compound annual growth rate of 3.5 percent over the five years).[58]

While banks differentiate from each other based on their pricing of various element of the retail banking relationship, there are significant similarities the offerings of major banks. Table 7 shows the basic free-checking account offered by 4 banks in the Miami metropolitan area. Other metropolitan areas would show similar results.

One of the results of this competition is that retail-banking customers have high churn rates. The American Bankers Association estimates that the average US bank experiences portfolio attrition rates of between 12 percent and 15 percent[59] while Bank Marketing News estimates the average rate to be about 12 percent.[60] These attrition rates typically are as high as 25-30 percent for customers in their first year of a relationship with a new bank.[61]

---

[52] The four above 1,800 were Pittsburgh, San Francisco, Minneapolis, and Cincinnati.
[53] Robin Prager, Antitrust in the U.S. Banking Industry (Presentation), Board of Governors of the Federal Reserve System November 30, 2007. Available at www.fdic.gov/bank/analytical/cfr/Prager.ppt.
[54] When the results of a proposed merger or acquisition does approach the deposit cap limits, (e.g. Bank of America/Fleet and Wells/Wachovia), banks typically will make commitments to either sell off component parts of the business or "run off" deposits in order to stay under the 10 percent cap. Deposit cap requirements do not apply to organic deposit growth.
[55] For example, see The Board's Statement on Wells Fargo and Wachovia.
[56] Ronald L. Spieker, "Future of Banking Study, Bank Branch Growth Has Been Steady- Will It Continue?" FDIC, August 2008.
[57] Allen N. Berger, Astrid A. Dick, Lawrence G. Goldberg, Lawrence J. White (2007), "Competition from Large, Multimarket Firms and the Performance of Small, Single-Market Firms: Evidence from the Banking Industry," *Journal of Money, Credit and Banking*, 39:2-3, pp. 331-68.
[58] FDIC Quarterly 2010-4, at p. 43.
[59] American Bankers Association, cited in "Start Banking on your current customers," Stellar Strategic Group, http://www.stellarstrategic.com/pdf/Relationship_Marketing.pdf ("ABA Stellar Strategic Group").
[60] "Deposit Growth Strategies in a Difficult Market," *Bank Marketing News*, January 29, 2009.
[61] ABA Stellar Strategic Group.

TABLE 7: Checking Account Features Offered by Selected Banks in Miami, Florida				
Feature	B of A	JPM Chase	Regions	Wells Fargo
Min. Opening Balance	None	$25.00	$100.00	$50.00
Minimum Balance	$0.00	$0.00	$0.00	$0.00
Free ATMs	Yes	Yes	Yes	Yes
ATM Rebates	No	No	No	No
Check Card Visa	Visa	Visa	Visa	
Telephone Banking	Yes	Yes	Yes	Yes
Online Banking	Yes	Yes	Yes	Yes
Overdraft Protection	Yes	Yes	Yes	Yes
Monthly Fee	$8.95, waived with a qualifying monthly direct deposit or an avg daily balance of $1,500 or more is kept.	$6.00, waived with a qualifying monthly direct deposit or at least 5 debit card purchases in a month.	$8.00, waived with a qualifying direct deposit, or 15 electronic trans per month, or a $1000 avg monthly balance.	$5.00, waived with a qualifying monthly direct deposit or an avg daily balance of $1,500 or more is kept.
Fraud Protection	Yes	Yes	Yes	Yes
Direct Deposit	Yes	Yes	Yes	Yes
Number Branches	5,700	3,108	2,518	2,087
Interest	0%	0%	0.01%	0%
FDIC protection	Yes	Yes	Yes	Yes

Source: www.checkingoptions.com, www.bankofamerica.com, www.chase.com, www.regions.com, www.wellsfargo.com

Given this degree of competition we would expect that banks and credit unions would tend to pass on cost savings to customers fully in the long term. The reverse is also true. Because competition reduces profitability we would expect that banks would pass on cost increases to customers fully in the long term. In practice, in the short term they would likely pass on less than 100 percent of significant cost changes because of the time it takes to revise pricing and product offerings and do market tests. The next part of this section examines the evidence on the extent to which banks increase or decrease prices in response to significant changes in costs.[62]

---

[62] The increase in interchange fee revenues from merchants can, for the pass-through discussion below, be treated equivalently as a reduction in cost.

B. The Pass-Through of Benefits and Costs to Consumers in Retail Banking

1. Improvements in the Value of Retail Banking Services in the 2000s

The last decade saw two important and related increases in revenue streams for depository accounts. First, banks and credit unions issued debit cards to more depository customers, and bank customers used these cards to make more transactions. As a result the average debit card interchange fee revenues for depository accounts increased considerably. Second, banks and credit unions increased revenues from fees charged to consumers when they incurred overdrafts, which became more common with the use of debit cards.

These increases in revenue were significant factors behind the expansion of retail banking services.[63] During the 2000s, consumers and small businesses received an increasing number of benefits from banks and credit unions through the expansion of services, many of which came without charges, and through reductions in fees.

- **Free checking**. The percentage of accounts at large banks that qualified for free checking[64] increased from 7.5 percent in 2001 to 76 percent in 2009.[65] That expansion resulted in part from a significant decline in the average minimum balance required to qualify for free checking from $440 in 2001 to $186 in 2009 (for no interest checking accounts).

- **Expansion of Consumer Access - ATMs and branches**. Over the decade banks made it easier to obtain money from accounts by expanding their deployment of ATMs and by opening more branches. Many banks also significantly expanded their operating hours both during evening and weekends to make banking more convenient for busy Americans. Despite lower revenues per ATM, banks continued to deploy ATMs throughout the 2000s as a service to drive competitive positioning with consumers. Total US ATM machine deployment has grown from 227,000 in 1999 to a total of 425,010 ATMs in 2008, driven heavily by bank ATM deployment by national players including Bank of America, JPMorgan Chase and Wells Fargo.[66] Similarly, bank branch coverage has increased steadily over time, reaching over 98,000 branches by 2010.[67]

---

[63] We have not conducted any empirical study that would demonstrate a causal relationship between these expansions in benefits and the expansion of revenues. However, the linkage is apparent from the basic economics of retail banking and conversations with executives in the banking industry confirm that linkage. At the same time we are not suggesting that all of the expansions in services and reductions in fees are related to debit cards. Banks have expanded ATMs and online banking in part to reduce to cost of having to maintain expensive branches and employer tellers.

[64] Free checking in this context means the percentage of accounts where there were no monthly service fees, or it was possible to waive monthly maintenance fees via a variety of methods, including minimum balances, direct deposit activity or number of debit card transactions per month.

[65] Bankrate, Checking Studies, 2001 – 2010, www.bankrate.com.

[66] Tyler Metzer, "ATM Use in the United States," CreditCards.com, March 2, 2010. Statistics referenced sources including ABA, ATM & Debit News, Dove Consulting and American Banker.

[67] SNL Financial estimate of bank branches, March 2010.

- **Online banking**. At the beginning of the decade most consumers did not have access to online banking, and if they did they had to pay extra for it. Over the decade banks invested in developing and improving online banking so that their customers could do most of their banking online. Forrester Research estimates that by 2011 76 percent of household will be banking online.[68] Virtually all banks now provide online banking to virtually all customers for free.[69]

- **Online bill payment**. At the beginning of the decade banks charged customers for online bill payment. By 2004 approximately two-thirds of the largest banks provided online bill payment as a free service to their retail deposit customers.[70] By the end of the decade free online bill payment was ubiquitous.

- **Mobile banking.** Mobile banking was introduced in 2007, and today serves 12 million consumers, a number which is expected to increase to 45 million consumers by 2014.[71] Consumers have also received this service for free.

The most significant benefit consumers received over the course of the 2000s was free checking, which reduced the barrier to getting basic retail banking services. Figure 1 shows the increase in free checking over the decade along with the increase in debit-card transactions.[72] Debit card interchange fees would have followed the same trend over this period since the change in the total fees was attributable mainly to the increase in the number of transactions rather than changes in debit card interchange fee rates.[73] We are not suggesting that we have demonstrated a causal relationship between these fees and the rise of free checking and, in fact, a number of other factors including overdraft fees were likely associated with the rise of free checking. Nevertheless, both the economics of competition in retail banking and anecdotal evidence indicates that debit card interchange fees were a major factor in the growth of free checking.

One of the most significant additional benefits that consumers and small businesses received with their checking accounts was a debit card that makes it more convenient to pay for things with funds from their accounts as well as to obtain cash. During the 2000s, banks reduced the cost of using debit cards, introduced rewards for using these cards, and increased the services that customers obtained with these cards.

---

[68] "US Online Banking: Five Year Forecast," Forrester Research, March 19, 2007.
[69] Banks have an incentive to offer this service for free in part because it reduces the cost of branches and tellers.
[70] "Pricing – The 'Fee vs. Free' Controversy," *Online Banking Report*, August 25, 2004. The article referenced a Fall 2003 Tower Group Report.
[71] Frost and Sullivan, cited by Constance Gustke "5 Reasons to Use Mobile Banking," Bankrate.com, March 10, 2010.
[72] The time series on the percentage of free checking accounts is based on Bankrate's survey of checking accounts. The methodology of Bankrate's survey is not reported in detail. While we cannot verify that the estimates are fully comparable across years, the significant trend toward free checking in the 2000s is consistent with our understanding from our conversations with industry participants.
[73] See Robin A. Prager, Mark D. Manuszak, Elizabeth K. Kiser, and Ron Borzekowski (2009), "Interchange Fees and Payment Card Networks: Economics, Industry Developments, and Policy Issues," *Finance and Economics Discussion Series*, Board of Governors of the Federal Reserve System, 2009-03, at figure 3 for evidence on the change in debit card interchange fees over this period of time.

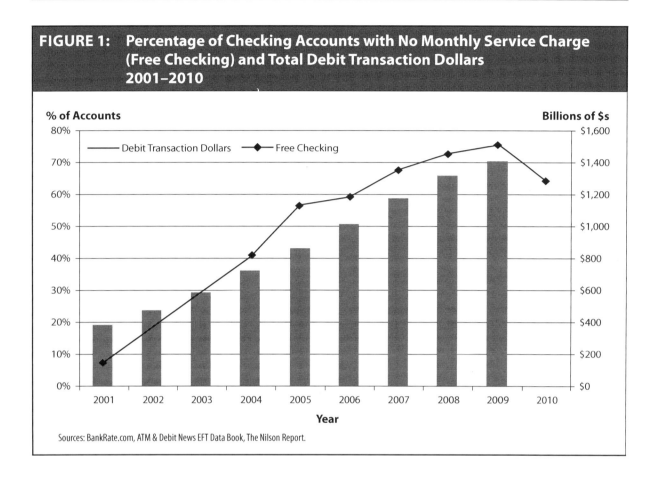

FIGURE 1: Percentage of Checking Accounts with No Monthly Service Charge (Free Checking) and Total Debit Transaction Dollars 2001–2010

Sources: BankRate.com, ATM & Debit News EFT Data Book, The Nilson Report.

Debit card fees. During the 2000s most banks eliminated fees for using debit cards. In the early 2000s many banks charged fees to some or all of their customers when they used PIN debit to make purchases, with fees ranging from $0.25 - $1.00. Some banks also charged annual fees for debit cards. By 2007, almost all large banks had eliminated these fees.[74] In a 2007 Bankrate survey, only 7 of the top 100 depository institutions had fees for debit usage.[75]

Debit card rewards. Few banks offered rewards for using debit cards at the beginning of the decade. By 2009 about two-thirds of debit cards had a reward program that provided a variety of benefits,[76] and approximately 45 percent of consumers were aware of these programs.[77] Debit card rewards participants receive points redeemable for airline miles, merchandise, charitable contributions, and cash back. Many banks also offer reward programs that provide incentives and bank matches for savings, such as Bank of America's Keep the Change program.

---

[74] Ellen Cannon, "Analysis: Check card fees gone," Check Card Survey 2007, Bankrate, 2007.
[75] Ibid.
[76] 2009 Debit Card Rewards – Consumer Insights," Consumer Loyalty Study, First Data, April 2009.
[77] Ibid.

Cash back at the Point of Sale. Over the decade banks increasingly made it possible for debit card users to obtain cash back at the point of sale. Consumers can usually receive cash back for free using their debit card at many merchant locations including supermarkets and drug stores; in many locations they would have to pay foreign ATM fees of $1.50 - $5.00 per transaction.

Fraud and Liability Protection. As consumers and small businesses switched from making purchases or paying bills with debit cards rather than checks over the 2000s they obtained increasing fraud and liability protection that was of considerable value to them. Because of real-time authorization and many sophisticated card security and risk management features, the use of debit cards is subject to very low rates of fraud compared with checks. Federal Law sets the maximum consumer fraud liability at $50 as long as the fraud is reported in a timely manner, but most banks have chosen to limit consumer liability to zero in most instances. Consumers were protected from $788 million in debit card fraud losses in 2008.[78]

During the 2000s total debit card interchange fees increased dramatically for banks and credit unions. These additional revenues from checking account customers led these banks and credit unions to compete for new checking account customers and to keep their existing customers from leaving for other financial institutions. The fee revenues, together with the forces of competition, led banks and credit unions to provide a number benefits to debit card users in particular and checking account customers generally. The loss of these fees and the same forces of competition would lead banks and credit unions to withdraw or curtail these benefits.

2. Bank Response to Regulation E Changes

Recent changes in Regulation E provide information on how banks respond to significant reductions in revenues and how quickly they do so. As mentioned, during the 2000s, banks earned increased net service fees ("NSF") in part from overdraft fees ("OD"). Concern over these fees led the Board, along with the Office of Thrift Supervision and the National Credit Union Administration, to exercise their authority under the Federal Trade Commission Act to make changes to Regulation DD that changed notification and opt-out requirements around NSF/OD fees. The final rules, which were announced in November 2009, were made to Regulation E, which implements the EFTA,[79] and came into effect on July 1, 2010. These regulations required banks to provide notice to consumers about NSF/OD fees, requiring them to "opt-in" in order for the bank to assess NSF/OD charges for ATM and debit transactions. Consumers who do not opt-in have their transactions that are over the limit declined. Although this change only applied

---

[78] "2009 Deposit Account Fraud Survey Report," American Bankers Association, November 2009. Check fraud numbers for the same period rose to $1.024 billion, despite declines in check usage.

[79] Federal Reserve System 12 CFR Part 205 [Regulation E: Docket No. R-1343]. The official staff commentary 12 CFR part 205 (Supp. I) interprets the requirements of Regulation E to facilitate compliance and provides protection from liability under Sections 915 and 916 of the Electronic Fund Transfer Act for financial institutions and other persons subject to the Act who act in conformity with the Board's official interpretations. 15 U.S.C. 1693m(d)(1). The commentary is updated periodically to address significant questions that arise.

TABLE 8:	Post Regulation E Checking Account Feature Changes		
Date	Financial Institution	Checking Account Fees Changes	Source
July 2010	Bank of America	Announced no more free checking for "basic accounts," $8.95/mo for teller access and paper statements. The fee is waived if customers make direct deposits in each period or maintain an average balance of $1,500. eBanking accounts are free.	Reuters News
July 2010	Wells Fargo	Eliminated free checking for new bank customers, introduced a $5 monthly fee on its most basic account. Fees are waived if a direct deposit of $250 or more is made or an average balance of $1,500 is kept.	Reuters News
September 2010	Citibank	Announced an $8/mo service fee. Customers must perform a combination of transactions to avoid service fees (direct deposits, any debit card purchase, bill payments, auto deductions, ACH payments, checks paid, cash withdrawals at any ATM)	Dow Jones Business News
December 2010	JPMorgan Chase	Basic account has a $6/mo fee waived if a direct deposit of $500 or more is made or 5 or more debit card purchases are made. "Chase Free Extra Checking" will be renamed "Chase Total Checking." with a $12 fee which will be waived with 1.) direct deposit of $500 or more, 2.) by keeping a daily balance of $1,500 or more, or 3.) keeping an avg balance of $5,000 or more in a combination of accounts at Chase.	The Record

to ATM and debit transactions, it had a significant impact on checking account fee revenue, as approximately 30-50 percent of NSF/ODs are associated with debit transactions.[80]

Starting within days after the new rules went into effect, banks began to announce changes to address the expected lost revenues by reducing the availability of free checking, raising other fees to recover the lost revenue and eliminating services.[81] By the fall of 2010, just a few months after the changes went into effect, most major banks had made significant changes. The percentage of accounts with free checking dropped 11 percentage points (roughly 20 million accounts) from 76 percent in 2009 to 65 percent in 2010. Table 8 summarizes changes in depository account

---

[80] Based on discussions with knowledgeable industry observers.
[81] We are not suggesting that these changes were entirely the result of the new Regulation E rules. Around this time banks were also responding to pressures from the financial crisis.

offerings for a selection of banks from July 2010-December 31, 2010 which were largely driven, according to analysts and banks, by the Regulation E changes.

The Regulation E experience shows that banks respond swiftly to significant costs increases or revenue reductions.[82]

C. Anticipated Reaction of Banks and Credit Unions to Reductions of Debit Interchange Fees

As shown above, the reductions in debit card interchange fees for banks and credit unions under the Board's proposals are large relative to depository account revenues and retail bank customer revenues. Given the highly competitive nature of the banking industry and the historical evidence presented above, we would expect that banks and credit unions would pass a significant portion of these costs on to retail banking customers in the form of higher fees or reduced services. As with the Regulation E changes, the change in fees and services would be expected to happen quickly, especially given the size of the impact. Over time we expect that banks and credit unions would reduce investment in various deposit-related services that benefit retail bank customers, since maintaining and attracting those customers would be less profitable.[83]

---

[82] To date we have been unable to find reliable, quantitative data to assess how much the banks and credit unions lost as a result of the Regulation E changes or how much of these losses were passed on to consumers in the former of higher fees or reduced services. Part of the complexity with the recent Regulation E changes is that banks were forced to eliminate a consumer service (and its associated costs) unless consumers opted in for the NSF/OD service. An unexpectedly large percentage of consumers chose to opt in, and many more have chosen to opt-in over time, making the determination of losses difficult.

[83] The Reserve Bank of Australia reduced credit card interchange fees November 2003. See Howard Chang, David S. Evans, and Daniel D. Garcia Swartz (2005), "The Effect of Regulatory Intervention in Two-Sided Markets: An Assessment of Interchange-Fee Capping in Australia," *Review of Network Economics*, 4:4, pp. 328 – 358, which estimates that Australian banks passed on 30-40 percent of the reduced credit card interchange fee revenues to cardholders in the short run (approximately the first year after the reduction). The Australian experience confirms that a reduction in interchange fees to merchant acquirers will result in an increase in other fees to cardholders. The estimated pass-through rate in Australia may not predict reliably what would happen in the United States in the event of a significant reduction in debit card interchange fee revenues. Predictions for debit cards may not apply to credit cards since they are very different products. Moreover the Australian credit card industry is highly concentrated, with the top four issuers accounting for 85 percent of all issuing, and predictions of pass-through from a highly concentrated market are likely to understate the pass-through that would occur in the highly competitive market for retail banking. Nevertheless, it is noteworthy that credit card fees continued to increase in later years. By 2006, for example, the average fee per account was about AU$40 higher than in had been in 2002 (prior to reforms), about the same as the decline in interchange fee per account that had resulted in the reforms. Without having done an extended analysis of these changes, it would still appear that the reduction in interchange fees was likely fully passed on to consumers in the form of higher fees. See http://www.rba.gov.au/payments-system/resources/statistics/rps.xls for the number of credit card accounts. See "Banking Fees in Australia," Reserve Bank of Australia, May 2008, available at http://www.rba.gov.au/publications/bulletin/2008/may/3.html; and "Banking Fees in Australia," Reserve Bank of Australia, May 2006, available at http://www.rba.gov.au/publications/bulletin/2006/may/2.html.

Shortly after the Durbin Amendment was passed as part of the Dodd-Frank bill, banks and credit unions started considering how to change their fees and services in response. These plans have accelerated since December 16th, when the Board proposed larger changes to debit card interchange fees than many observers had anticipated.

Based on our review of various sources we have found that banks and credit unions have been considering the following changes to offset the reductions in revenues in the two months since the Board announced its proposed reductions:[84]

- Increased monthly maintenance fees on DDAs
- Transaction fees for debit card usage
- Annual fees for debit cards ranging from $25-$30/year
- Fees for cash back at the point of sale
- Lower interest rates on funds in DDAs
- Limits to number of debit card transactions
- Limits to dollar amount of debit card transactions
- Increases to ATM fees for non-customers
- Reduction or elimination of debit card rewards programs, including savings programs
- Increased balance requirements and direct deposit amounts
- Reductions in interest spreads for consumers

Banks and credit unions would decide which of these changes to implement in the marketplace based on competitive dynamics and market research on the response of consumers to these various changes. There is, however, widespread agreement that the combination of radical debit card interchange fee reductions and the Regulation E changes of 2010 would lead to the elimination of free checking for most individuals and small businesses.[85]

We do not believe that it is likely that most banks and credit unions would impose significant fees on debit card transactions because, as discussed earlier, consumers can use cash, checks, and credit cards instead—each of which is free for making transactions.[86] However, it is likely that

---

[84] Robin Sidel, "At Banks, New Fees Replacing Old Levies," *The Wall Street Journal*, January 5, 2011; and Robin Sidel, "Checking Isn't Free at More Branches," *The Wall Street Journal*, February 19, 2011.

[85] Ibid. Also see, "New fees could drive millions to join the 'unbanked' // Some say the end of free checking could lead many to drop accounts. Others say big banks are using scare tactics as part of a lobbying effort," *Minneapolis Star Tribune*, February 13, 2011; and Karen Blumenthal, "Why Checking Fees Keep Going Up," *The Wall Street Journal*, December 4, 2010.

[86] Consumers spend at least $.075 per check ($5.96 + shipping and handling for a box of 150 checks at Walmart). www.walmartchecks.com.

banks and credit unions would curtail the supply of debit cards to consumers and small business customers in a number of ways.

As a result of increased checking account fees fewer consumers and small businesses would have checking accounts and therefore fewer would have debit cards.

Banks and credit unions would be likely to reduce the supply of debit cards services for transactions that have unusually high costs because of risk or customer service calls. That would likely involve banks and credit unions prohibiting the use of debit cards in certain high-cost situations or possibly surcharging for those transactions.

Banks, credit unions, and card networks would be likely to modify some of the features of debit cards, either eliminating them or charging for them separately. For example, banks and credit unions could charge consumers for cash back at the point of sale, impose fees for chargebacks to merchants, charge for customer service calls, and reduce fraud protections; the networks could also change features of the debit cards that benefit merchants such as the faster settlement of funds relative to checks.

The Board's proposed limits would decrease the profitability of debit cards relative to checks, credit cards, and exempt forms of prepaid cards. We would therefore expect that banks and credit unions would reduce the supply of debit card services and expand the supply of these alternative payment services.

IV. IMPACT OF PROPOSED FEE REDUCTIONS ON MERCHANTS

Merchant processors would be the direct beneficiaries of the reductions in debit card interchange fees. They book these fees as expenses and seek to recover them from merchants.

Based on discussions with people familiar with the merchant processing and acquiring business, approximately 25 percent of the merchants that accept cards, typically the larger merchants who collectively account for roughly 75 percent of payment card volume, have negotiated "interchange-fee plus" contracts with their processors. These contracts result in their paying merchant fees plus the interchange fees for transactions at their stores. The remaining 75 percent of merchants are typically smaller merchants who collectively account for roughly 25 percent of card volume. These smaller merchants pay processing charges without any specific assessment for interchange fees; the merchant processor factors in the interchange fee when it negotiates the price schedule for the merchant.[87]

The interchange-fee plus merchants would receive a penny-for-penny reduction in debit-card interchange fee costs. The first several parts of this section focus on determining the extent to

---

[87] There are no reliable data available to our knowledge on the total number of unique merchants that accept payment cards. Published data count merchant locations, which substantially exceeds the number of unique merchants since larger merchants operate from many locations.

which these larger merchants would reduce prices to consumers as a result of the decreases in the debit card interchange fees they would have to pay. We find that they would receive very small reductions in their costs as a percentage of sales (less than 0.2 percent) and would pass little of these savings on to consumers quickly. It is uncertain how much they would pass on to consumers in the form of lower prices over the longer run. The last part of this section considers the smaller merchants that have blended pricing. We find that merchant processors would not pass much of the reduction in interchange fees to these smaller merchants quickly. These smaller merchants would therefore not realize material cost reductions in the near term that they would be able to pass on to consumers.

For the purposes of this section "large merchants" refers to the merchants that have interchange-fee plus pricing and account for roughly 25 percent of all merchants. "Small merchants" refers to the merchants that have blended discounts and account for 75 percent of all merchants.

A. Estimated Magnitude of Debit Card Interchange Fee Reductions for Large Merchants

Merchants incur a variety of costs that result from taking payments from consumers that depend on the particular method of payment that consumers use. These costs include direct costs such as handling cash, the cost of returned checks, and merchant processor fees as well as indirect costs such as the time it takes cashiers to handle payments and the inconvenience that customers experience as a result of the payment choices made by other customers in line.[88] Debit card interchange fees are one of the elements of costs that determine how much merchant processors[89] charge the merchant when a customer uses a debit card for payment.

As a percentage of sales, the savings that merchants would receive from the debit card fee reductions is equal to the reduced debit card interchange fees they would pay divided by their total sales. We do not have access to the data to calculate this figure exactly but present a rough approximation.

According to the Board the average debit card transaction was $38.58 in 2009. Under the Board's proposals, debit card interchange fees would decline by 32 cents under the 12 price cap proposal or by roughly 37 cents under the 7 cent safe harbor proposal for a debit card transaction. Approximately 18.9 percent of the dollars that consumers spent were on debit cards in 2009[90] and 29.3 percent of

---

[88] Daniel D. Garcia-Swartz, Robert W. Hahn, and Anne Layne-Farrar (2006), "The Move Toward a Cashless Society: A Closer Look at Payment Instrument Economics," *Review of Network Economics*, 5:2.

[89] In order to accept cards, merchants must have a relationship with a merchant acquirer, a bank that accepts liability for merchant risk and sponsors the merchant. In practice, many merchant acquirers outsource the actual processing of merchant card transactions to an acquirer processor that sets the discount rate to the merchant, and assesses ancillary processing fees associated with card acceptance.

[90] Equal to the total debit card transaction volume ($1.45 trillion, as reported in The Proposed Rules) divided by the total US expenditure volume on goods and services (7.68 trillion, as reported in Nilson Report Issue #962).

transactions were made on debit cards in 2009.[91] Based on this information, the average purchase at merchants in 2009 was approximately $59.89.[92] Using these figures we find that the average savings for a large merchant would be 10.8 cents for the average purchase (0.18 percent) for the 7 cent safe harbor proposal or 9.4 cents for the average purchase (0.16 percent) for the 12 cent cap proposal.

The actual savings would vary across merchant categories depending on the interchange fees that the networks charge for that category (for example, grocery stores have lower rates than average);[93] the rate structure adopted in that category for signature or PIN debit (some merchant categories have a mixture of flat rate and proportional fees); and the share of dollars that are spent on debit cards (the percentage is higher at grocery stores and lower for bill payment). The actual savings would also vary across large merchants because many networks provide different interchange fees to merchants based on how much volume they process on that network, and many merchants have negotiated additional rate discounts directly from the networks.

For the purposes of our discussion we are going to assume that the typical large merchant would realize a 10 cent reduction in cost on an average purchase, amounting to 0.18 percent of overall sales. The 10 cent figure is for the purchase of a basket of goods by consumers. Merchants set prices on individual goods. We do not have data available to determine the average price of a good. But by way of illustration merchants would realize cost savings of less than 2 cents on a $10 item.

It is likely that these savings overstate the actual savings that merchants would realize. As mentioned earlier banks and credit unions would likely reduce the supply of debit card services including some services such as one-day settlement that merchants currently benefit from. In addition, banks and credit unions would likely take actions that would result in consumers and small businesses using debit cards less and alternative forms of payment such as checks, credit cards and exempt prepaid cards more. Banks and credit unions may also raise the cost to consumers of withdrawing cash at the point of sale which would reduce the supply of this form of payment which merchants at least claim is low cost to them. Merchants may, on the other hand, take steps to encourage the use of debit cards at the point of sale which could offset these changes to some degree.

B. The Extent to Which Merchants Pass Small Cost Changes on to Consumers

Merchants would be unlikely to change prices in response to the very small reduction in costs that would result from the proposed reductions in debit card interchange fees for three reasons we describe here.

---

[91] Schuh November 2010 Presentation.
[92] $38.58*(.293/.189)
[93] See "Visa U.S.A. Interchange Reimbursement Fees," Visa Inc., 2010, available at http://usa.visa.com/download/merchants/october-2010-visa-usa-interchange-rate-sheet.pdf; and "MasterCard Worldwide U.S. and Interregional Interchange Rates," MasterCard, 2010, available at http://www.mastercard.com/us/merchant/pdf/MasterCard_Interchange_Rates_and_Criteria.pdf.

Menu costs: It takes time and money for merchants to change the prices they charge consumers. Economists refer to these as "menu costs" because they are similar to the costs that restaurants incur when they change the prices on their menus.[94] Retailers would weigh the benefits and costs of changing prices. The benefits of reducing prices in response to a cost reduction would include persuading consumers to shop at their store instead of competing stores. Given that stores compete on many dimensions, including location, convenience, and service, it is hard to imagine that price changes in response to the small reductions contemplated here would result in a competitive edge. Merchants also reduce prices to drive sales. It is hard to believe that the handful of penny changes involved here would do that either.

Focal price points: Retailers tend to set prices based on focal "price points" such as $9.99.[95] When they change prices they tend to change them to another focal point that they believe will be appealing to consumers. A 2 cent change in cost on an item would not be likely to persuade retailers to move to a different focal point by itself. They would be likely to leave prices where they are or move the price to another focal point based on a number of cost and demand changes.

Price predictability: Retailers tend not to change prices frequently in part because consumers like predictability in prices. Retailers are particularly hesitant to reduce prices because consumers are resistant to increases in prices tomorrow that reductions today may make necessary.[96]

In fact, most merchants do not change prices frequently in response to changes in the continual changes in demands and costs that occur in the market. Economists have conducted a number of studies that document that prices are "sticky" in many markets:

Former Board Vice Chairman Blinder and co-authors conducted a survey of 200 firms in 1998. They found that the median firm changed prices about once a year.[97]

Nakamura and Steinsson found that the average duration of a price for consumer goods was 11 months. They found that the average ranged from 0.5 months for vehicle fuel, 1.9 months for travel, 3.5 months for unprocessed food, 9.0 months for processed food, 16.1 months for household furnishing, 16.3 for recreation goods, and 27.3 months for apparel.[98]

MacDonald and Aaronson found that restaurants kept the same prices for around one year.[99]

---

[94] Daniel Levy, Mark Bergen, Shantanu Dutta, and Robert Venable (1997). "The Magnitude of Menu Costs: Direct Evidence from Large U.S. Supermarket Chains." *Quarterly Journal of Economics*, 112:3, pp. 791–825.

[95] Edward S. Knotek II (2010), "The Roles of Price Points and Menu Costs in Price Rigidity," Federal Reserve Bank of Kansas City, Research Working Paper.

[96] Eric T. Anderson and Duncan I. Simester (2010). "Price Stickiness and Customer Antagonism." *Quarterly Journal of Economics*.

[97] Alan S. Blinder, Elie R. D. Canetti, David F. Lebow, and Jeremy B. Rudd (1999). "Asking About Prices: A New Approach to Understanding Price Stickiness," *Review of Industrial Organization*, 15:1, pp. 97-101.

[98] Emi Nakamura and Jon Steinsson (2008), "Five Facts about Prices: A Reevaluation of Menu Cost Models," *Quarterly Journal of Economics*. This excludes temporary price changes for promotions and price changes resulting from the substitution of a new product for an existing product. See tables 2 and 4.

[99] James M. MacDonald and Daniel Aaronson (2006), "How Firms Construct Price Changes: Evidence From Restaurant Responses To Increased Minimum Wages," *American Agricultural Economics Association*.

A 1995 study by Kashyap found there was an average of 14.7 months between price changes for mail-order catalog goods.[100]

The price stickiness literature suggests that on average it would take about a year for cost changes to work their way down to changes in the prices that consumers pay.

Given the very small size of the debit card interchange fee reductions on a per transaction and per product basis, the disincentives for changing prices quickly, and the evidence on price stickiness, we believe that it is unlikely that consumers would see materially lower prices quickly following the proposed interchange fee reductions on July 21, 2011. Some merchants that are changing prices for other reasons might adjust prices in light of these changes, but others would likely wait for a future date to consider changing prices.

C. Pass-Through of Debit Card Interchange Fee Reductions to Consumers

Merchants eventually change their prices in response to changes in costs, demand, competition, and other factors. We would expect that one of the factors they would consider in changing their prices would be the cost reductions that would result from debit card interchange fee reductions. Economists have found that it is difficult to predict how much of a cost change will be passed on to consumers except in those markets that are intensely competitive, in which all of it is likely to be passed on in some form. The degree of pass-through depends on the precise nature of the demand facing firms,[101] how firms compete with each other, and other factors.[102]

The nature and degree of competition in a market requires a detailed analysis. In the case of banking we relied on the work by the Board that found that retail banking was the relevant product market and that the metropolitan statistical area was the relevant geographic market. We presented an analysis above that indicated that competition was intense within those retail banking markets and relied on a number of independent studies that supported this. There is no similar presumption that the merchant categories that would receive the bulk of the debit interchange fee reductions are intensely competitive and would therefore pass on most of the savings to consumers in the form of lower prices. For the banking analysis we were able to rely on published concentration statistics (the HHIs) for the geographic areas that the Board has determined to be the relevant geographic market. We were not able to find similar published data on merchant categories where

---

[100] A. K. Kashyap (1995), "Sticky prices: new evidence from retail catalogs," *The Quarterly Journal of Economics*.

[101] As a technical matter the rate of pass-through depends on the second-derivative of the demand schedule (i.e. the change in the change in demand in response to changes in prices). Different demand conditions can lead to very different rates of pass-through.

[102] Carl Shapiro and Joseph Farrell have observed that pass through rates are hard to estimate. See Joseph Farrell and Carl Shapiro (2010), "Antitrust Evaluation of Horizontal Mergers: An Economic Alternative to Market Definition," *The B.E. Journal of Theoretical Economics*, 10:1, at Section 3.B. Shapiro and Farrell are the chief economists respectively of the Antitrust Division of the U.S. Department of Justice and the U.S. Federal Trade Commission.

the antitrust authorities have identified local geographic markets that differ substantially from the metropolitan statistical area as we discuss below.

Supermarkets account for a significant portion of debit card use. The Federal Trade Commission has reviewed a number of supermarket mergers.[103] In the course of doing so it has found that there is a relevant product market for large supermarkets that can provide a full array of grocery and related products to consumers and that this market includes the grocery portion of supercenters. Other stores that sell food—such as club stores, premium natural and organic supermarkets, "mom & pop" stores, specialty food stores, and convenience stores—are generally not viewed as competitors in the relevant market.[104] The Federal Trade Commission has also found that the geographic market is local and depends mainly on how long it takes to drive to different supermarkets.[105] Based on examining data for a number of cities and admittedly casual inspection it appears that most people have the choice between a few supermarkets as defined by the antitrust authorities. A downtown resident of Boston, Massachusetts would find 4 supermarkets chains within the city limits (5 if we included Whole Foods which the FTC would not); based on the experience of two of the authors most people would find only one or two of these convenient to use on a regular basis for major shopping.

Big box retailers also account for a significant portion of debit card use. The Federal Trade Commission has found that there are local markets for big box retailers. In *Staples/Office Depot* the FTC argued and a court agreed that these office superstores faced little competition from other stores that sold office supplies and that the geographic markets were local. In 15 metropolitan areas, Staples and Office Depot were the only competitors.

Debit cards are used in a variety of merchant categories. In most of these categories the relevant product and geographic markets for assessing the degree of competition, and thus any presumption concerning full pass through, are much smaller than the overall category. Take first-run movie theaters, which are part of the entertainment services category. In *AMC/Loews*, the Justice Department found that there are local markets for first-run movie theaters and that first-run movie theaters do not face competition from second-run or specialist movie theaters, home movie viewing or other forms of entertainment.[106] In three local markets (the northern part of Chicago,

---

[103] We are not necessarily endorsing the conclusions reached by the antitrust agencies and we are not suggesting that there are any antitrust concerns in the merchant categories we discuss here. Our analyses are solely focused on predicting the degree of pass through from small cost reductions and not on any other competition issue. These analyses however do indicate that it would be at least premature to conclude that any of the categories we discuss are intensely competitive to the extent that would be required for full pass-through of cost reductions.

[104] Complaint, *In the Matter of The Great Atlantic & Pacific Tea Company, Inc., and Pathmark Stores Inc.*, ¶13, November 2007, available at http://www.ftc.gov/os/caselist/0710120/0710120cmplt.pdf. In the proposed merger between Whole Foods and Wild Oats the FTC concluded that for the purposes of assessing price competition these premium and natural organic supermarkets were in a separate product market from regular supermarkets.

[105] In the proposed merger between Whole Foods and Wild Oats the FTC concluded that for the purposes of assessing price competition these premium organic stores were in a separate product market than regular supermarkets.

[106] Complaint, *U.S. v. Marquee Holdings, Inc. and LCE Holdings, Inc.*, ¶¶ 14-27, December 2005, available at http://www.justice.gov/atr/cases/f213800/213861.htm.

downtown Boston and downtown Seattle), the parties to the merger were the only two competitors. The Justice Department sought and obtained divestitures in those and other local markets.

We conclude from these analyses that there is no presumption that all or most of the merchants retailers that would receive the debit-card interchange fee reductions operate in the sorts of intensely competitive product and geographic markets that would tend to drive the full pass through of cost changes.

What portion of a cost change these larger retailers would pass on to consumers is uncertain in the absence of research on the market conditions faced by these retailers. We have not found any empirical studies that would allow us to predict the effect of the very small industry-wide reduction in costs involved here. To the extent economists have conducted empirical studies of pass through the evidence indicates that the pass through rate is roughly 50 percent (for cost changes that are generally significantly larger than the ones applicable here) but could be lower or higher across businesses and industries.[107]

D. Estimated Windfalls Received by Large Merchants

As noted earlier, estimates from knowledgeable industry sources indicate that 25 percent of the merchants that accept cards account for 75 percent of card transactions and have agreements under which their merchant processors would pass on all of the debit-card interchange fee reductions to them. We have estimated how much revenue these large merchants would likely keep under the assumption that these merchants also account for 75 percent of debit card interchange fee revenues.[108] In the first 24 four months after the Boards regulations come into effect the large merchants would receive cost savings of $25.0 billion under the 12 cent cap proposal and $28.9 billion under the 7 cent safe harbor proposal.

Based on the analysis above we believe that it is likely these large merchants would not pass on a significant portion of these cost savings to consumers in the form of lower prices in the first 12 months given that these cost savings are a very small percentage of sales and the evidence on price stickiness reported above. For the purposes of a rough estimate, we assume that they would pass on 10 percent of the cost saving in the form of lower prices in the first year. We believe that it is highly speculative how much overall the large merchants would pass on in the next 12 months. For the purposes of a rough estimate we assume they would pass on 50 percent of the cost savings

---

[107] Empirical studies on pass-through by supermarkets and other retailers of manufacturer discounts to consumers suggest pass-through is approximately in the 50-70 percent range. See Vincent Nijs, Kanishka Misra, Eric T. Anderson, Karsten Hansen, and Lakshman Krishnamurthi (2009), "Channel Pass-Through of Trade Promotions," *Marketing Science*, at p. 8; and Sergio Meza and K. Sudhir (2006), "Pass-Through Timing," *Quant Market Econ*, at p. 352. Empirical studies on the pass through of changes in the costs of goods imported to the US due to exchange rate fluctuations finds that approximately 40-60 percent of cost shocks are passed through. See Pinelopi Goldberg and Michael Knetter (1997), "Goods Prices and Exchange Rates: What Have We Learned?" *Journal of Economic Literature*, at pp. 1249-50; and Jose Manuel Campa and Linda S. Goldberg (2005), "Exchange Rate Pass-Through Into Import Prices: A Macro Or Micro Phenomenon?," *Review of Economics and Statistics*, at p. 679.

[108] We have no reason to believe the proportion for debit cards would be substantially different.

in the form of lower prices in the second 12 months (about the average pass-through rate for the studies cited above). Based on these assumptions the large merchants would receive a windfall over the first 24 months of $17.2 billion in the case of 12 cent price cap proposal and $19.9 billion in the case of the 7 cent safe harbor proposal.

We believe that it is likely that after 24 months banks and credit unions which operate in highly competitive retail banking businesses would have passed on roughly 100 percent of the revenue losses from debit card interchange fee reductions in the form of increased fees or reduced services. We believe that it is also likely that after 24 months large merchants would pass on significantly less than 100 percent of their cost savings to consumers. Therefore, we would anticipate that the proposed debit card interchange fee reductions would continue to harm consumers and small businesses well beyond the initial 24 month period.

Proponents of the claim that merchant would pass on savings fully to consumers rely entirely on the economic proposition that firms in highly competitive industries will pass on all cost savings to consumers and the claim that retailing is highly competitive. For example, the Reserve Bank of Australia has reported no empirical evidence that retailers in that country passed on *any* cost savings to consumers following the reductions in credit and debit card interchange fees in that country.[109] They nevertheless claim that consumers have benefited from lower prices because economists would expect firms to lower prices under competition.[110] As we have discussed above, the evidence—much of it based on the analysis by antitrust authorities—demonstrates that the categories that account for significant portions of debit card transactions are not the kinds of highly competitive markets for which 100 percent pass through would ordinarily take place.[111] As far as we are aware, proponents of the claim that merchants would pass through the cost savings have not presented any empirical evidence to support it.

E. Impact of Debit Card Interchange Fee Reductions on Smaller Card Accepting Merchants on Blended Pricing

There are several reasons to doubt that the small merchants would receive significant cost savings quickly as a result of the proposed reductions in debit card interchange fees or that their prices would fall eventually by the full amount of the debit-card interchange fee reductions.

---

[109] "Reform Of Australia's Payments System Preliminary Conclusions Of The 2007/08 Review," Reserve Bank of Australia, April 2008, at pp 22-23, available at http://www.rba.gov.au/payments-system/reforms/review-card-reforms/pdf/review-0708-pre-conclusions.pdf .

[110] Ibid.

[111] Retail markets in Australia are even more concentrated than in the United States which makes the RBA claim even more difficult to accept. For example, in Australia two national supermarket chains account for more than 75 percent of the market for supermarkets. See National Association of Retail Grocers of Australia Pty Ltd letter dated July 20, 2010 citing market share figures from ACNielson and Retail World, available at http://www.pc.gov.au/__data/assets/pdf_file/0012/102072/sub047.pdf; and Andrew Jacenko and Don Gunasekera (2005), "Australia's retail food sector," Australian Bureau of Agricultural and Resource Economics, conference paper.

Because they pay blended pricing to their merchant acquirers, small merchants cannot easily tell how changes in debit card interchange fees should affect the merchant discounts they are charged. They also have less incentive to switch to another merchant processor that reduced merchant discounts in response to the interchange fee reductions because the costs of doing so are likely to outweigh the savings. They would incur costs for looking for a new processor, negotiating a contract, and completing paperwork. A merchant with sales of $1 million would only save between $1,565 and $1,809 per year if they found a merchant processor that fully passed on the cost reduction, while a merchant with sales of $250,000 would only save $391 and $452 per year.[112] Their incentives to switch would be even lower if merchant processors did not pass on all of the interchange fee reductions. Finally, for some smaller merchants it can be especially difficult to switch merchant processors. A significant portion of the process of entering into an agreement with a merchant processor is a determination of the risk that the merchant presents to the acquirer. Small merchants in particular can have high rates of chargeback and fraud or face other financial difficulties that could impose costs on the acquirers. There is typically significant paperwork and time required for entering into an agreement with a processor for a small merchant.

Merchant processors are unlikely to offer lower prices to the small merchants that receive blended pricing because, for the reasons just discussed, they recognize that by doing so they may not attract many merchants from competitors and that by not doing so they are unlikely to lose many accounts to competitors. Merchant processors have much less pricing flexibility with large merchants, who usually have the track record to easily switch processors, have accounting departments that can handle the paperwork, and have bargaining power because of their size.

Analysts are forecasting that large merchant processors will realize increases in earnings in part because they will retain some portion of the debit card interchange fee reductions. These increased earnings would come largely from the reductions in interchange fee expenses incurred for smaller merchants with blended fees who would not receive a corresponding reduction in fees. For example, the analyst group Baird recognizes that interchange fee pass-through will not be complete for direct merchants under bundled pricing and ISOs (agents of the merchant processors who particularly sign up small merchants) would have the opportunity to keep a portion of interchange fee reductions.[113] Similarly, Aite Group concluded that in the short run merchant processors and ISOs that offer bundled pricing to merchants will be able to bring down fees at a slower rate even though the debit interchange reduction impact will be immediate.[114]

---

[112] The calculation of the potential interchange fee cost reductions is based on the average debit interchange fees paid per transaction in 2009 (1.14%) and assumes that the portion of merchant sales volume transacted on debit cards is equal to the percentage of US total expenditure volume that debit card transaction made up (18.9%). Debit card transaction volume as a percentage of total expenditure volume is based on the total personal consumption expenditures of 7.68 trillion for 2009 as reported by The Nilson Report (Issue #962) and total debit card transactions of 1.45 trillion as reported in The Proposed Rules, at p. 81725.

[113] Business Process Outsourcing, Thoughts on Debit Interchange/Exclusivity Regulations, Robert W. Baird & Co., December 17, 2010.

[114] The New Order: How Interchange Regulation Will Change the U.S. Payment Industry, Aite Group, December 2010.

V. IMPACT OF PROPOSED FEE REDUCTIONS ON LOWER INCOME CONSUMERS, SMALL BUSINESSES, AND SMALL BANKS AND CREDIT UNIONS

Section 904 of the EFTA obligates the Board to conduct specified economic analyses whenever it proposes new regulations under the EFTA. Among other things, the Board must analyze the "costs and benefits to financial institutions, consumers, and other users of electronic fund transfers" and how the proposed regulation affects "competition in the provision of electronic banking services among large and small financial institutions and the availability of such services to different classes of consumers, particularly low income consumers."[115] The RFA also requires the Board to consider how proposed regulations would affect small financial institutions and as well as small businesses more generally.[116]

The previous sections document how the proposed regulations of debit card interchange fees would, in the aggregate, harm consumers. This section examines how the proposed regulation would affect lower-income consumers, small businesses, and small financial institutions. We hope the Board finds this material useful in preparing the analyses required by the EFTA and RFA.

A. Lower Income Consumers

Over the last several decades, lower-income segments of the population—including many individuals who belong to groups considered to be disadvantaged for various reasons—have been brought into the financial system. The likely effect of the proposed rate caps would be the withdrawal of many of those households from the mainstream market for banking services. In general, the proposed regulation would affect those households in particular because their relatively low average account balances mean that the profitability of existing relationships with them is likely to depend in large part on debit interchange fees and net service fees.

A checking account gives a household numerous benefits. Most obviously, it is a safe and liquid place to keep its funds. Research on lower-income households in the United States and other parts of the world shows that the ability to put money aside and access it easily is important for pulling these households up the economic ladder.[117] These accounts also provide the basic building blocks for household management of finances, the touchstone of financial competence. Finally, a checking account is the steppingstone for developing a credit record and the ability to borrow money. A FDIC survey of people that did not have bank accounts found that people want to open

---

[115] 15 U.S.C. § 1693b(a)(2)-(3).
[116] 5 U.S.C. § 603(a).
[117] Tyler Desmond and Charles Sprenger (2007), "Estimating the Cost of Being Unbanked," Federal Reserve Bank of Boston. Caskey et. al (2006), "The Urban Unbanked in Mexico and the United States," World Bank Policy Research Working Paper.

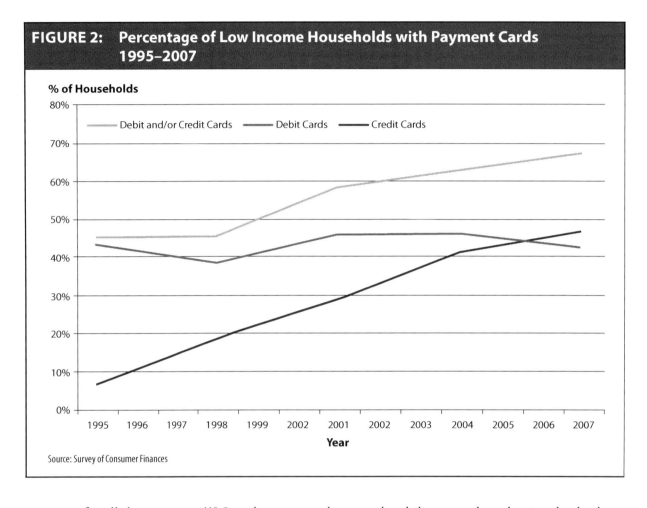

FIGURE 2: Percentage of Low Income Households with Payment Cards 1995–2007

Source: Survey of Consumer Finances

accounts for all these reasons.[118] Simply put, people covet the ability to cash and write checks, have a safe place for their money, and save.

One important benefit that has flowed from checking-account access has been the ability of lower-income households to obtain debit cards. Many of these households did not qualify for credit cards and therefore getting a checking account has been the main way for them to get plastic.[119] The percentage of low income households with access to a payment card increased from 45 percent to 67 percent between 1995 and 2007 as shown in Figure 2.[120] Crucially, much of the increase resulted from debit cards. The percentage of low income households with access to a credit card has remained fixed at around 43 percent through that time period, but the percentage

---

[118] "FDIC National Survey of Unbanked and Underbanked Households," FDIC, December 2009 ("FDIC Survey of Unbanked and Underbanked").

[119] In recent years they have been able to get prepaid cards. Although these cards often offer many of the same benefits, they are also relatively expensive (and thus less satisfactory as a general policy option for lower-income households).

[120] Low income is defined as households with an income that is 50 percent or less than the median.

of households with a debit card increased from 7 percent to 47 percent. Because modern debit cards are full-purpose payment cards, households that obtained those cards thereby gained access to mainstream financial activities like paying online, paying over the phone, renting a car, and all of the other transactions that customarily require a full-purpose payment card.

Lack of access to checking accounts, related banking services and debit/ATM cards has severe economic consequences for lower income households. Unbanked households have to rely on expensive check-cashing services when they are paid with checks, manage their cash between paychecks often in unsecure environments, and rely on payday lenders and other sources of borrowing when their cash does not stretch through the month. Their dependence on those more expensive services is exacerbated by the limited likelihood that they will have access to credit cards to manage minor liquidity events.

The FDIC estimates that as of 2009 more than 25.6 percent of American households were unbanked or under-banked.[121] Nine million households had no banking relationship, and 21 million households relied on high-cost check cashing or other expensive financial service providers.[122] The unbanked and underbanked consist disproportionately of low and moderate income Americans, including high percentages of African-Americans, Hispanics and Native Americans.[123]

Revenues from debit card interchange and other services spurred banks to provide free depository accounts to households. Many of these households were lower income households, as the *The Wall Street Journal* reported in June 2010:

The offers of free checking without any minimum balance requirements attracted a new wave of low-income customers, who previously went to check-cashing stores. Some consumer advocates have warned that the elimination of free checking could drive some of those customers out of the banking system.[124]

The proposed debit-card interchange fee reductions can be expected to push a significant number of lower-income households out of the banking system and thereby increase the number of unbanked households. Debit card interchange fee revenues and net service fees help defray the other costs of the accounts including the costs of complying with regulations, posting, processing and sending statements, and fraud costs. As a result of the combined loss of revenues from overdraft fees and debit-card interchange, banks are now eliminating, or considering eliminating, free checking and imposing higher fees on accounts. As noted earlier, the Regulation E limitations have already resulted in banks reducing the percentage of free checking accounts from 76 percent

---

[121] See FDIC Survey of Unbanked and Underbanked. Unbanked households are those without a checking or savings account, and under-banked households are those that have either a checking or savings account, but have used non-bank financial alternatives (e.g. check cashers or payday lenders) in the last 30 days.
[122] FDIC Survey of Unbanked and Underbanked, cited in "Obama Administration Pushes "Bank on USA" to Help Unbanked and Under-banked Americans," Worldpress.com, September 2, 2010.
[123] Ibid.
[124] Robin Sidel and Dan Fitzpatrick, "End Is Seen to Free Checking," *The Wall Street Journal*, June 16, 2010 ("WSJ: End Is Seen to Free Checking").

in 2009 to 65 percent in 2010.[125] The elimination of debit-card interchange revenues is likely to accelerate the discontinuation of free checking[126] and result in increased fees for many customers, especially those who do not maintain high balances.[127]

We were not able to forecast the number of accounts that households would abandon as a result of the higher checking account fees that would be imposed in the event that the Board adopted the proposed debit card interchange fee regulations. On JPMorgan Chase's 4Q 2010 earning conference call, however, Jamie Dimon, the bank's CEO, stated that the fee increases that would result from the loss of debit card interchange fee revenues would make banking service too expensive for as many as 5 percent of Chase's customers.[128] We would expect that a significant portion of the customers that would abandon checking accounts would be lower-income households since those are the ones most likely not to be able to want to pay for the more expensive accounts. To get an understanding of the potential significance of these closures we note that a one percent decline in checking accounts would result in the loss of checking access for roughly 1 million households; an increase in the number of households by 1 million would increase the percent of unbanked individuals by 12 percent.[129] While we are not in a position to offer a precise forecast of the impact of the Board's proposed rules on the number of unbanked households, based on the information we have seen we believe increases in this order of magnitude—1 million or more—are plausible. For example, if Mr. Dimon is correct that 5 percent of accounts would be closed and 20 percent of those accounts were closed by households in the bottom quintile of the income distribution, then the reduction of low income household with a checking account would be approximately 1 million. We urge the Board to investigate this further.

B. Small Businesses

We estimate that roughly 15.4 million small businesses have checking accounts.[130] These likely include most active small businesses that are engaged in the sales of goods and services and there-

---

[125] BankRate.com.
[126] See WSJ: End Is Seen to Free Checking; and "US Debit Market and the Durbin Amendment: Worse Than The Worse-Case Scenario," Oliver Wyman, December 22, 2010.
[127] See Table 8.
[128] "US debit fee caps may hurt poorest customers-Dimon," *Reuters News*, January 14, 2011.
[129] Based on 1 percent loss in checking relationships from 105.4 million households with a checking account. In this illustration, the number of unbanked households would increase from 9.00 million to 10.05 million.
[130] There were an estimated 198 million consumer and small business accounts in 2010 as we discussed in footnote 29. Based on data we have received from knowledgeable industry observers roughly 9.1 percent (18 million) of checking accounts are held by smaller businesses. This figure is adjusted downward by 14.7 percent to account for small business that had a checking account at more than one financial institution (see the 2003 Survey of Small Business Finances which shows that approximately 14.6 percent of small businesses had a checking account at more than one financial institution and the average number of financial institutions used for checking accounts by small business was 1.17). The total number of small businesses was 27.5 million in 2009 but many of these small businesses are part-time businesses, inactive, or have small receipts.

fore the preponderance of small businesses (those with fewer than 500 employees) based on the percentage of sales or employment. Approximately one-eighth of the $15.7 billion ($1.96 billion) of debit-card interchange fee revenue that the Board reported for 2009 came from purchases made by the owners of small business accounts.[131] Indeed, the average debit-card interchange revenue is higher for small business accounts than for consumer accounts because small businesses tend to spend more on their debit cards than do consumers. Specifically, the estimated debit card fee revenue per small business account for 2009 is roughly $109 ($1.96 billion in interchange fees divided by 18 million small business accounts). The proposed reductions in debit-card interchange fees would reduce that by between $79 and $92 per account. Based on estimates of the fraction of debit-card fee revenues due to small business accounts, we estimate that banks and credit unions would lose $4.2-$4.8 billion in revenues from small business accounts over the first 24 months after the proposed regulation went into effect.[132]

Our analysis of how banks and credit unions would respond to the loss of the debit-card interchange fee revenues indicates that they would promptly pass on much of the lost revenue relatively quickly to checking account holders in the form of higher fees or reduced services. As a result, the average small business account holder could expect to face higher fees or reductions in services that would account for a significant portion of the $79-$92 of debit card interchange fees that banks and credit unions would lose per account. In the aggregate then, small businesses would suffer a loss in the first 24 months of proposed rate caps approaching the $4.2-$4.8 billion of debit card interchange fee revenues that the regulation would remove from small business accounts.

Some small businesses also accept debit cards for payment and would obtain offsetting benefits to the extent that their merchant processors passed on reductions in debit card interchange fees in the form of lower blend payment card prices. As we discussed above, however, we find it unlikely that merchant processors would lower blended prices quickly to smaller businesses or do so by anything approaching the full amount of the reduced debit card interchange fees.

We present an illustrative calculation of the possible overall impact on small businesses. Suppose banks and credit unions consistently passed on 75 percent of the lost revenue in first year and 100 percent in the second year. Then the total loss to small businesses would be between $3.7 and 4.3 billion over the first 24 months. Suppose merchant processors reduced fees to merchants with blended prices by 10 percent of the reduction in interchange fees in the first 12 months and 50 percent in the second twelve months. In this scenario, merchant debit card

---

[131] The estimate of the percentage of interchange fees from small business accounts is based on information from knowledgeable industry observers concerning the fraction of checking accounts held by small businesses. We have excluded prepaid cards, which accounted for $500 million of the total $16.2 billion of interchange fees in 2009, because most prepaid cards are exempt from the proposed regulations.

[132] The estimated revenue reduction figures of $4.2-$4.8 billion are based on the assumption that small businesses will continue to make up roughly 1/8th of the total debit interchange fees during the first two years following the implementation of the proposed fee reductions.

charges would fall by between $2.6 and $3.0 billion in the first 24 months. The net impact on small businesses would be between $1.1 and $1.3 billion. These figures are likely to understate the net harm to small businesses because they do not include the higher fees for small business owners that use a personal checking account for their business. The smallest businesses, in particular, are likely to be the worst off, as they will receive little benefit from lower fees for debit card transactions if they have modest sales volume, while all small businesses will experience increases in checking account fees.

C. Small Financial Institutions

As discussed earlier, we also doubt that banks and credit unions with assets of less than $10 billion would receive materially higher interchange fees than banks and credit unions with assets of $10 billion or more. The networks would face market pressures from large debit-card issuers and large merchants to reduce the debit card interchange fees received by exempt institutions to a level similar to the level that covered institutions receive. Moreover, merchants could discriminate against cards from small issuers by refusing to accept these cards or steering consumers away from them. Exempt institutions might also prefer to accept lower interchange fees than risk having their checking account customers discouraged by retailers from using their cards.

Indeed, the community banks themselves are convinced that the Board's proposed interchange fee regulations will harm them. The Independent Community Bankers of America (ICBA) noted that "the so called 'carve out' for institutions with less than $10 billion in assets included in the Durbin amendment simply won't work primarily because merchants will now control the entire transaction process, driving customers to cheaper price-controlled cards instead of cards issued by their local community bank."[133]

The Board's proposed interchange fee caps are likely to be more severe for smaller institutions because these institutions have considerably higher average total costs for debit cards – because they incur fixed costs that they recover over small volumes of transactions and because they face higher variable costs of transactions than larger institutions. We have examined this issue in particular with respect to the average variable costs of authorization, clearing and settlement that the Board has used as the basis for its proposed safe harbor and cap. According to the Board the median per transaction variable cost for the 89 large institutions included in its survey was 7.1 cents.[134] However, the average variable cost weighted by transaction volume was 4.0 cents.[135] The difference between the median and the weighted average demonstrates that larger institutions have significantly lower average variable costs than larger institutions.

---

[133] Independent Community Bankers of America, "Survey: Fed Debit Card Rule Will Harm Community Bank Customers," Press Release, February 14, 2011.
[134] The Proposed Rules, at 81725.
[135] Ibid., at 81737.

In fact, even among the institutions in the Board's survey the differences are striking. For the weighted average to be 4.0 cents large institutions must have average variable costs less than 4.0 cents. Yet 20 percent of the large institutions had average variable costs in excess of 12 cents according to the Board.[136] Small banks and credit unions outsource their debit card processing to card processors. Based on conversations we have had with knowledgeable industry observers it is our understanding that the average processing cost (the equivalent of authorization, clearing and settlement) is 15 cents and higher for institutions with assets less than $10 billion. We would expect other costs related to debit cards would be higher for smaller banks and credit unions than for larger ones.

Smaller institutions may also face more difficulties recovering lost revenues than larger institutions. Although they emphasize close relationships with their customers for the product lines that they do offer, they tend to provide retail customers with fewer services such as insurance, mortgages, and other financial services products than do larger institutions. As a result, it is possible that the operating margins of smaller institutions could decline even after they undertake efforts to raise fees and reduce services. That in turn would reduce their operating capital and their ability to extend loans. The impact on these smaller institutions could exacerbate the negative effects discussed above for small businesses. Notably, although small banks have less than a quarter of the industry's assets, they make more than half of small business loans.[137]

We have not had access to sufficient data to assess what the overall financial impact of the proposed rules would be on small banks and credit unions and their small business customers who need credit. We would urge the Board to conduct further research, as we understand it is required under EFTA and RFA, to assess more fully the impact of its proposed rules on small banks and credit unions.

VI. CONCLUSION

The Board's proposed debit card interchange fee regulations would likely have the following effects over the 24 month period between July 21, 2011 and July 20, 2013:

- Consumer and small business owners would face higher retail banking fees and lose valuable services. We estimate that these losses would equal a large fraction of the $33.4-$38.6 billion that banks and credit unions would lose over those 24 months.

- Small businesses would lose a large fraction of the $4.2-4.8 billion that banks and credit union would lose on debit card interchange fees from small business accounts over those

---
[136] Ibid.
[137] FDIC Call Report Data as of September 30, 2010.

24 months. Most of these businesses do not accept debit cards and would not have any offset from lower fees. Given that smaller merchants that do accept cards are unlikely to receive significant reductions in the blended pricing they pay, we would anticipate that small businesses overall would lose.

- The number of unbanked individuals would likely increase, possibly by more than 1 million households under plausible assumptions, as a result of lower-income individuals not being able to afford checking accounts.

- Large retailers would receive a windfall that based on some plausible assumptions could equal $17.2-$19.9 billion dollars in the first 24 months.

chapter 5

HOW CHANGES IN PAYMENT CARD INTERCHANGE FEES AFFECT CONSUMERS FEES AND MERCHANT PRICES: AN ECONOMIC ANALYSIS WITH APPLICATIONS TO THE EUROPEAN UNION

By

David S. Evans and Abel Mateus

I. INTRODUCTION

This paper presents an economic analysis of how changes in interchange fees for payment cards are passed through to final consumers. It shows that a decrease in the interchange fee would tend to increase the fees charged by banks that issue cards to consumers but would tend to decrease the prices charged to consumers by merchants that accept cards. The net effect on consumers depends on the magnitude of these countervailing effects. The paper shows how an analysis of competitive conditions in markets can provide some guidance on the likely overall effect.

Although some previous studies of interchange fee regulations have recognized these competing effects there has been little rigorous analysis of the question.[1] That is unfortunate since the sign and magnitude of the overall effect on consumers is relevant for the debate over interchange fee regulation. It is generally accepted that antitrust should benefit consumers, at least in the long run. Government intervention is often justified on the grounds that it is needed to correct some "market failure" that prevents competition from maximizing consumer welfare. Competition authorities take consumer interests as paramount in enforcing the competition laws.[2] Evidence that a particular reduction in interchange fees increases consumer welfare could confirm the desirability of that reduction, while evidence that the reduction decreases consumer welfare raises questions on the amount of the reduction and possibly the desirability of the intervention.[3]

---

[1] In the United States, Federal Reserve economist, Mark Manuszak, in response to questions posed regarding the impact of recently proposed debit card interchange fee regulations reported to the Federal Reserve Board of Governors that, "any savings that consumers might realize at point of sale could be offset by fee increases at their banks, as well as changes in terms that debit cardholders face for card use and deposit accounts. So, specifically, account holders at covered institutions may face higher fees for debit card use or additional account fees .... [I]t's hard to anticipate what the overall [e]ffect on consumers will be." "Federal Reserve Board of Governors Holds an Open Meeting," CQ Financial Transcripts, December 16, 2010, at pp. 10-11 of 28. The Reserve Bank of Australia simply asserted that merchants would pass on all of the their savings on interchange fees to consumers: "[n]o concrete evidence has been presented to the Board regarding the pass-through of these saving, although this is not surprising as the effect is difficult to isolate… [d]espite the difficulties of measurement, the Board's judgment remains that the bulk of these savings have been, or will eventually be, passed through into savings to consumers." See "Reform of Australia's Payments System Preliminary Conclusions Of The 2007/08 Review," Reserve Bank of Australia, April 2008, at pp 22-23, available at http://www.rba.gov.au/payments-system/reforms/review-card-reforms/pdf/review-0708-pre-conclusions.pdf. The European Commission estimated the extent to which banks pass on interchange fee revenues to consumers in the form of lower prices from data on a panel of European countries; See "Interim Report I Payment Cards," European Commission, April 12, 2006, ("Interim Report I"). However, there are severe econometric issues with the methods that it used which render its estimates unreliable, as we discuss further below.

[2] Joaquín Alumina, the European Commission's Commissioner of Competition, has stated: "[C]ompetition policy is a tool at the service of consumers. Consumer welfare is at the heart of our policy and its achievement drives our priorities and guides our decisions. Our objective is to ensure that consumers enjoy the benefits of competition, a wider choice of goods, of better quality and at lower prices." See "Competition and Consumers: the Future of EU Competition Policy," a speech delivered by Joaquín Almunia on European Competition Day, May 12, 2010, available at http://europa.eu/rapid/pressReleasesAction.do?reference=SPEECH/10/233&format=HTML&aged=0&language=EN&guiLanguage=en.

[3] It is possible that a horizontal agreement could be permitted under Article 101(3) TFEU if that agreement provides sufficient benefits that are shared with consumers.

This paper is related to and complements several strands of the literature on interchange fee regulation. First, there is a large theoretical literature on the socially optimal level of interchange fees and on whether card schemes have an incentive to set these fees too high. We do not address that literature, but simply provide a local analysis of a further reduction of the fees already set in Europe, and consider if that reduction would improve overall consumer welfare.[4] Furthermore, it provides a check on indirect empirical approaches towards designing socially optimal interchange fees such as the tourist test.

Second, there is an empirical literature on how interchange fee reductions have altered consumer fees and merchant prices in jurisdictions that have lowered fees.[5] This paper makes advances in the economic framework for assessing the pass-through and likely effects of reductions.

Third, there is a recent literature, which is closely related to this paper, which uses evidence on market structure and historical fluctuations in interchange fees to assess the likely net effect on consumers.[6] This paper provides a more detailed analysis of the economics of pass-through as applied to the payments card industry and explores its relevance to the situations in the highly diverse Member States of the European Union.

The paper reaches three main conclusions.

1. Government authorities can obtain considerable insights into the impact of interchange fee reductions on consumers by applying the "economics of pass-through" literature to the particular circumstances of the payment card systems, banking, and retail markets in their jurisdictions.

2. The analysis confirms the general finding of the two-sided markets literature that the ability to improve consumer welfare through government regulation of the interchange fee is very dependent on the specific empirical facts of the market. One

---

[4] We do not present an analysis of social welfare. To move from our analysis to an analysis of social welfare one would have to further consider, and quantify, producer surplus and dynamic efficiencies resulting from improved performance on payment methods. Nevertheless, when policies harm consumers there should be an exceptionally strong showing that there are countervailing economic efficiencies that would warrant this. Moreover, our analysis suggests that the net effect of interchange fee reductions is to transfer wealth from consumers to merchants and that this policy is more consistent with rent-seeking behavior on the part of merchants than with sound public policy.

[5] See Howard Chang, David S. Evans, and Daniel D. Garcia Swartz, "The Effect of Regulatory Intervention in Two-Sided Markets: An Assessment of Interchange-Fee Capping in Australia," *Review of Network Economics*, 4:4 (2005); Robert Stillman, William Bishop, Kyla Malcolm, and Nicole Hildebrandt , "Regulatory intervention in the payment card industry by the Reserve Bank of Australia," CRA International, (2008) ("CRA International Report"); and Santiago Carbo Valverde, Sujit Chakravorti, and Francisco Rodriguez Fernandez, "Regulating Two-Sided Markets: An Empirical Investigation," ECB Working Paper No. 1137, (2009), available at http://ssrn.com/abstract=1522023.

[6] David Evans, Robert Litan, and Richard Schmalensee , "The Net Effects of the Proposed Durbin Fee Reductions on Consumers and Small Businesses," *Lydian Journal*, Issue 5(2011), available at http://www.pymnts.com/assets/Lydian_Journal/LydianJournal-March-2.pdf and David Evans, Robert Litan, and Richard Schmalensee, "Economic Analysis of the Effects of the Federal Reserve Board's Proposed Debit Card Interchange Fee Regulations on Consumers and Small Businesses," Submission to the Federal Reserve Board of Governors, (2011), also available at http://ssrn.com/abstract=1769887.

would reach very different conclusions on the impact of regulation on consumers in a jurisdiction with highly competitive retail industries and highly concentrated retail banking (consumers likely to benefit from a reduction) than with very concentrated retail industries and highly competitive retail banking (consumers unlikely to benefit from a reduction).

3. A review of the competitive circumstances in many European countries suggests that it is unlikely that significant reductions in interchange fees would result in an improvement in the situation of consumers at least through price effects. The impact of interchange fee reductions on consumer banking fees is likely to be large and quick. Banks would experience a significant reduction in revenue for their current accounts. The evidence strongly suggests that banks would increase fees to largely compensate for this loss. The reductions in merchant prices to consumers are likely to be small and delayed. Merchants would receive a small decrease in their overall costs. The evidence suggests that they would not pass on much of this savings to consumers in the short run and on average only about half in the long run.

The paper is organized as follows. Section II describes the economics of four-party systems. Section III summarizes what economists have learned about the pass-through of cost changes to final consumer prices. Section IV applies this to assess the impact of interchange fee reductions on retail banking prices, while Section V applies it to merchant pricing. Section VI reports estimates of the overall effect of an interchange fee reduction under alternative assumptions. Section VII concludes.

II. ECONOMICS OF FOUR-PARTY PAYMENT SYSTEMS

Payment card systems are two-sided platforms that facilitate transactions between consumers and merchants by providing a means of payment for both parties. Some payment card systems are the sole intermediary between merchants and cardholders and are known as three-party (or three-corner) systems. Most payment card systems have additional intermediaries that stand between the card network and the merchant (merchant acquirers) and between the card network and consumers (card issuers). They are traditionally called four-party (or four-corner) systems—merchant, acquirer, issuer, and cardholder—even though they are technically five-party systems after including the network. This paper focuses on four-party systems.[7]

---

[7] The analysis is similar for three-party systems in which case the issuing and acquiring functions are integrated with network thereby eliminating two of the five arms-length contracts discussed below.

Economic models of the payment card industry typically focus on the four-party model and make a variety of simplifying assumptions.[8] These may include assuming that one side of the platform (typically the acquiring side) is perfectly competitive and that the card network is a monopolist. These models then analyze the determinants of price levels and price structure. Of particular interest, in many of these models, is the interchange fee that determines the relative prices paid by merchants versus cardholders for the payment transaction services provided by the platform. The network charges the interchange fee to acquirers and pays the interchange fee to issuers.[9] Under perfect competition on the acquiring and issuing side the interchange fee is fully passed through as a cost to merchants and received as a benefit by cardholders. It thus determines the prices paid by merchants and cardholders. While these are useful modeling assumptions that make the mathematics tractable, the actual economics of the four-party systems is more complex in ways that can affect the impact of interchange fees on consumer fees and merchant prices. This section explains these details, which can vary greatly across countries and across payment systems within countries.

A. Card Issuing

In most countries the card network contracts with banks to issue cards under its brand. For many countries the debit card is the predominant type of card that is issued. The debit card provides a method that a checking account customer can use for accessing funds in her checking account. She can use the debit card to withdraw cash at cash machines that are connected to the bank or to pay with funds in her checking account at merchants that accept the debit card brand for payment.[10] There is no direct competition among issuers for consumers to take debit cards. Rather, banks compete for checking account customers and the debit card is included in the bundle of services provided by the bank.

Credit cards, on the other hand, are not necessarily linked to the checking account. Consumers have the choice of paying off their charges over the course of month in full, often by making a payment from their bank account, or taking out a loan for some or all of these charges. Credit cards are sometimes provided by the bank to its retail banking customers and in other cases provided by banks that specialize in offering credit cards to consumers regardless of whether they have a checking account at that bank.

---

[8] See Jean-Charles Rochet and Jean Tirole, "Cooperation among Competitors: Some Economics of Payment Card Associations," *The RAND Journal of Economics*, 33:4 (2002), pp. 549-570 and Julian Wright, "The Determinants of Optimal Interchange Fees in Payment Systems," *The Journal of Industrial Economics*, 52:1 (2004), pp. 1-26.

[9] The models do not assume that the acquirer necessarily pays the fee to the issuer; the direction of the payment is determined by profit maximization. Although the acquirer does pay the fee to the issuer in most payment systems in reality there are some—such as the Australian domestic debit scheme—in which the issuer pays the acquirer.

[10] In some countries the bank provides a "deferred debit card" in which case the funds are swept from the checking account periodically, say at the end of the month, and which provide a line of credit.

B. Card Acquiring

Typically the acquirer and its sales agents sign up merchants to accept card payments.[11] In some markets the acquirer signs up merchants to accept only one card brand, whereas in most markets, the merchant is signed up to accept multiple card brands. The acquirer then works with the merchant to get the appropriate equipment and communications systems installed to accept cards and transmit the relevant information to the acquirer when a payment card transaction occurs. The acquirer typically has a contract with the merchant that determines the services that the acquirer will provide the merchant and the prices the merchant will pay for those services.

The most important service the acquirer provides is acting as an intermediary between the merchant and the network, whereby the acquirer assumes ultimate responsibility for merchant settlement risk.[12] The acquirer is compensated by a per-transaction charge for handling the acquiring services; while there may be fixed transaction charges most of the fees collected by merchants come from charges that are based on a percent of the transaction amount. In some cases the acquirer charges merchants its own fee plus the applicable interchange fee for the transaction, which varies by card brand, type of card, kind of transaction, and possibly other factors. This is known as "interchange plus pricing" and is common for acquirer contracts with large merchants. In other cases, particularly for small and medium size enterprises, the acquirer charges the merchant a single all-inclusive fee. With "blended rate pricing" the merchant acquirer does not distinguish between different brands and types of cards.

The acquiring side of the business exhibits considerable variety across countries. There are several major ways in which acquiring is structured.

1. Competitive non-exclusive acquiring. In this case the card networks enter into contracts with multiple acquirers who compete with each other for merchants. The acquirers can represent multiple systems and present merchants with the ability to take cards from multiple brands. Card issuers can also act as acquirers.

---

[11] Acquirers may delegate some of these tasks to other firms. In some countries such as the United States acquirers are financial institutions are participating members in a networks such as MasterCard or Visa and have the unique ability to enter into contracts with merchants on behalf of the card network. But many of these acquirers then either delegate most of processing, risk management and other work to other companies or in some cases in effect rent their licenses to larger firms.

[12] When the consumer pays with their card an electronic communication is sent from the merchant via the acquirer to the card network and then back to the card issuer to authenticate the cardholder and determine if funds are available. Once a successful transaction takes place and it is time for settlement, the acquirer receives the funds on behalf of the merchant and ultimately deposits those fees less any "off the top" service charges in the merchant account. In the event of a fraudulent transaction, return or other standard exception, the acquirer facilitates appropriate reversal of the transaction, and assessment of any chargeback or exception fees according to the rules established by the network. In the event of merchant fraud or bankruptcy, the acquirer—either on its own or as a result of a requirement by the network—will assume the risk of outstanding merchant transactions that require refunds to consumers. In addition, the acquirer is typically accountable to the networks for ensuring that merchant business practices do not result in excessive reversals or chargebacks, and as such often levy fines against acquirers when merchants exceed certain fraud, risk or other exception thresholds.

2. Competitive exclusive acquiring. The acquirer only works for one card system and as a result merchants have to contract with multiple acquirers to accept the brands of multiple networks.

3. Sole acquirer. The banks in a country, or an individual card network, grant a single acquiring license. In one variation of this model the banks hold an equity interest in the acquirer and receive dividends based on the profitability of the acquirer.

Bank issuers may participate directly or indirectly in the acquiring business in some countries. Banks that issue cards may also acquire merchants. This situation gives rise to "on-us" transactions where the merchant and the cardholder are both serviced by the same bank. The interchange fee in this case nets out since the bank that pays the fee and the bank that receives the fee are one in the same. In other countries, as noted above, banks may receive a dividend or some other form of compensation from the merchants. We do not treat these varied organizational arrangements in detail in our analysis below but we would recommend that regulators consider them carefully in their particular jurisdictions to estimate the impact on consumers accurately.

C. Card Schemes

The card networks typically earn money through fees they charge merchant acquirers and merchant issuers. Public information on these is usually not available. In the United States, however, a study by the Federal Reserve Board found that on average payment networks charge acquirers 4.1 cents per transaction and issuers 4.5 cents per transaction; those figures compare to an average of 44 cents for interchange fees. Thus the networks earned 48 percent of their net network fees revenue from acquirer assessments and 52 percent from issuer assessments.

The organization of the card networks varies across jurisdictions. Historically, most card systems were membership organizations in which the system was owned by the issuers and acquirers or sometimes just the issuers.[13] The two global networks, MasterCard and Visa, became publicly owned equity corporations in 2006 and 2008 respectively; although some banks have equity the issuers and acquirers do not have majority ownership.[14]

D. Flow of Funds among Parties

With this background in mind let us now consider a card network that has a 1.0 percent interchange fee and explore how that fee flows to the various parties based on a €100 transaction. The €1 interchange fee is paid by the acquirer to the issuer. The acquirer charges the merchant for its

---

[13] In some countries such as Brazil the card system is owned by some of the banks that issue cards while other banks are licensed to issue cards but do not have an ownership position.
[14] Visa Europe is not owned by Visa International and has continued as an association of banks.

services using either on an interchange-fee plus (in which case the merchant pays €1) or a blended rate contract (in which case the acquirer has selected a rate that reflects its interchange fee cost). The card network does not receive anything from the interchange fee but assesses its own separate fees to the acquirer (which would become part of the cost basis for the acquirer) and the issuer.[15]

E. Interchange Fees and Contracts between Payment System Participants

The remainder of this paper will focus on the impact of changing the interchange fee exogenously through government-imposed price caps. A four-party system involves five "contracts" between the parties that involve prices and the delivery of services. In some cases the contract is explicit: acquirers generally have a formal contract with the merchant. In other cases it may be informal: banks may tell consumers what they are getting with their bank accounts but there may be no formal agreement. Importantly, these contracts spell out a price, a variety of services that will be provided, and rights and obligations of the parties. A price cap that lowers the interchange can affect the contracts between

1. the acquirer and the merchant as a result of the acquirer's costs going down;
2. the merchant and the consumer as a result of the merchant's costs going down;
3. the network and the acquirer as a result of the acquirer's costs going down;
4. the issuer and the cardholder as a result of the issuer's revenue going down; and,
5. the network and the issuer as a result of the issuer's revenue going down.

A proper accounting of the effects of an interchange fee change has to consider all of these contracts. In each case the parties can adjust both the prices and the services provided. In the remainder of this paper we focus only on the price recognizing that in reality the parties could also adjust services and therefore the "quality-adjusted prices" being paid between the parties in the system. We further assume that the network does not change its assessments on acquirers and issuers as a result of the change in the interchange fee and therefore focus on contracts 1, 2, and 4.[16]

---

[15] That does not mean, however, that the network is indifferent to the interchange fee. The card network uses the interchange fee to affect the incentives faced by merchant acquirers and card issuers and through them merchants and consumers. A lower interchange fee encourages more merchant acceptance by effectively lowering the cost to the acquirer and ultimately the merchant; a lower interchange fee also reduces the revenue that issuers receive from cards and therefore reduces their incentives to issue cards and in turn increases the prices that consumers have to pay for cards. As is well known in the two-sided market literature the card network will balance these considerations to maximize the volume of transactions on the network since it will make more money if there are more transactions. It is actually a bit more complicated and depends in part on the ownership structure of the network (in particular whether the issuers or acquirers are owners).

[16] The incentive for the network to change its fees has not been explored in the literature and is beyond the scope of this paper.

When the interchange fee changes, the costs and revenues of the various parties in the system change. The "economics of pass through" is the framework used by economists to evaluate how these sorts of changes ultimately affect the final prices to consumers.

III. THE ECONOMICS OF PASS-THROUGH

Beginning students of economics often learn a simple and elegant result. When there is perfect competition among firms and there are constant unit costs of production 100 percent of a change in costs will be passed on to consumers in the form of higher or lower prices. The situation is shown in Figure 1. DD reflects the demand schedule facing consumers. CC is the constant average and marginal cost of production; CC also reflects the industry supply curve since firms will be willing to supply as much output as the market wants at that price which covers costs. The competitive price and output level is at the intersection of CC and DD. If CC increases by €1.00 to C'C' then it is apparent from the diagram that the price increases by €1.00 as well. If, for example, the government imposed a €1.00 tax on each unit of output that the producer had to pay, the price to consumers would simply rise by this €1.00. It is easy to verify that the result does not depend on the shape of the demand schedule; replacing the linear schedule in the diagram with any proper nonlinear demand schedule would give the same result.

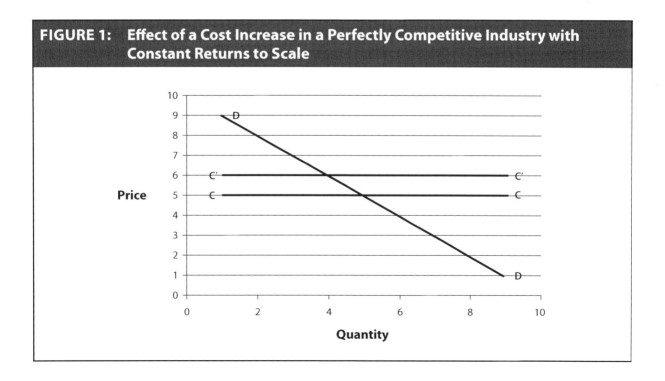

FIGURE 1: Effect of a Cost Increase in a Perfectly Competitive Industry with Constant Returns to Scale

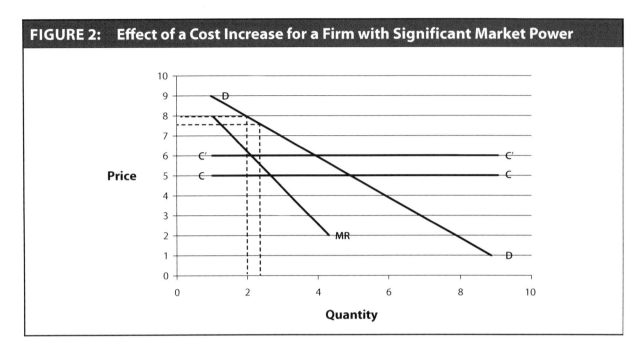

FIGURE 2: Effect of a Cost Increase for a Firm with Significant Market Power

Economics does not provide such a specific conclusion about the pass-through of costs when markets deviate from perfect competition with constant returns to scale. The percent of the cost change that is passed through to consumers in price changes depends on details such as the market structure, extent of product differentiation, the competitive interactions among the firms, and the precise shape of the demand schedule around the profit-maximizing price and output level before the cost change.[17]

As a general matter, we would expect that when firms are not in a competitive industry with constant returns to scale they would only pass on a portion of a cost change to consumers—and thereby share both the pain and gain of cost changes with consumers. We can motivate this result by considering the situation for a firm that faces a downward sloping demand curve and therefore has some market power to set its own price. Consider the situation in which the government imposes a €1.00 tax on each unit of output sold by the firm. Figure 2 shows how this affects the setting of the profit-maximizing price. At least in the case of linear demand the firm will increase its price by less than €1.00.[18] The firm passes through only a portion of the cost increase to consumers and absorbs a

---

[17] See E. Glen Weyl, "Pass-Through as an Economic Tool," Working Paper, (2008), available at http://economics.uchicago.edu/pdf/weyl_110308.pdf ("Weyl 2008").

[18] As Weyl observes the impact of a cost change on final prices depends critically on the precise shape of the demand schedule around the equilibrium from which prices are changing in addition to the nature of competition and costs. While economists write down linear demand schedules for convenience there is no reason to believe that schedules are linear in the real world. If the demand schedule is non-linear then, depending on the curvature around the equilibrium, a cost increase could result in varying degrees of pass-through including possibly more than 100 percent (what is known as cost amplification).

portion through reduced profit. There is a similar result when the firm has a cost decrease. Consider the case in which the tax falls by €1.00. The firm will lower its price to consumers.

This result exposes two common fallacies. The first is that a monopolist would keep the benefits of a cost reduction for itself; it will not because with lower costs it can make more profits by lowering price and increasing sales. The second is that a monopolist would just take a cost increase from its profits; it will not because it can lower the reduction in profits by raising prices somewhat.

A number of economists have studied empirically the extent to which cost changes have affected final prices. Many of these studies have looked at situations in which the government imposed a tax that producers had to pay, or the extent to which changes in foreign exchange rates effect have on import prices and the prices of domestic goods. The studies are summarized in Appendix A.[19] Overall these studies find that the pass-through rate varies in real-world markets from 22-74 percent in the long run with a median of approximately 50 percent in the long run.[20] For studies that focused on Europe the pass-through rates range from 19 to 66 percent in the long run with a median of approximately 53 percent. We will use 50 percent as the long-run pass-through rate on the merchant side for our illustrative calculations below.

The previous studies have focused on long-run price changes as a result of cost changes. Economists have also studied the degree to which prices are sticky—how long does it take for firms to changes their prices in response to cost shocks. These studies, summarized in Appendix B, have found that merchants do not adjust prices quickly.[21] These studies typically find that prices stay constant for about a year or more. Moreover, prices appear to be particularly sticky in Europe.[22]

The cost and other shocks analyzed in the price-stickiness literature are large enough to enable the researchers to measure their effects on prices. Dhyne et al. calculated the average price decrease in the ten European countries they analyzed was 10 percent.[23] Nakamura and Steinsson calculated the median price reduction in their analysis to be 9.2 percent.[24] Klenow and Kyrstov observed a median price change of 9.7 percent and found that only 12.1 percent of all price changes were less

---

[19] We have reported recent significant papers on pass through that we have identified in searching the literature, that cover a range of products, and that provide an estimate of the pass-through rate.

[20] We took the median of the estimates reported in Appendix A. For papers reporting a range, we took the midpoint of the range. For the Campa and Goldberg paper, we used the (larger) estimate reported for the one year rather than one quarter pass-through rate.

[21] We have reported recent significant papers on price stickiness that we have identified in searching the literature, that cover a range of products, and that have an estimate of the duration over which prices are sticky.

[22] One study found that in Europe only about 40 to 64 percent of the equilibrium price adjustment needed take place within two years, in contrast to about 58 to 80 percent in the United States. See Rita Duarte and Carlos Robalo Marques, "Wage and Price Dynamics in the United States and the Euro Area," *Banco de Portugal Economic Bulletin*, Autumn 2009, pp. 173-189. The shocks that necessitate price adjustments in this paper relate to demand and technological shocks, so the paper is not directly estimating the pass-through of costs.

[23] Emmanuel Dhyne, Luis J. Álvarez, Hervé Le Bihan, Giovanni Veronese, Daniel Dias, Johannes Hoffmann, Nicole Jonker, Patrick Lünnemann, Fabio Rumler and Jouko Vilmunen, "Price Changes in the Euro Area and the United States: Some Facts from Individual Consumer Price Data," *Journal of Economic Perspectives*, 20:2 (2006), pp. 171-192.

[24] Emi Nakamura and Jón Steinsson, "Five Facts About Prices: A Reevaluation of Menu Cost Models," *Quarterly Journal of Economics*, 123:4 (2008), pp. 1415-1464.

than 1 percent in absolute value.²⁵ These studies may not therefore accurately predict what happen for very small changes in costs. It turns out that this is important for our discussion of merchant pass through since the reduction in the average cost for merchants, as a percent of price, from even drastic interchange fee reductions is small in percentage terms (typically less than 0.5 percent) and tiny in absolute terms (typically less than 4 cents on a typical €50 purchase by a consumer). The price-stickiness literature finds that firms appear to try to minimize menu costs by avoiding the types of small price changes that could result from the very small per item cost changes resulting from changes in interchange fees.²⁶

Several conclusions emerge from the theoretical and empirical literature on pass-through

1. For highly competitive industries with constant returns to scale, firms would pass through 100 percent of a change in cost to buyers.

2. For other situations, the rate of pass through as a theoretical matter depends on the precise shape of the demand schedule, market structure, costs and the nature of the competitive interaction among firms. It is therefore case specific.

3. Studies of actual industries undergoing cost shocks find pass-through rates ranging from 22 to 74 percent with a median of 50 percent.

4. Firms are unlikely to pass small cost changes along in the short run (about a year) as a result of menu costs and other factors that tend to make prices sticky.

5. There is little empirical evidence on how quickly and how much of very small cost changes will be passed on but we would expect they would be passed on more slowly than larger ones.

IV. THE IMPACT OF CHANGES IN INTERCHANGE FEES ON RETAIL BANKING FEES

Changes in interchange fees result in effective cost changes for acquirers and issuers. When the interchange fee declines the cost that acquirers incur for a transaction declines as well. There are then two pass-through issues: how much of the cost decrease does the acquirer pass on to the

---

[25] Peter J. Klenow and Oleksiy Kryvtsov (2008), "State-Dependent or Time-Dependent Pricing: Does it Matter for Recent U.S. Inflation?," *Quarterly Journal of Economics*, 123:3, pp. 863-904.

[26] Jeffrey R. Campbell and Bejamin Eden, "Rigid Prices: Evidence from U.S. Scanner Data," Federal Reserve Bank of Chicago Working Paper WP 2005-08, (2010); Alberto Cavallo, "Scraped Data and Sticky Prices: Frequency, Hazards, and Synchronization," Working Paper, (2010); Alberto Cavallo and Roberto Rigoborn, "The Distribution of the Size of Price Changes," Working Paper, (2010); Saul Lach and Daniel Tsiddon, "Small Price Changes and Menu Costs," *Managerial and Decision Economics*, 28 (2007), pp. 649-656; Fredrik Wulfsberg, "Inflation and Price Adjustments: Evidence from Norwegian Consumer Price Data 1975-2004," Working Paper, (2010).

merchant and how much of the cost decrease received by the merchant does the merchant pass on to the consumer. When the interchange fee declines the revenues that issuers receive from acquirers for transactions increases; this decrease in revenue from acquirers is equivalent to a cost increase for serving cardholders. The pass-through question for the issuer is: how much of the cost increase for serving cardholders gets passed on to the consumer? This section addresses the retail-bank pass through and the next section the final merchant pass through, focusing in both cases on the European Union.

A. Overview of Payment Cards in the European Union

Most payment card transactions in the European Union involve debit cards rather than credit cards although the relative shares vary considerably across countries. Overall, debit cards accounted for about two-thirds of payment card spending and credit cards including deferred debit cards account for one-third in 2009.[27] Credit and debit cards are provided through four-party card systems in most countries. Most of these schemes are national networks that have an affiliation with an international scheme to facilitate card use outside of the countries; some of the domestic schemes are run by one of the international schemes.

Most of the credit and debit card networks provide for interchange fees that are charged to the acquirer and paid to the issuer. The interchange fee rates vary considerably across countries and between credit and debit schemes within countries.[28] Data on total interchange fees for domestic and cross-border payment card schemes in the EU are not available. However, based on some rough calculations, in 2009, European card issuers received around €9.2 billion in interchange fees of which roughly €3.7 billion were for credit cards including deferred debit cards and €5.5 billion were for debit cards.[29]

---

[27] "Payment Statistics," European Central Bank, September 2010, available at http://sdw.ecb.europa.eu/reports.do?node=1000001440. The reported percentages excludes France for which there was no subtotals provided for the categories credit, debit, and delayed debit.

[28] The European Commission reported a wide range of rates across countries in 2004. See Interim Report I, Graphs 7, 10, and 11, at pp. 25, 29, and 30. The current published rates for Visa and MasterCard also differ significantly across countries. For Visa's current interchange rates in individual European countries, see the country links at "Visa Europe Interchange Fees," http://www.visaeurope.com/en/about_us/what_we_do/fees_and_interchange/interchange_fees.aspx. For MasterCard's current interchange rates in individual European countries, see the country links at "MasterCard Intra-Country Interchange Fees," http://www.mastercard.com/us/company/en/whatwedo/interchange/Country.html. Current rates for the domestic debit systems in individual European countries are not generally publicly available.

[29] These estimates are based on the following. The European Central Bank reports that payment card volume in 2009 was €1,632 billion. For a subset of transactions, the ECB reports the type of transactions. Of these transactions, we classify 32.7% of the volume as credit (consisting of the categories "delayed debit," "credit," and "credit and/or delayed debit"). We assumed a weighted average interchange fee of 0.50 percent for debit and 0.70 percent for on credit based as very rough illustrative numbers based on discussions with knowledgeable industry observers. Our understanding is that the interchange fees for many domestic card systems are confidential and not necessarily known publicly and also that interchange fees vary widely across countries. We emphasize that we are using the 0.50 and 0.70 percent figures for illustrative purposes only.

In recent settlement discussions with MasterCard and Visa the European Commission has agreed to allow interchange fees for debit cards of 0.20 percent and interchange fees for credit cards of 0.30 percent (applicable only to MasterCard). These rates have been based in part on an application of the "tourist test" to assess the appropriate interchange fee. If interchange fees declined to this amount across the European Union the debit interchange fee rate would decline by roughly 60 percent and the credit interchange fee by 57 percent.[30] Such a change would reduce approximately €5.4 billion of costs payments made by acquirers to retail banks that issue debit and credit cards based on 2009 information and on our rough estimates of aggregate interchange fees. We are going to evaluate how this reduction would be passed-through in both sides of the markets.

B. The Retail Banking Industry in Europe

We are going to focus on debit cards which, including deferred debit cards, account for more than two-thirds of transaction volume on payment cards in Europe.[31] Debit cards are part of the suite of products and services that retail banks provide customers who open checking accounts with them. To understand how changes in interchange fees could be pass through to customers it is necessary to examine how these fees relate to the overall retail banking business.

Although there are differences across countries, retail banks typically provide consumers with a suite of services that includes a current account into which consumers deposit funds (usually from their paychecks) and then access those funds to make payments by withdrawing cash from the bank or ATMs, writing checks, or using debit cards. Some banks require customers that take out a mortgage, a personal loan or small business loan to open a current account. Banks typically charge consumers monthly or annual fees for these accounts as well as charges for specific services such as withdrawing money from an ATM, using a debit card, or making a direct debit. They also earn revenue from lending available funds; in some countries banks pay consumers some interest on their funds while in others banks do not pay interest on funds (and are sometimes legally prohibited from doing so).

Retail banks incur fixed costs for building and maintaining bank branches and ATM networks. They also incur incremental costs for providing various services. They recover these costs and earn profits from the fees mentioned above as well as the interchange fees they receive from acquirers. While published data are not readily available, our understanding from knowledgeable industry participants is that interchange fees account for about 10 percent of revenues from core retail banking services (including account payments, account management, and cash utilization, and

---

[30] This is based on 0.50 percent for debit and 0.70 percent for credit. See, *supra* note 29.
[31] If deferred debit cards were included in debit cards the fraction of transaction volume on debit cards would be even higher than two-thirds.

excluding loans and mortgages).[32] Although the amount would vary across country and bank, typical bank would experience a roughly 6 percent reduction in customer account revenue as a result of a 60 percent reduction in the debit card interchange fee rate.

To assess the extent to which retail banks would increase fees to customers we consider several sources of evidence which together suggest that retail banks would likely pass on a significant portion of the cost increases to consumers in the form of higher fees. That finding is based on two principle sources of evidence, which we preview here. The first is that retail banking is fairly competitive in many EU countries and there is evidence that retail banking has roughly constant returns to scale. That would tend to suggest that retail banks would pass on most of the cost increase in the long run; price stickiness would temper that in the short run. The second is based on what happened in Australia following the interchange fee reductions that started about a decade ago. Although Australia has a relatively concentrated banking industry the short-run pass through was around 40 percent and it appears that there was close to full pass through in the long run.

C. The Extent of Retail Bank Competition

As noted earlier we would expect 100 percent pass through of a cost change to consumers only in the case of perfect competition with constant returns to scale. It is therefore useful to examine the extent of competition in retail banking. The European Commission constructed and analyzed the concentration ratios for the top 3 and top 5 retail banks in each of the European countries and determined that, "European retail banking markets in general are moderately concentrated at national level."[33] The population-weighted average five-firm concentration level is around 60 percent (they did not report data on the more commonly used HHI measure). This is a relatively low concentration level in our experience based on that measure.

The European Central Bank completed a similar analysis of institutions that provided credit based on total assets in 2008s. The average (unweighted) HHI for the EU27 in 2008 was 1,120 and, after weighting for population in each country, 677.[34] The HHIs for each individual country are reported in Table 1 on next page. We would expect that some of these HHIs would have increased in some countries as a result of bank failures and consolidations during the financial

---

[32] This compares with estimates that the originally proposed debit card interchange fee regulation in the United States of about 80 percent would decrease deposit account related revenues by 21 to 24 percent. See Evans, David S., Robert E. Litan & Richard Schmalensee, "Economic Analysis of the Effects of the Federal Reserve Board's Proposed Debit Card Interchange Fee Regulations on Consumers and Small Businesses," Submission to the Federal Reserve Board of Governors, (2011), p. 21, also available at http://papers.ssrn.com/sol3/papers.cfm?abstract_id=1769887.

[33] European Commission, Report on the Retail Banking Sector Inquiry, Commission Staff Working Document, SEC (2007) 106, at p. 19.

[34] "Structural Indicators for the EU Banking Sector," European Central Bank, January 2010, available at http://www.ecb.int/pub/pdf/other/structralindicatorseubankingsector201001en.pdf. Population data from Eurostat, available at http://epp.eurostat.ec.europa.eu/tgm/web/_download/Eurostat_Table_tps00001HTMLDesc.htm.

Table 1: Banking HHIs by Country

	HHI for Credit Institutions (Total Assets)					Share of the 5 largest Credit Institutions (Total Assets)				
	2004	2005	2006	2007	2008	2004	2005	2006	2007	2008
Belgium	2,102	2,112	2,041	2,079	1,877	84.3	85.3	84.4	83.4	80.8
Bulgaria	721	698	707	833	834	52.3	50.8	50.3	56.7	57.3
Czech Republic	1,103	1,155	1,104	1,100	1,000	64	65.5	64.1	65.7	62
Denmark	1,146	1,115	1,071	1,120	1,229	67	66.3	64.7	64.2	66
Germany	178	174	178	183	191	22.1	21.6	22	22	22.7
Estonia	3,887	4,039	3,593	3,410	3,120	98.6	98.1	97.1	95.7	94.8
Ireland	500	600	600	600	800	43.9	45.7	44.8	46.1	55.7
Greece	1,070	1,096	1,101	1,096	1,172	65	65.6	66.3	67.7	69.5
Spain	482	487	442	459	497	41.9	42	40.4	41	42.4
France	623	727	726	679	681	49.2	51.9	52.3	51.8	51.2
Italy	230	230	220	328	344	26.4	26.8	26.2	33.1	33
Cyprus	940	1,029	1,056	1,089	1,024	57.3	59.8	63.9	64.9	63.9
Latvia	1,021	1,176	1,271	1,158	1,205	62.4	67.3	69.2	67.2	70.2
Lithuania	1,854	1,838	1,913	1,827	1,714	78.9	80.6	82.5	80.9	81.2
Luxembourg	304	312	294	276	278	29.7	30.7	29.1	27.9	27.3
Hungary	798	795	823	840	822	52.7	53.2	53.5	54.1	54.5
Malta	1,452	1,330	1,185	1,177	1,236	78.5	75.3	71.4	70.2	72.8
Netherlands	1,726	1,796	1,822	1,928	2,168	84	84.5	85.1	86.3	86.8
Austria	552	560	534	527	454	43.8	45	43.8	42.8	39
Poland	692	650	599	640	562	50	48.5	46.1	46.6	44.2
Portugal	1,093	1,154	1,134	1,098	1,114	66.5	68.8	67.9	67.8	69.1
Romania	1,111	1,115	1,165	1,041	922	59.5	59.4	60.1	56.3	54
Slovenia	1,425	1,369	1,300	1,282	1,268	64.6	63	62	59.5	59.1
Slovakia	1,154	1,076	1,131	1,082	1,197	66.5	67.7	66.9	68.2	71.5
Finland	2,680	2,730	2,560	2,540	3,160	82.7	82.9	82.3	81.2	82.8
Sweden	854	845	856	934	953	54.4	57.3	57.8	61	61.9
United Kingdom	376	399	394	449	412	34.5	36.3	35.9	40.7	36.5
Unweighted average	1,114	1,134	1,104	1,103	1,120	58.5	59.3	58.9	59.4	59.6
Population-weighted average	649	667	656	674	677	44	45	45	46	45

Source: "Structural Indicators for the EU Banking Sector," European Central Bank, January 2010, available at http://www.ecb.int/pub/pdf/other/structralindicatorseubankingsector201001en.pdf. Population data from Eurostat, available at http://epp.eurostat.ec.europa.eu/tgm/web/_download/Eurostat_Table_tps00001HTMLDesc.htm.

crisis.³⁵ Nevertheless, the figures point to a generally unconcentrated banking industry in many of the EU countries measured on a national basis.

Since retail banking competition tends to be primarily local the national HHIs could provide a distorted picture of the choices available to individuals. Some data are available based on the regional coding system known as NUTS used by the EU for 2004. Not surprisingly Germany has a higher concentration at the regional level than it appears to have at the national level because of the system of Sparkassen and Volksbanken that do not compete nationally. Nevertheless, according to our estimates about 83 percent of the regions have an HHI below 1,400 and 55 percent below 1,200.³⁶

Of course, even these regions may provide a distorted picture because people still typically go to branches for banking near where they live or work. We have not found systematic data on local levels of concentration. However, we have identified the number of banking alternatives in three cities that we are personally familiar with—Brussels, Lisbon, and Toulouse—as well as an illustrative UK city—Manchester. A consumer in Brussels would find at least 14 different retail banks to choose from within a 10-minute drive from the city center; Lisbon (14); Toulouse (11); and Manchester (18).

Of course, HHIs and other concentration measures have only limited ability to predict the extent of marketplace competition. Several economists have also studied the extent of competition in banking in the EU. An economic study by Bikker and Haaf analyzes competition in nine EU countries (Belgium, France, Germany, Italy, the Netherlands, Portugal, Spain, Sweden and the UK) using a measure of market power, based on earlier work by Bresnahan, of the average bank in each of the markets for two core product groupings: deposits and loans. The authors conclude that, "[t]he measure of competition from the Bresnahan model indicates for both the deposit and loan markets in all nine EU countries under consideration that the degree of competition is high."³⁷

There is some evidence that these estimates may, in fact, understate the competitiveness of European banking markets. Carbo et al. reviewed the banking markets in 14 European countries between 1995

---

³⁵ Recent instances of bank consolidation in Europe include the acquisition of Fortis by BNP Paribas, the acquisition of HBOS by Llyods TSB, the merger of Banques Populaires and Caisses d'Epargne, the acquisition of Commerzbank by Dresdner, and the acquisition of an interest in Postbank by Deutsche Bank. "BNP Paribas Completes the Acquisition of Fortis Bank and Forms a Strategic Partnership in Insurance with Fortis," *BNP Paribas Press Release*, , May 12, 2009; BBC News, "Lloyds HBOS Merger Gets Go-Ahead," January 12, 2009; "Merger Between Groupe Banque Populaire and Groupe Caisses d'Epargne," *Banque Populaire Press Release*, June 23, 2009; "Commerzbank Successfully Concludes the Bankwide Project to Integrate Dresdner Bank," *Commerzbank Press Release*, May 27, 2011; "Postbank Welcomes Deutsche Bank as Major Shareholder," *Postbank Press Release*, November 26, 2010. In Spain the Cajas, regional banks owned by regional governments, have been consolidated in about half of the number and some major ones are in the process of being privatized. In the United Kingdom, HHIs for banks have increased from 2008 to 2010. See Independent Commission on Banking, Interim Report: Consultation on Reform Options, April 2011 ("Independent Commission on Banking Interim Report"), available at http://s3-eu-west-1.amazonaws.com/htcdn/Interim-Report-110411.pdf, at p. 28.

³⁶ Using data on current accounts. See EC, Interim Report 2, 2007. The regional data reports to 2004.

³⁷ J.A. Bikker and K. Haaf, "Competition, Concentration and Their Relationship: An Empirical Analysis of the Banking Industry," Journal of Banking and Finance, 26 (2002): pp. 2191–2214.

and 2001 by analyzing five different commonly used measures of competition.[38] The authors complete an adjustment of each measure for country-specific factors such as banking market-specific differences in cost efficiency, non-traditional activities, real output growth and inflation. They find that when they adjust for these market-specific factors, the estimate of the degree of competition increased.

Overall, the evidence suggests that retail banking is a reasonably competitive industry in much of Europe although there are variations across countries and locales. There is also evidence that the assumption that retail banking has constant costs of production is roughly true.[39] Under these circumstances, we would expect that retail banks would pass on much of any increase in cost in the long run in the form of higher fees or reduced services. Of course, we are not suggesting that this evidence means that banking is literally perfectly competitive or immune from competition problems.[40] Several competition authorities have brought investigations and cases. A recent banking commission report in the UK suggested that there were serious competition issues in that country in part resulting from the banking consolidation following the financial crisis.[41] It is therefore useful to look at other sources of evidence.

1. *Evidence of Pass-Through from Other Banking Markets*

Although there are differences in banking across countries, in particular concerning the regulation of prices and services, there are also many similarities. It is therefore useful to

---

[38] The five measures were net interest margin/total asset ratio (NIMTA), Lerner Index, the ratio of bank net income to the value of total assets (ROA), the Panzar-Rosse H-statistic, and the HHI. Santiago Carbo, David Humphrey, Joaquin Maudos, and Philip Molyneux, "Cross-Country Comparisons of Competition and Pricing Power in European Banking," *Journal of International Money and Finance*, 28 (2009): pp. 115–134.

[39] The early literature on bank cost functions found constant returns to scale. For a survey, see Jeffrey A. Clark, "Economies of Scale and Scope at Depository Financial Institutions: A Review of the Literature," *Federal Reserve Bank of Kansas City Economic Review*, 3 (1988): 16-33. The more recent literature has found some evidence of increasing returns to scale in both the United States and in Europe, particularly for small banks, but the magnitude of the scale economies tend to be small and/or sensitive to the exact assumptions made about the shape of the production function. For example, Maggi and Rossi (2003) estimate three versions of their model. In one version, they find constant returns to scale at all bank sizes. In another, they find increasing returns to scale for small banks, constant returns to scale for medium-sized banks, and decreasing returns to scale for large banks. In the third version, they find slightly increasing returns to scale at all bank sizes. Bernardo Maggi and Stefania P.S. Rossi, "An Efficiency Analysis of Banking Systems: A Comparison of European and United States Large Commercial Banks Using Different Functional Forms," University of Vienna Department of Economics Working Paper No. 0306, (2003). Other studies of returns to scale at European banks have similar findings. Yener Altunbas and Phil Molyneux, "Economies of Scale and Scope in European Banking," *Applied Financial Economics*, 6:4 (1996): 367-375; Jaap W.B. Bos and James W. Kolari, "Large Bank Efficiency in Europe and the United States: Are There Economic Motivations for Geographic Expansion in Financial Services?" *Journal of Business*, 78:4 (2005), 1555-1592; and Laura Cavallo and Stefania P.S. Rossi, "Scale and Scope Economies in the European Banking Systems," *Journal of Multinational Financial Management*, 11:4-5 (2001): 515-531.

[40] Six of the 25 largest metropolitan areas including Los Angeles, Chicago, and Washington DC had HHIs below 1,000 in 2010; two other metropolitan including Boston and Denver had HHIs slightly above 1,000 (below 1,100). Eighteen of the 25 largest metropolitan areas including New York City had HHIs below 1,500. Twenty-one of the 25 largest metropolitan areas had HHIs below 1,800, with the median HHI for the 25 at 1,270.

[41] See Independent Commission on Banking Interim Report.

consider the evidence on the extent to which interchange fee changes have been passed through in other countries.

The clearest evidence, and the most extensively studied situation, involves Australia. In 2003, the Reserve Bank of Australia (RBA) mandated a reduction in credit card interchange fees in Australia.[42] The RBA imposed cost-based regulation that took effect in November 2003 and resulted in a reduction of the credit card interchange fee from about 0.95 percent to about 0.55 percent. This substantial reduction represented an annual loss of about AU$40 per card and about AU$490 million per year for all banks.

A study of the impact of the RBA's interchange fee regulations estimated that Australian banks passed on 30-40 percent of the reduced credit card interchange fee revenues to cardholders in about the first year after the start of the reduction.[43] It is difficult to estimate long-run pass through as there are likely other changes in market conditions that affect prices. But it is notable that credit card fees continued to increase in later years following the intervention. By 2006, for example, the average fee per account had increased by roughly the decline in interchange fees per account when the new regulations were implemented at the end of 2003; in addition banks had effectively increased prices by reducing reward programs.[44] Without having performed a detailed analysis, the Australian experience therefore suggests that the reductions in interchange fees were likely largely or fully passed on to consumers in the form of higher fees in the long run. It is notable that that Australian credit card issuers largest four issuers have accounted for about 85 percent of all issuing and it is therefore, based on concentration measures, seemingly less competitive than many EU banking markets.

---

[42] "Payment System Board Annual Report," *Reserve Bank of Australia*, November 2004, available at http://www.rba.gov.au/publications/annual-reports/psb/2004/pdf/2004-psb-ann-report.pdf. The RBA also imposed regulation of debit card interchange fees in Australia effective November 2006, which mandated a slight decrease in the interchange fees paid by issuers to acquirers for domestic Australian PIN debit transactions, which accounted for the substantial majority of debit usage in Australia. See "Update on Payment System Issues," *Reserve Bank of Australia*, September 13, 2006, available at http://www.rba.gov.au/media-releases/2006/mr-06-06.html. Note that this interchange fee flowed from issuers to acquirers—that is, in the opposite direction from interchange fee payments for most credit and debit card transactions worldwide, so that the decrease in interchange fees would be an increase in interchange fees when defined in the usual direction of being paid by acquirers to issuers. At the same time, the RBA mandated a decrease in the Visa and MasterCard debit card interchange fees (which were paid by acquirers to issuers). Given the relatively small size of the debit card interchange fee changes and the potentially offsetting effects between higher issuer costs resulting from the regulation of the Visa and MasterCard interchange fee and the lower issuer costs resulting from the regulation of the domestic debit interchange fee, an assessment of the impact of those reforms on fees for debit cards and/or deposit account would be difficult, and no one has done an empirical study to our knowledge.

[43] Howard Chang, David S. Evans, and Daniel D. Garcia Swartz, "The Effect of Regulatory Intervention in Two-Sided Markets: An Assessment of Interchange-Fee Capping in Australia," *Review of Network Economics*, 4:4 (2005), pp. 328 – 358.

[44] Credit card usage continued to increase from 2003 to 2006, so that the increase in annual fees smaller (roughly three-quarters) relative to the reduction in interchange fees per account in 2006 (based on the interchange fees rates before and after the RBA's intervention). See http://www.rba.gov.au/paymentssystem/resources/statistics/rps.xls for the number of credit card accounts. For fee data, see "Banking Fees in Australia," Reserve Bank of Australia, May 2008, available at http://www.rba.gov.au/publications/bulletin/2008/may/3.html; and "Banking Fees in Australia," Reserve Bank of Australia, May 2006, available at http://www.rba.gov.au/publications/bulletin/2006/may/2.html. See also CRA International Report, at p. 20.

Although there have been no systematic studies it appears that the experience in Spain was directionally similar. As a result of an agreement with merchants the Spanish card systems reduced payment card interchange fees from 1.54 percent on average in 2002 to 0.64 percent in 2009.[45] Following that decrease, Spanish banks increased account fees to consumers. Our understanding from knowledgeable industry executives is that the increase in account fees largely compensated for the decrease in interchange fees.

Carbo et al. claim, however, to have found evidence that Spanish efforts to reduce interchange fees enhanced consumer welfare.[46] This study, however, suffers from some flaws that lead us to put little weight on it. First, it attempts to measure consumer welfare solely by the volume of transactions conducted by consumers. The study does not consider whether consumers are paying more to conduct those transactions through account fees which, as we saw above, increased after the reduction in interchange fees. Therefore it does not assess the true impact on consumer welfare. Second, the study claims that output increased as a result of decrease in interchange fees, but it does not control for the rapid growth of the Spanish economy during that timeframe. From 2002-2007, the number of payment card transactions grew at an average annual rate of 13 percent in Spain. While this is a faster growth rate than some European countries, it is not an exceptional for a country with rapid economic growth and starting with a less than fully mature payment card infrastructure. For example, the corresponding growth rates in payment card volume were 14 percent in Ireland and 31 percent in Poland, which did not have significant interchange fee reforms over that time period.[47] Third, the authors do not analyze the net effect of an increase in interchange fees on card volume. That is, their analyses if correct would show that a decrease in interchange fees increases merchant acceptance and that an increase in merchant acceptance increases card usage, which almost all economists would likely agree *a priori*. But they did not address the other side of the market: the potential impact of an increase in interchange fees that could lead to an increase in cardholder fees and a decrease in card ownership and usage. The negative impact on the cardholder side could be smaller, similar, or greater than the impact of lower interchange fees on the merchant side. Finally, the authors recognize that their econometric estimates could be flawed because of endogeneity. They, in fact, test for whether their results are subject to this flaw and find conclusively that they are.

---

[45] Banco de España, Bank Payment Cards Statistics, http://www.bde.es/webbde/es/sispago/estadisticas_ingles.pdf. Figures are for domestic intra-system payment card transactions (debit and credit). For domestic inter-system payment card transactions, the corresponding figures are 1.87% in 2002 and 0.88% in 2009. Beginning in 2006, Banco de España began reporting interchange separately for debit and credit transactions. Interchange on domestic intra-network transactions declined from € 0.32 in 2006 to € 0.24 in 2009. The corresponding figures for inter-network transactions were € 0.36 in 2006 and € 0.31 in 2009.

[46] Santiago Carbó Valverde, Sujit Chakravorti, and Francisco Rodriguez Fernandez, "Regulating Two-Sided Markets: An Empirical Investigation" *Federal Reserve Bank of Chicago*, Working Paper 2009-11 (2010).

[47] Carbo et al. include a linear time trend in their analysis. Any non-linear effects would likely be captured in their regulatory dummy variables.

Evans, Litan, and Schmalensee have also examined the extent to which US banks pass through increases in total debit interchange revenues to their customers.[48] The US retail banking industry is generally acknowledged to be fairly competitive. The average HHI for the top 25 metropolitan areas in the US is only 1,329.[49] Banks started issuing debit cards in significant numbers in the mid-1990s. Since then the volume on transactions, and the associated interchange fees, have grown considerably. Evans et al. show that the expansion of debit card interchange fee revenues was associated with a significant decline in the fees that banks charged for checking accounts. By 2009 about three quarters of banking customers paid essentially no annual fees for their accounts. (A contributing factor in this was the expansion of overdraft fees.) They also show that banks have quickly responded to regulation of overdraft fees and anticipated reductions in debit card interchange fees with increases, or announcements of planned increases, in customer fees.

The Australian, Spanish, and US experience with changes in interchange fees provides strong support that banks tend to pass on significant changes in interchange fees quickly and substantially.

2. European Commission's Analysis of Interchange Fees and Rates

The European Commission reported a statistical analysis of the relationship between interchange fees and customer fees based on data it collected from banks for its Sector Inquiry. The Commission reports that the estimated pass-through rate is 25 percent.[50] Unfortunately, we believe that the Commission's estimates are not reliable because of some serious statistical problems. Most importantly, the analysis is likely to be subject to severe simultaneity bias. The theory of two sided markets tells us that interchange fees are set by the card scheme as a function of consumer and merchant demand, issuer and acquirer marginal costs, and the externalities between cardholders and merchants. Cardholder fees in turn depend on the interchange rate, consumer demand, and issuer marginal costs. As a result, the interchange rate and the cardholder fee are *simultaneously* determined by these underlying factors. Analysis that fails to account for this simultaneity will be biased and not reliable.

The following example illustrates what can go wrong. Suppose that issuer marginal costs decrease due to improved anti-fraud technology. This will affect cardholder fees in two ways. First, the direct effect of reducing issuer costs leads to lower cardholder fees. Second, the reduction in issuer costs leads the platform to reduce the interchange rate and what merchants have to pay. But, now, the reduction in the amount paid by the acquirers in interchange fees to the issuers

---

[48] David Evans, Robert Litan, and Richard Schmalansee, "The Net Effects of the Proposed Durbin Fee Reductions on Consumers and Small Businesses," *Lydian Journal*, Issue 5 (2011), available at http://www.pymnts.com/assets/Lydian_Journal/LydianJournal-March-2.pdf.
[49] FDIC Quarterly," FDIC, 2010, 4:4 (2010), at p. 46 ("FDIC Quarterly 2010-4").
[50] Interim Report I, Annex 5.

leads to an offsetting effect, and an increase in the cardholder fees. The Commission's analysis needs to isolate the effect of interchange rates on cardholder fees, which requires netting out the offsetting direct effect. If the analysis fails to do so, it will tend to understate the true rate of pass through. This problem is not limited to this specific example, but occurs with any change that has both a direct effect on cardholder fees and an effect on interchange rates. Unless the analyst perfectly controls for all such factors or uses some other appropriate technique, the estimates will be worthless.[51]

3. Summary of Findings on Retail Banking Pass Through

The evidence described above suggests that we would expect a priori that banks would pass on a relatively large portion of the lost interchange fees to consumers in the form of higher prices or less service. Economic theory suggests that competitive industries with constant returns to scale will tend to pass on cost changes go consumers and those characteristics seem to describe retail banking competition in many countries in the EU. The actual experience of countries with dramatic changes in interchange fee revenues also points towards significant pass through. That was the case with Australia—and Spain, though it is less well documented—from an interchange fee revenue decrease following the interchange fee cuts. It is also appears to be the case in the United States from an interchange fee revenue increase following the expansion in the use of debit cards. There is some tension between the theory and the experience in Australia, which appears to have had significant pass through even though it had a relatively concentrated issuing market. The Australian result could result from idiosyncratic features of that market or it could indicate that there is something about the demand and cost structure of banking that results in high pass through.[52]

The pass-through rate for changes in interchange fees is likely to vary across countries depending on the details of retail banking competition including the structure of the industry and the nature of consumer demand. Retail banking is a relatively competitive industry in many European countries based on structural indicia, thus the rate of pass-through should be relatively high. However, in countries with less competitive retail banking the rate may be lower. The evidence of Australia (a low competitive system on the acquiring side) and the United States (highly competitive on the acquiring side) on the relationships between customer fees and interchange fee revenues is consistent with customer fees changing considerably in response to changes in interchange fees revenues.

---

[51] In its analysis of the pass-through of interchange rates into merchant discount rates, the Commission recognizes this problem and uses dynamic panel methods in response. This method is not perfect, but in principal it can handle the simultaneity problem. The Commission did not use these methods for its interchange fee analysis.

[52] Once one deviates from perfect competition with constant unit costs and form imperfect competition with linear demand schedules the pass through rate could be less than or greater than 100 percent. See Weyl 2008, *supra*. The empirical studies suggest that on average pass through is 50 percent but for any particular industry it could be much higher with particular demand conditions.

We would also expect that retail banks would change customer fees relatively quickly in response to a significant change in fees. Interchange fees account for a relatively large fraction of retail bank revenues for current accounts. The experience in Australia, Spain, and the United States are consistent with that. Significant changes in consumer offers took place quickly after the change in interchange fee revenues.

We would like to emphasize, however, that the purpose of analysis is not to predict how much interchange fee reductions would be passed on to retail bank consumers in any particular country. That really depends on the circumstances in that country. However, we would suggest that regulatory authorities study this issue by, for example, estimating pass-through rates from historical changes in retail banking costs. To highlight the importance of this exercise we are going provide a rough estimate of the EU-wide increase in fees based on some plausible assumptions. Before we do that we turn to the merchant side.

V. MERCHANTS AND INTERCHANGE FEE PASS-THROUGH

A reduction in interchange fees would result in merchant acquirers passing some portion of those cost savings on to merchants and those merchants in turn passing some portion of those cost savings on to consumers. This section begins by examining the acquirer-merchant relationship to assess the portion of the interchange fee reductions that merchants could expect to receive. It then considers the competitive situation in various industries that accept payment cards to assess the extent to which firms in these industries would pass cost savings on to consumers.

A. Pass-Through from Acquirers to Merchants

Merchants in most European countries have access to few acquirers and sometimes only one. Some merchants are, however, very large firms that account for a significant portion of the sales in their category. These merchants have countervailing buyer power that would likely restrain the prices that merchant acquirers can charge. In these circumstances it is difficult to predict the extent to which merchant acquirers would pass along reductions in interchange fees without undertaking a careful examination of the dynamics between the merchants and acquirers, and their relative bargaining power, in each particular country. To the extent that large merchants have negotiated interchange-fee plus contracts they would receive full and quick pass through of interchange fee reductions.

Smaller merchants are another matter. They have less bargaining power and that is reflected in part by the fact that they often have blended-rate merchant fee contracts for which the interchange fee is not transparent. The economics of pass through would suggest that, a priori, acquirers would pass on only a portion of their interchange fee cost savings to small and medium size merchants.[53]

The actual pass-through of interchange fees from acquirers to merchants for a country depends on the competitive structure of its acquiring business, the types of contracts in use, and the share of larger versus smaller merchants that accept cards.

B. Pass-Through from Merchants to Consumers

Merchants that take payment cards operate across many industries with highly diverse competitive conditions. There is no reason to believe that there is a single answer to how much of the interchange fee reduction would be passed on to consumers in the form of lower prices. The answer might be quite different for restaurants versus supermarkets versus department stores versus online sellers. Even within industries the answer may vary since firms differentiate themselves and some larger firms within an industry may have more market power than small ones. Of course, the answer is likely to vary across countries.

The pass-through literature discussed above provides, however, some preliminary insights for Europe. As noted earlier, we identified studies for European countries and then considered those that examine the impact of cost changes, or exchange rate fluctuations, on consumer prices. The median long-run pass-through rate for those studies was 53 percent which is similar to the overall median of 50 percent.

These pass-through rates are not surprising given the market structure of leading retail categories in many countries.[54] Some categories such as restaurants are highly competitive. Consumers have many choices; can easily switch between restaurants; and easy entry disciplines prices. Other categories such as large supermarkets are relatively concentrated in some

---

[53] The European Commission's Sector Inquiry of Retail Banking reported that there was a low correlation between merchant service charges and concentration. However, as the report acknowledges, this correlation analysis does not control other variables that affect the level of merchant service charges. In particular, economic theory predicts that concentration should affect acquirers' markups over costs, so at a minimum the analysis would have to control for interchange fees and other acquirer costs. If these costs are higher in countries with greater than average concentration, the raw correlation will understate the true impact of concentration on merchant service charges. In the United States analysts expect that the proposed approximately 80 percent reduction in debit-card interchange fees would result in increased profits for acquirers at least in the near term because they would not pass on all of the savings to small merchants who have blended fee contracts. See David Evans, Robert Litan, and Richard Schmalensee, "Economic Analysis of the Effects of the Federal Reserve Board's Proposed Debit Card Interchange Fee Regulations on Consumers and Small Businesses," Submission to the Federal Reserve Board of Governors, (2011), at p. 44, available at http://ssrn.com/abstract=1769887. In Australia, the Reserve Bank of Australia reported that acquirers passed on all of the interchange fee cost savings within a year. See "Payments System Board: Annual Report 2006," *Reserve Bank of Australia*, pp. 11-12. Note that Australia has a highly concentrated retail sector.

[54] We are not arguing that any of these categories are markets for the purposes of assessing dominance under Article 102 TEFU and have not undertaken that analysis.

countries.⁵⁵ The French competition authority, for example, found that in many areas consumers only had one or two supermarket chains available to them.⁵⁶ The UK competition authority reached a similar conclusion.⁵⁷

Using the same four illustrative cities as we used above to consider the availability of different banks—Brussels, Lisbon, Manchester, and Toulouse—we considered the number of supermarkets available to consumers within a 10 minute drive of the city center. In each case, we found that there were far fewer supermarkets than banks: 3 supermarkets versus 14 banks for Brussels; 2 versus 14 for Lisbon; 6 versus 18 for Manchester; 3 versus 11 for Toulouse.

These pass-through rates likely overstate the extent to which retail businesses would lower prices in the short run because the cost changes for merchants are small and merchants would tend not to lower prices quickly as a result of the price stickiness issues that we discussed earlier. To estimate the cost savings to the merchant, we make the following assumptions. We assume as above that the average debit card interchange is 0.50 percent and consider a decline to 0.20 percent, which is the rate Visa and MasterCard agreed to assess as a result of their respective settlements with the European Commission. If the merchant acquirer passed on the full interchange fee cost savings to a merchant the merchant would pay 60 percent less in interchange fees on a debit card transaction. Visa reports that the average value for a card transaction in Europe was about €50 in the mid-2000s before the recent recession.⁵⁸ Using that figure, and assuming that the merchant acquirer passes on 100 percent of the reduced interchange fee to the merchant, the merchant would save interchange fee costs of €0.15 on a €50 purchase that paid for with a debit card. Merchants, however, typically charge the same price for all transactions regardless of the payment method and therefore we would need to assess the average cost savings for all consumers who purchase from a merchant and not just those who pay with a debit card. We were not able to obtain data on the fraction of retail transactions that are paid for with cards in Europe. In the United States approximately 29 percent of consumers' payments are made with debit cards.⁵⁹ We assume the same fraction applies in Europe. In that case the average debit card interchange fee savings for a merchant would be a little over €0.04 on a €50 purchase. Given the results of the price stickiness literature we would not expect that merchants would pass on this savings quickly.

---

[55] See Peter Freeman, Jayne Almond, Barbara Donoghue, Alan Gregory, Alan Hamlin, Bruce Lyons, "The Supply of Groceries in the UK Market Investigation," Competition Commission, April 30, 2008 ("UK Competition Commission Grocery Investigation") and Stéphane Turolla, "Spatial Competition in the French Supermarket Industry," Working Paper, (2010), available at http://www.sfer.asso.fr/content/download/3698/32881/version/1/file/B4+-+Turolla.pdf.

[56] République Française Autorité de la concurrence, "Avis n° 10-A-26 du 7 décembre 2010 relatif aux contrats d'affiliation de magasins indépendants et les modalités d'acquisition de foncier commercial dans le secteur de la distribution alimentair," 10-A-26, December 7, 2010, available at http://www.autoritedelaconcurrence.fr/pdf/avis/10a26.pdf.

[57] UK Competition Commission Grocery Investigation.

[58] "Annual Report 2010," Visa Europe, available at http://www.visaeurope.com/en/annual_report/annual_report.aspx.

[59] Kevin Foster, Erik Meijer, Scott Schuh, and Michael A. Zabek, "The 2009 Survey of Consumer Payment Choice," *The Federal Reserve Bank of Boston*, (2011).

Based on this analysis we conclude that across all merchants:

- Merchants would obtain less than 100 percent of an interchange fee reduction from merchant acquirers. Very large ones would be likely to obtain 100 percent pass while smaller ones would get less than 100 percent.

- Merchants would pass on roughly 50 percent of their savings to consumers in the long run if the experience for the very small cost decreases from interchange fee reductions was similar to the much larger cost changes studied by economists. There would be great variation across merchant categories in the degree of pass through with some highly competitive merchant categories passing on all of the savings and other less competitive segments passing on less than 50 percent.

- Merchants would not reduce prices quickly in response to an interchange fee reduction given that the reduction would be very small for any particular item or for typical purchases overall.

VI. OVERALL ASSESSMENT OF THE IMPACT ON CONSUMERS

Consumers could gain or lose from a reduction in interchange fees depending on the particular competitive situations of the retail banking, the structure of the merchant acquiring market, and card accepting industries in their country. There are two extremes.

Consumers are more likely to benefit when their retail banks have significant market power, the merchant acquirers have little market power, and card-accepting merchants have little market power. In this case retailers would receive most of the interchange fee reduction and would pass most of it on to consumers at least in the long run. Meanwhile banks might not pass on all of the cost increases in the form of higher fees even in the long run.

Consumers are less likely to benefit when their retail banks are pretty competitive, the merchant acquires have significant market power, and card-accepting merchants consumers have significant market power. In this case, banks would likely pass on most of the cost increases to bank customers in the form of higher fees in the long run and a large portion even the short run. Meanwhile, merchants would obtain only a part of the cost decrease from acquirers and then would only pass on a portion of those decreases to consumers even in the long run.

In our view regulators should carefully study the circumstances in their jurisdictions to see where they are between these extremes and thereby assess whether interchange fee reductions are likely to harm final consumers. The remainder of this section provides an admittedly rough calculation for the EU overall based on plausible assumptions. We claim only that the results are indicative that drastic reductions in interchange fees could pose significant harm to end consumers in the EU and that regulators should therefore examine this issue carefully.

In order to simulate the long-run impact of a roughly 60 percent reduction in interchange fees in the European Union we started by estimating the annual impact of such reduction under two extreme sets of parameters:[60]

Simulation A: For countries and regions with a competitive retail banking system and small sector of competitive merchants we made the following assumptions:

- In 2009, total interchange was €9.2 billion.

- Issuers pass-through 70 percent of the reduction in interchange fees to cardholders in the form of additional fees.

- Acquirers pass-through 100 percent of the reduction in interchange fees to large merchants, which comprise 75 percent of card sales.

- Acquirers pass-through 50 percent of the reduction in interchange fees to small merchants, which constitute 25 percent of card sales.

- Large merchants pass-through 50 percent of their cost reduction to consumers.

- Small merchants pass-through 80 percent of cost reduction to consumers.

Simulation B: For countries and regions with a concentrated retail banking system and large sector of competitive merchants we make the following hypothesis:

- In 2009, total interchange was €9.2 billion.

- Issuers pass-through 50 percent of the reduction in interchange fees to cardholders in the form of additional fees.

- Acquirers pass-through 100 percent of the reduction in interchange fees to large merchants which comprise 50 percent of card sales.

- Acquirers pass-through 50 percent of their reduction in interchange fees to small merchants which comprise 50 percent of card sales

- Large merchants pass-through 50 percent of cost reduction to consumers

- Competitive merchants pass-through 80 percent of cost reduction to consumers.

---

[60] For these illustrative purposes, we assume a reduction in the credit card interchange fee from 0.70 percent to 0.30 percent and a reduction in the debit card interchange fee from 0.50 percent to 0.20 percent, which is a reduction of about 59 percent on a blended basis. See also *supra* note 29.

Table 2: Annual Impact on Consumers (€ Millions)			
Scenario	Consumer Fees	Consumer Prices	Consumer Net
AA	−3,793	+2,573	−1,219
AB	−3,793	+2,492	−1,300
BA	−2,709	+2,573	−135
BB	−2,709	+2,492	−217

We now combine these two simulations in four variants, considering each side of the market: AA is simulation A, BB is simulation B, AB takes the issuer-consumer impact from simulation A and the merchant-consumer prices effect from B, and BA the converse combination. Table 2 reports the results in millions of Euros.

The estimates of the annual cost to European consumers of a 60 percent reduction in interchange fees vary from a low of €135 million from a high of a €1.3 billion. We present these not as definitive estimates but as illustrative calculations based on plausible assumptions that demonstrate the importance of regulators developing more refined estimates based on the circumstances of their jurisdictions.

We have also estimated the impact for the period of 2012-2021 of a mandated reduction in interchange fees, under the following assumptions of the distribution of the impact over time:

1. Total interchange fees for the EU were €9.2 billion in 2009 and transaction volume grows by 5 percent a year over the next decade.

2. Interchange revenues experience a roughly 60 percent decline starting in 2012.[61]

3. Retail banks will pass on 50 percent of the reduced interchange revenues to consumers in the form of higher prices in the first year, 65 percent in the second year, and 70 percent after that.

4. Merchant acquirers pass on 80 percent of the interchange fee cost savings to merchants in the first year, 90 percent in the second, and 100 percent after that.

5. Merchants pass on 10 percent of their cost savings in the first year, 20 percent in the second, and 50 percent after that.

6. Future values are discounted back at a rate of 2.0 percent.

---

[61] This assumes, as discussed above, that debit card interchange fees currently average 0.50 percent and decline to 0.20 percent and that credit card interchange fees currently average 0.70 percent and decline to 0.30 percent.

Under these assumptions a 60 percent EU-wide reduction in interchange fees would result in consumers incurring net higher costs between 2012 and 2021 with a net present value of €17.5 billion. Again, we are not presented this figure as an estimate of the actual cost to European consumers but as an illustration, based on plausible assumptions, of the potential impact of a pan-European reduction of interchange fees on European consumers. The point is that the wealth transfer under these assumptions from merchants to consumers is significant. It would therefore be desirable for regulators to develop more refined calculations of the impact of interchange fee reductions on consumers.

VII. CONCLUSIONS

The net effect of a reduction in interchange fees on consumers depends on the relative magnitudes of the increase in banking fees and the reduction of merchant prices. If the pass-through rates of cost changes for merchants and retail banks were symmetric and both sides passed on changes just as quickly consumers would just break even. The higher fees they would pay to banks would be just offset by the lower prices they would pay to merchants.

This paper has shown that it is more likely that there are asymmetric effects that result in consumers incurring net losses as a result of interchange fee reductions. Banks are likely to pass along the much costs of revenues they have lost from merchants to consumers in the form of higher fees (or reduced services) based on the theoretical and empirical evidence we have reported. Banks are likely to impose those increases quickly given that they would lose a significant portion of retail banking revenue as a result of the decreased fees. Although there would be great variation across merchant categories on average merchants would be likely to pass on only half of the cost savings in the long run. They would pass on little in the short run because prices are sticky and the cost savings on a per-product basis are tiny.

We have conducted rough calculations based on plausible assumptions that show that a roughly 60 percent reduction in interchange fees would cost European consumers about €17.5 billion, in present discounted value terms, over a decade. We are not putting this number forward as an actual estimate of the cost of an interchange fee reduction since it is ultimately based on many assumptions that would require verification. However, we do believe that the evidence we have reported suggests that significant reductions in interchange fees would likely impose substantial costs on European consumers.

APPENDIX A

SUMMARY OF PASS-THROUGH LITERATURE

Study	Location(s)	Product(s)	Source of Cost Changes	Pass-Through
Pinelopi Koujianou Golberg and Michael M. Knetter (1997), "Goods prices and exchange rates: What have we learned?" *Journal of Economic Literature*, 35(3), 1243-1272.	United States	Imported goods	Exchange rate fluctuations	40 to 60 percent
José Manuel Campa and Linda S. Goldberg (2005), "Exchange rate pass-through into import prices," *Review of Economics and Statistics*, 87(4), 679-690.	23 OECD countries	Imported goods	Exchange rate fluctuations	46% (quarter) 64% (year) 48% (European countries, quarter) 66% (European countries, year)
Ehsan U. Choudhri, Hamid Faruqee, and Dalia S. Hakura (2005), "Explaining the exchange rate pass-through in different prices," *Journal of International Economics*, 65, 349-374.	G-7 countries excluding the US	Imported goods	Exchange rate fluctuations	22 to 73 percent (overall) 19 to 64 percent (European countries)
David Besanko, Jean-Pierre Bube, and Sachin Gupta (2005), "Own-brand and cross-brand retail pass-through," *Marketing Science*, 24(1), 123-137.	United States	Supermarket products	Trade Promotions	74 percent (median pass-through rate for product categories with pass-through less than 100%)
Gita Gopinath and Roberto Rigobon (2008), "Sticky borders," *Quarterly Journal of Economics*, 123(2), 531-575.	United States	Imported Goods	Exchange rate fluctuations	22 percent

Study	Location(s)	Product(s)	Source of Cost Changes	Pass-Through
Vincent Nijs, Kanishka Misra, Eric T. Anderson, Karsten Hansen, and Lakshman Krishnamurthi (2010), "Channel pass-through of trade promotions," *Marketing Science*, 29(2), 250-267.	United States	Consumer Products	Trade Promotions	60 to 70 percent
Mikael Carlsson and Oskar N. Skans (forthcoming), "Evaluating microfoundations for aggregate price rigidities: evidence from matched firm-level data on product prices and unit labor cost," *American Economic Review*.	Sweden	Manufactured goods	Firm-level costs	33 percent
John Beirne and Martin Bijsterbosch (2011), "Exchange rate pass-through in central and eastern European EU Member States," *Journal of Policy Modeling*, 33(2), 241-254.	Nine Central and Eastern European countries	Imported goods	Exchange rate fluctuations	50 to 60 percent
Lian An and Jian Wang, "Exchange rate pass-through: Evidence Based on Vector Autoregression with Sign Restrictions," Federal Reserve Bank of Dallas Globalization and Monetary Policy Institute, Working Paper No. 70.	Nine OECD countries	Imported goods	Exchange rate fluctuations	44 percent (Overall) 56 percent (European countries)

APPENDIX B

SUMMARY OF PRICE STICKINESS LITERATURE			
Study	**Location(s)**	**Data**	**Price Duration**
Alan S. Blinder, Elie R.D. Canetti, David F. Lebow, and Jeremy B. Rudd, *Asking About Prices: A New Approach to Understanding Price Stickiness*, New York: Russell Sage Foundation, 1998.	United States	Survey of executives	12.0 months
Anil K. Kashyap (1995), Sticky Prices: New Evidence from Retail Catalogs," *Quarterly Journal of Economics*, 110(1), 245-274.	United States	Mail order catalogs	14.7 months
Emmanuel Dhyne, Luis J. Álvarez, Hervé Le Bihan, Giovanni Veronese, Danial Dias, Johannes Hoffman, Nicole Jonker, Patrick Lünnemann, Fabio Rumler, and Jouko Vilmunen (2006), "Price Changes in the Euro Area and the United States: Some Facts from Individual Consumer Price Data," *Journal of Economic Perspectives*, 20(2), 171-192.	Ten Euro Area countries (Austria, Belgium, Finland, France, Germany, Italy, Luxembourg, the Netherlands, Portugal, and Spain) and the United States	Consumer Price Index	Europe: 13.0 months United States: 6.7 months
James M. MacDonald and Daniel Aaronson (2006), "How Firms Construct Price Changes: Evidence from Restaurant Responses to Increased Minimum Wages," *American Journal of Agricultural Economics*, 88(2), 292-307.	United States	Consumer Price Index (Restaurants)	12.0 months
Denis Fougè, Hervé Le Bihan, and Patrick Sevestre (2007), "Heterogeneity in Consumer Price Stickiness: A Microeconometric Investigation," *Journal of Business and Economic Statistics*, 25(3), 247-264.	France	Consumer Price Index	8.2 months

Study	Location(s)	Data	Price Duration
Emi Nakamura and Jón Steinsson (2008), "Five Facts About Prices: A Reevaluation of Menu Cost Models," *Quarterly Journal of Economics*, 123(4), 1415-1464.	United States	Micro Consumer Price Index	11.0 months
Peter J. Klenow and Oleksiy Kryvtsov (2008), "State-Dependent of Time-Dependent Pricing: Does it Matter for Recent U,S, Inflation?" *Quarterly Journal of Economics*, 123(3), 863-904.	United States	Micro Consumer Price Index	7.2 months

chapter 6

PAYMENTS INNOVATION AND INTERCHANGE FEE REGULATION: HOW INVERTING THE MERCHANT-PAYS BUSINESS MODEL WOULD AFFECT THE EXTENT AND DIRECTION OF INNOVATION

By

David S. Evans

I. INTRODUCTION

In most parts of the world, when a person pays a merchant with a card the bank that issued that card receives a payment from the acquirer that processes transactions for that merchant. These "interchange fees" have come under increasing scrutiny by governments around the world. Antitrust authorities, central bank regulators, and legislatures in various jurisdictions have imposed price caps on these fees often leading to a decrease of around 50 percent as discussed below. Some commentators and merchant groups have argued for even larger decreases including interchange fees of zero.[1]

Most of the work on interchange fees has focused on static models that examine how the payment system sets the profit-maximizing interchange fee, whether the interchange fee deviates from the interchange fee that would maximize social welfare, and how to regulate prices.[2] Little work has considered the relationship between interchange fees and the level and type of innovation. Yet getting innovation right is likely to be far more important than getting prices right. Innovation generates new products that provide considerable improvements in social welfare while changing prices for existing products typically leads to marginal improvements in social welfare.[3]

This topic is especially important given the recent experience of ISIS in the United States. ISIS is a joint venture of the three largest mobile operators in the US (AT&T, T-Mobile and Verizon). It said on its formation last year that it was going to develop a mobile payments system in US working with the Discover Network and with BarclayCardUS as its first issuer.[4] Recent reports indicate that ISIS has abandoned this plan because the sharp reductions in debit-card interchange fees proposed by the U.S. Federal Reserve Board in December 2010 made its original business model untenable.[5] It was going to distinguish itself by having a low merchant fee model but the proposed price caps would eliminate that source of differentiation. There are similar concerns in Europe over the impact of interchange fee caps on the incentives for starting new payment schemes. Although some banks are interested in starting a new EU card scheme to challenge MasterCard and Visa Europe, it is unclear whether these schemes would be viable if the European Commission required them to adopt the same low interchange fees as MasterCard and Visa have agreed to.[6]

Any economist who opines on innovation must be humble. Innovation is an extraordinarily complex process. After years of research economists have not found that it is possible to make

---

[1] See below at p. 18 and notes 33-36 for more detail.
[2] For summary, see Marianne Verdier, "Interchange Fees in Payment Card Systems: A Survey of the Literature", *Journal of Economic Surveys*, 25:2 (2011): 273-97.
[3] For the classic study on new products see Jerry A. Hausman, "Valuation of New Goods under Perfect and Imperfect Competition," in *The Economics of New Goods*, Chicago: University of Chicago Press, 1997.
[4] See Troy McCombs, "AT&T, T-Mobile and Verizon Wireless Announce Joint Venture to Build National Mobile Commerce Network," Verizon Wireless, November 16, 2010, available at http://news.vzw.com/news/2010/11/pr2010-11-16.html.
[5] See Robin Sidel and Shayndi Raice, "Pay-by-Phone Dialed Back," *The Wall Street Journal*, May 4, 2011; Maria Aspan, "Dodd-Frank Hurt Mobile Payment System Plans: AT&T," *Reuters News*, May 13, 2011.
[6] John B. Frank, "Monnet Could Challenge V/MC with Introduction of European Debit System," *ePaymentNews*, July 10, 2009, available at http://epaymentnews.blogspot.com/2009/07/monnet-could-challenge-vmc-with.html#axzz1OXiNepsF

many definitive statements either as a matter of theory or empirical evidence. Moreover, there has been no significant work concerning innovation involving multi-sided platforms. Nor have economists conducted much research on innovation in the payments industry.[7]

The aims of this paper are correspondingly modest. The focus is on examining how the interchange fee model—and what is referred to as the "merchant pays model" more generally for reasons explained below—has influenced innovation in the payments industry and conjecturing how skewing it to a consumers pay model, as a result of low price caps on interchange fees, would alter innovation. A driving observation for the analysis is that interchange fee regulation that caps these fees a low level—as was originally proposed by the US Federal Reserve Board and has been advocated by some—does not simply regulate prices but inverts the business model from one in which merchants bear most of the cost of the system (a merchant-pays model) to one in which consumers do (a consumers-pay model).

The paper argues that the merchant-pays model has resulted in drastic innovation that has resulted in considerable benefits to merchants and consumers and has been behind significant incremental innovation as well. While it is not possible to prove that these benefits could not have come without interchange fees, or with much lower ones, one should be at least mindful of these benefits in considering a radical change to the business model that was relied on by the entrepreneurs who created these benefits.

The paper also considers how adopting a consumer-pays model would alter the direction and pace of innovation. It would go much too far to suggest that sharply reducing interchange fees would eliminate innovation. Entrepreneurs will adapt to the new regime and adjust the types of payments innovation they develop accordingly. In fact, there will likely be a flurry of innovation resulting from such radical change in business models. Nevertheless, the amount of innovation and investment in payments could decline if there was switch to a consumer pays model for the simple reason that the amount of profits that payments systems can obtain from the consumer side is less than what it can obtain from the merchant side. It is simply less interesting to invest in innovation in an industry that is smaller and less profitable all else equal.

It is also likely that adopting the consumer-pays model would hinder new payment systems, such as ISIS in the US and some of the new proposed schemes in the EU, from starting or reaching critical mass, and shift the direction of innovation away from increasing payment card transactions and towards other types of improvements for which it is possible to charge and earn profits. (These considerations go beyond the usual concern that government regulation—and price caps in particular—deter innovation.[8])

---

[7] For a descriptive review of what is happening in payments innovation and why, see David S. Evans and Richard Schmalensee, "Innovation in Payments," in *Moving Money: the Future of Consumer Payments*, Washington: Brookings Institution Press, 2009.

[8] See Paul L. Joskow and Nancy L. Rose, "The Effects of Economic Regulation," *Handbook of Industrial Organization*, 2 (1982):1449 - 1506 and the extensive literature they discuss; Also see W.Kip Viscusi, John M. Vernon and Joseph E. Harrington Jr., *Economics of Regulation and Antitrust*. Cambridge: MIT Press, 2005.

The next section explains the merchant-pays model and describes how most payment systems have adopted this model from the beginning of the general-purpose payment card industry. Section III documents the social welfare that has resulted from the merchant-pays systems. Section IV describes how inverting the business model from merchant to consumer pays would affect the amount and direction of innovation. Section V concludes.

II. THE MERCHANT-PAYS MODEL

The merchant-pays model has been the basis for general-purpose payment card networks since these systems were first introduced in the 1950s. Before the invention of these networks consumers could pay with "store cards" that merchants issued. Consumers used those cards to identify themselves to the merchant who would put charges on a house account. Consumers could then pay those charges off at the end of the month or finance them. Some groups of merchants developed standard identification cards that could be used at any of the merchants in that group. The merchants bore the costs of running their payment and financing programs and managing the risk associated with those activities. Many merchants did not offer payment cards, which were, at that time, largely confined to department stores.

Diners Club introduced the first general-purpose payment card in 1950 in the United States. Unlike the store cards it was possible for cardholders to use these cards to pay at any merchant that had joined the Diners Club network. Initially, Diners Club signed up restaurants but then expanded to hotels, airlines, car rentals, and other parts of what was called "travel and entertainment." The new network also quickly expanded internationally. American Express and Carte Blanche entered eight years later and also became internationally used cards primarily for travel and entertainment.[9]

These three-party[10] systems all adopted the merchant-pays model to cover the costs of operating this network and earn a profit. They charged merchants a fee—this was initially 7 percent of the transaction but declined to about 5 percent by the end of the 1950s. Cardholders did not bear much of the direct cost of these systems. They paid a modest annual fee but that roughly covered value of the float they received as a result of delaying their payments until the end of the month. Moreover, they did not have to pay any transactions fees—fees associated with using the card. As is well known, these card systems were examples of two-sided platforms that helped facilitate exchange between two groups that needed each other—in this case merchants and customers.[11]

---

[9] Bank of America also entered in 1958 with a card program in California. Interstate banking restrictions in the US prevented in from operating outside of California.

[10] They are call three party because they involve the merchant, network, and consumer.

[11] Rochet, Jean-Charles and Jean Tirole, "Platform Competition in Two-Sided Markets," *Journal of the European Economic Association*, 1:4(2003): 990-1029; David S. Evans and Richard Schmalensee, *Catalyst Code: The Strategies Behind the World's Most Dynamic Companies*, Cambridge: Harvard Business School Press, 2007.

Like many two-sided platforms they charged a low price to one side (the "subsidy" side) and a higher price to the other side (the "money" side).[12]

A number of banks tried to enter the payment card business in the 1950s in the US. Bank of America introduced a credit card in 1958 in California that was particularly successful in part because it could promote this card to merchants and consumers statewide in a state with a large population. The credit card provided a personal line of credit that enabled consumers to finance their purchases. The finance charges to consumers who used it provided an additional stream of income to the issuer beyond merchant fees.

Interstate banking regulation prevented Bank of America and most banks from operating nationally while state regulation sometimes prevented them from operating even beyond a single location. These government-imposed restrictions therefore limited their ability to scale. Banks formed two national associations in 1966 that evolved into MasterCard and Visa in response to these restrictions. Many of the members were initially banks that had their own local card programs. Like American Express, they signed up merchants and cardholders and charged both sides. As part of becoming associations, the banks agreed to allow consumers to pay with the card of any bank that belonged to the association at any merchant that had been signed up by any bank that belonged to the association. Eventually, the card associations adopted "interchange fees" to pay the bank that issued the card a fee when the card was used at a participating merchant. The interchange fee determines in large part how much of the overall revenue (and profits) for the system come from the consumer versus the merchant side. It does this by influencing the prices merchant acquirers—the companies that sign up merchants and process merchant transactions—charge to merchants and card issuers charge to consumers for using the card.

The card association—or four-party system[13]—model was adopted around the world. In some countries MasterCard and Visa organized bank associations.[14] In many countries domestic schemes emerged which affiliated with MasterCard or Visa for the purpose of international card acceptance. Banks in these four-party systems issued credit cards, debit cards, or both. Countries quickly diverged, however, on the relative issuance of credit versus debit cards. Credit cards became the leading card type in the United States initially while debit cards became the leading card type in most of continental Europe. Debit cards started taking off in the US in the mid 1990s and today account for 45 percent of payment card volume.[15] Credit cards have grown

---

[12] This distinction between the "money side" and the "subsidy side" is used in the business strategy literature. Given joint costs and indirect network effects it is often not strictly correct to say that one side provides a "subsidy" to the other. Rather one side is more important for generating profit than the other. For evidence on the prevalence of low and zero prices though see David S. Evans, "Some Empirical Aspects of Multi-sided Platform Industries," *Review of Network Economics*, 2:3 (2003):191-209.

[13] They are called four-party systems because they have merchant, acquirer, issuer, and cardholder although strictly speaking they are five-party systems that include the network.

[14] Some multinational card schemes also emerged, such as Eurocard which eventually was merged into MasterCard. See "MasterCard Completes Europay Merger," *Electronic Payments International*, July 26, 2002.

[15] "The Nilson Report #948," *The Nilson Report*, May 2010.

slowly in most other parts of the world with the exception of the Commonwealth and some of the Nordic countries.

PayPal provided another significant innovation by serving as an intermediary between consumers and merchants who wanted to transact online. Buyers provided PayPal with a means of payment (a payment card or their bank account number), which PayPal billed; sellers did the same and PayPal credited their cards or their bank accounts. Following its early acquisition by eBay, it mainly provided this service to buyers and sellers on eBay. Later it promoted its service more broadly to merchants off of eBay so that consumers could pay anyplace that took PayPal. PayPal is free to payers and it makes its money from charges to recipients of funds.

While it is not possible to obtain precise figures it would appear most payment card systems are based on a merchant pays model in which the preponderance of the cost of the provision of payment transaction services is borne by merchants.[16] On the merchant side, almost all countries have interchange fees in which the bank that issued the card to a consumer receives a fee—often a percent of the transaction amount—from the merchant's acquirer when the consumer pays with her card.[17] Merchant acquirers pass on some or all of these fees to merchants either as a separate interchange fee assessment or as part of the overall merchant service fee. The three-party systems collect these charges directly from merchants usually. Therefore, merchants almost always pay some percent of the transaction amount. Merchants incur other costs as well to accept cards including obtaining terminals, training staff, and paying merchant processing fees on top of interchange fees.

On the cardholder side, people pay little directly for using payment cards. Debit cards account for the preponderance of card transactions around the world. The bank usually provides these cards to customers as part of their checking account. Banks normally do not impose transaction fees for using these cards.[18] In some countries, credit cards account for a significant share of card transactions. Credit card customers do not pay transaction charges (and in fact sometimes receive rewards for using their cards). They do pay annual fees but the cost of these is offset in part by the free float that they receive as a result of not having to pay charges until the end of the month. About half of the people who use these cards, at least in the US, pay off their charges in full every month and do not finance. For them the annual fee is the only cost of using

---

[16] Two other payment systems are notable. Cash is provided by the government and is financed in effect from payers and payees from seigniorage and general tax funds. Checks are provided through a complex set of institutions and regulations at least in the United States. We discuss this more below.

[17] A small number of card schemes have zero interchange fees or have systems in which the merchant acquirer is paid by the card issuer. The European Commission's first interim report listed four EU countries in which banks participated in a debit payment network without interchange fees. In all the report listed 16 major domestic debit networks. Also, the primary credit card networks in Europe operate in a non-zero interchange fee structure. See "Interim Report I Payment Cards," European Commission, April 12, 2006. Card networks in other markets such as China, Singapore, and the United States operate with a non-zero interchange fee.

[18] Of course, banks could charge indirectly for debit cards as part of the overall banking relationship.

credit cards. The other half finances their charges; the finance fees cover at least in part the cost of providing risky lending to customers.[19]

Payment card systems act as intermediaries between consumers and merchants. As it turns out, the merchant-pays business model appears to be common not just for payment card systems, but also for most businesses that serve as intermediaries between consumers and merchants. The three leading examples of well-developed industries that provide intermediation services between consumers and merchants are shopping malls, e-commerce sites, and advertising-supported media.

1. Shopping mall owners usually charge merchants store rental fees and sometimes a percent of transaction volume; they usually provide consumers with free access to the malls.

2. e-Commerce sites such as amazon.com and ebay.com charge merchants fees for access to their sites and a "referral fee" or "final value fee" that are typically a percentage of the transaction price of the goods sold.

3. Advertising-supported media usually attracts viewers or listeners by providing them with valuable media content for free or for a fee that usually would not be sufficient to cover the cost of developing and delivering the content. They then sell access to these viewers to advertisers. Variants of the advertising-media model include search engines, social networking, and yellow pages.

Two recent innovative businesses that were started in the United States represent new variants of the merchant pays model.

OpenTable has a web-based platform that provides reviews and information on participating restaurants and enables consumers to make reservations at those restaurants. Consumers do not pay anything for the service. However, restaurants pay $1 per patron they get in addition to a monthly fee for reservation management software and a one-time set up fee.[20] TopTable, which OpenTable acquired in September 2010, provided similar services to restaurants in a number of European countries.[21]

---

[19] In the four-party systems the network also charges the acquirers and the issuers directly and the acquirers may pass on some of these costs to merchants. In the United States, debit networks collected 48 percent of network fees from acquirers and 52 percent from issuers; these fees are small relative to interchange fees, however, and therefore the interchange fees largely determine the overall cost to the merchant versus the consumer side of the business.

[20] Randall Stross, "The Online Reservations That Restaurants Love to Hate," *The New York Times*, December 11, 2010, available at http://www.nytimes.com/2010/12/12/business/12digi.html.

[21] Interestingly, OpenTable has attracted the same sort of complaints from restaurants that the payment card systems received early in their existence. Compare Randall Stross, "The Online Reservations That Restaurants Love to Hate," *The New York Times*, December 11, 2010, available at http://www.nytimes.com/2010/12/12/business/12digi.html to David S. Evans and Richard Schmalensee, "System Wars," in *Paying with Plastic: The Digital Revolution in Buying and Borrowing*, Cambridge: MIT Press, 2005.

Groupon helps businesses obtain traffic to their stores by providing coupons to people at heavily discounted prices for the products or services offered by the business. Groupon does not charge consumers anything for access to its discounting platform. It collects all of its revenues from merchants who pay 50 percent of the face value of the coupon as a commission to Groupon.[22] Groupon has expanded into 43 countries.[23] A number of other companies have started similar businesses in the US or other countries.

It would appear, then, that over long periods of time and in diverse countries that payment cards have been using the merchant-pays model, and the same is true for other businesses that provide intermediation services between merchants and consumers.[24] The merchant-pays model was also adopted by new businesses that had no market power at all. It is possible that a different pricing structure—one more balanced or tilted towards consumers—could enable the consumer-merchant intermediary businesses, including payment cards, to start, grow and sustain themselves profitably. But it would seem more likely that there is some fundamental market dynamic about the demand and costs for these businesses that has led them to structure themselves this way.

III. THE ROLE OF THE MERCHANT-PAYS MODEL IN INNOVATION

Over the last 60 years consumers and merchants have been able to participate in a number of innovative payment systems that were based on business models in which the merchant paid for most of the cost of the system. This section describes this innovation and the social welfare that they provided.

New businesses fail in part because it is very difficult to persuade customers to change their existing behavior. When a new venture succeeds there is a strong presumption that it is providing significant value to its customers. This statement is a strong version of the revealed preference theorem in economics: the best way to determine what consumers value, and by how much, is to observe what they choose relative to the alternatives. Over the last 60 years individuals and merchants (the customers of the two-sided payment systems) have flocked to new payments methods that they have determined provide them value.[25] The focus here is in explaining the sources of that value.

---

[22] Bari Weiss, "Groupon's $6 Billion Gambler," *The Wall Street Journal*, December 20, 2010.
[23] Groupon's registration of securities (Form S-1) filed on June 2nd, 2011, available at http://sec.gov/Archives/edgar/data/1490281/000104746911005613/a2203913zs-1.htm.
[24] I have not conducted any systematic surveys of business models for advertising, shopping malls, or e-commerce businesses around the world but my impression from the countries that I am familiar with is that it is generally the case that the merchant pays.
[25] Some of the advocates of interchange fee regulation claim that merchants do not have a choice. But all merchants need to enter into contracts to accept cards and then must install equipment and train staff to take payment cards. In the United States MasterCard and Visa have lowered interchange fees to various segments that did not accept cards. As prices declined merchants changed from making the business decision of not accepting cards to accepting them. In some countries that have high merchant discounts many merchants choose not to accept cards.

Generally there is an opportunity for the creation of a multi-sided platform when the provision of intermediation services to the different customers of the platform generates enough value to cover the cost of the platform itself as well as any subsidies that need to be paid by one side or the other. For example, for advertising-supported media, merchants obtain enough value from advertising that the media entity can charge enough money to cover the costs of operating the platform as well as to cover the cost of the content that is used to lure consumers to come to the platform where they will, in turn, be exposed to advertisements.[26]

When Diners Club started in 1950 consumers and merchants both faced imperfections in transactions. Merchants incurred expenses from maintaining their own charge programs. They had to issue cards, manage their books, collect money, and so forth. The cards they issued were mainly relevant for repeat customers since occasional customers would probably not spend the time applying for a card and giving an occasional customer even temporary credit was likely risky. The merchant cards were also not relevant for travelers. At the same time many merchants obviously found that, despite the availability of cash and checks for payment, it was profitable to establish a charge card program. It was presumably a valuable service to their customers and increased sales even though it must have been more costly than accepting cash or checks. Cash and checks were inconvenient in some cases for consumers. Especially in the days before ATM machines it was inconvenient to carry cash for payment especially for occasional large purchases. Check books were more convenient but because they were not a secure method of payment for merchants not all merchants accepted them and did not accept them from all people.

Diners Club and subsequent entrants created three-party payment systems to solve these transaction problems by adopting a merchant pays model as described above. Diners Club charged a 7 percent commission on transactions to the merchant; it charged cardholders an annual fee that roughly compensated it for the cost of the float and did not charge cardholders any transaction fees. Although consumers clearly obtained value from the charge cards Diners Club chose a strategy that did not seek to extract a significant payment for that value. Diners Club grew quickly in the United States and around the world.

Having demonstrated that there was merchant and consumer demand for a general-purpose card system that enabled multiple merchants and consumers to transact with each other, Diners Club soon faced competition from other firms including American Express. By the early 1960s eighteen thousand merchants including most travel and entertainment businesses accepted cards from the three-party systems and a million consumers had and used these cards.[27]

In the United States, MasterCard and Visa were particularly important for solving another problem for merchants and consumers: the provision of credit. Before the advent of credit cards,

---

[26] Simon Anderson and Jean Gabszewicz, "The Media and Advertising: A Tale of Two-Sided Markets," *Handbook on the Economics of Art and Culture*, 1 (2006):567-614.

[27] David S. Evans and Richard Schmalensee, "More Than Money," in *Paying With Plastic: The Digital Revolution in Buying and Borrowing*, Cambridge: The MIT Press, 2005.

merchants—especially large ones and ones that sold consumer durables—offered financing to their customers.[28] Often these merchants allowed consumers to buy on an installment plan that enabled them to spread the cost of their purchases, and therefore finance them, over time. Consumers sometimes availed themselves of these plans or took out personal loans from their banks. This, of course, was an extremely cumbersome system. The scale of lending operations was limited by the size of the merchant's customer base. Consumers faced high implicit interest charges from installment loans and had to apply separately at each store they patronized. They could obtain better rates from their banks, but securing a personal loan each time a new purchase was desired was a time consuming and inconvenient process. Credit cards provided a more efficient method of financing for both merchants and cardholders. Not surprisingly, over time these programs displaced merchant lending programs including store cards and enabled consumers to avoid applying to their banks for personal loans when they wanted to make large purchases.

The four-party system itself was a major innovation. Banks had obvious skills in facilitating payments and lending money. However, no single bank had the scale in most countries to start its own card system. By standardizing on a single brand and having interoperable cards they made it possible to generate network effects quickly as a result of pooling merchants and cardholders and making it possible for them to transact with each other regardless of which bank had issued their card. The four-party system created by MasterCard and Visa provided a business model that banks around the world could imitate.

Most of these payment systems appear to have adopted an interchange model that required merchant acquirers to pay a percent of the transaction amount to the card issuer. That resulted in these four-party systems having a merchant-pays model that was similar to what the three-party systems had. These four-party systems then helped spread the use of debit and credit cards around the world.

The introduction of debit cards outside of the US starting in the 1970s and in the US starting in the late 1990s was another major innovation. In many countries, these cards helped merchants, consumers, and banks reduce the use of checks which of course are cumbersome on many dimensions. Data for the United States and the European Union indicates that debit cards have become the preferred non-cash method of payment for consumers. In the United States debit cards accounted for 35 percent of all non-cash transactions in 2009 and were the most commonly used non-cash payment method.[29] In Europe, cards with a debit function made up over 28 percent of all non-cash payment transactions and were second only to credit transfers in terms of the most commonly used form of payment.[30]

---

[28] Lendol Calder, *Financing the American Dream: A Cultural History of Consumer Credit*, Princeton: Princeton University Press, 2001.

[29] "The 2010 Federal Reserve Payments Study: Noncash Payment Trends in the United States: 2006 – 2009," The Federal Reserve System, April 5, 2011, available at http://www.frbservices.org/files/communications/pdf/press/2010_payments_study.pdf

[30] "Payment Statistics," European Central Bank, September 2010, available at: http://sdw.ecb.europa.eu/reports.do?node=1000001440. The reported percentages excludes France for which there was no subtotals provided for the categories credit, debit, and delayed debit.

The merchant-pays model and the interchange-fee based four-party system model were therefore behind the development of an industry that, sixty years after its start, provides one of the leading payment methods in the world. Millions of merchants around the world have chosen to accept cards for payment and hundreds of million consumers use these cards to make purchases. The theory of revealed preference implies that merchants and consumers are obtaining value from using these cards. Otherwise merchants would not accept these cards and consumers would not use them. There also does not seem to be any serious question about the overall value of payment cards. It is generally acknowledged that they have reduced the use of paper-based methods of payment and therefore moved society to the use of more efficient payment mechanisms.[31]

It is possible as a matter of theory that society could have gotten the benefits of these innovations if the entrepreneurs behind the payment card industry had chosen the consumer-pays model that would result with drastically lower interchange fees. That seems quite implausible though. It is hard to imagine that most entrepreneurs in the payments industry, over extended periods of time, in varying market circumstances, and in most countries stumbled upon the wrong model to starting payments systems. If the inverted consumer-pays model could have lead to the innovations described above, then we would have expected that more than a handful of entrepreneurs in a few countries would have adopted it.

This is not to say that the particular pricing adopted by the merchant-pays model is the socially efficient pricing that an all-knowing social planner would adopt. The two-sided markets literature has identified a variety of reasons why interchange fees, for example, could be set too high or too low relative to the socially efficient benchmark. It would be quite extreme, and inconsistent with the evidence, however, to assert that almost every payment system in almost every country over six decades is upside down in having a merchant-pays rather than a consumer-pays model.

IV. THE IMPACT OF A CONSUMER PAYS MODEL ON INNOVATION AND INVESTMENT

Competition authorities and regulators have imposed reductions in interchange fees of around 50 percent thus far. The Reserve Bank of Australia, for example, reduced the credit card interchange fee from .95 percent to .55 percent (a 42 percent reduction) during the 2000s.[32] The European

---

[31] See, e.g., William Poole, "President's Message: Checks Lose Market Share to Electronic Payments – and the Economy Gains," Federal Reserve Bank of St. Louis, January 2002, www.stlouisfed.org/publications/re/articles/?id=451 ("Replacing checks with electronic payments is good for the economy; electronic payments are just plain more efficient."); "Federal Reserve Study Shows More Than Three-Quarters of Noncash Payments Are Now Electronic," Federal Reserve Financial Services Policy Committee, December 8, 2010, available at http://www.federalreserve.gov/newsevents/press/other/20101208a.htm ("The results of the study clearly underscore this nation's efforts to move toward a more efficient electronic clearing system for all types of retail payments.")

[32] "Payment System Board Annual Report, 2004," Reserve Bank of Australia, November 2004, available at http://www.rba.gov.au/publications/annual-reports/psb/2004/pdf/2004-psb-ann-report.pdf.

Commission, in settlements with MasterCard and Visa Europe, reduced the interchange fee by about 60 percent.[33] The Federal Reserve Board originally proposed a 73 to 84 percent reduction in debit card interchange fees but ultimately reduced it by about 45 percent.[34] Some commentators in the US and Europe have argued that interchange fees should be zero which would largely eliminate the costs of payment cards for the merchant side of the business.[35]

Such regulation is much more radical than the price regulation that governments usually impose on public utilities or former state-owned enterprises. Traditional regulation typically results in marginal adjustments in prices within the confines of a well-established business model. Interchange fee regulation results in an inversion of the business model. The two-sided market literature has recognized that interchange-fee regulation results in determining the "pricing structure"—the relative prices for the two sides—rather than the overall pricing level. But it has not focused on the inversion issue and the radical departure it would result in from existing ways of doing business.[36]

One would expect that such an inversion would have consequential results including on innovation as this section describes in more detail.

A. Impact on Profits and Return on Investment

The theory of two-sided platforms finds that the relative prices for the two sides of the platform depend, in part, on the elasticities of demand.[37] The platform charges a higher price to the side with a more inelastic demand and a lower price to the side with a more elastic demand, all else equal. It seems plausible in the case of payment cards that consumers have a relatively elastic demand since they can use free payment methods such as cash for many transactions or other relatively low-cost substitutes such as checks. It likewise seems plausible that merchants have a relatively inelastic de-

---

[33] See "Antitrust: Commission Makes Visa Europe's Commitments to Cut Interbank Fees for Debit Cards Legally Binding," European Commission, December 8, 2010, available at http://europa.eu/rapid/pressReleasesAction.do?reference=IP/10/1684 and "Commissioner Kroes Takes Note of MasterCard's Decision to Cut Cross-Border Multilateral Interchange Fees (MIFs) and to Repeal Recent Scheme Fee Increases," European Commission, April 1, 2009, available at http://europa.eu/rapid/pressReleasesAction.do?reference=IP/09/515.

[34] The debit card interchange fee was reduced from 44 cents for an average $38.58 transaction to 21 cents, plus 1 cent for fraud losses, a 5 basis points for fraud prevention efforts. This works out to 24 cents for an average $38.58 transaction. See "Debit Card Interchange Fees and Routing; Final Rule," The Federal Reserve System, 12 CFR Part 235, Regulation II; Docket No. R-1404, June 29, 2011, at p. 41, available at http://www.federalreserve.gov/newsevents/press/bcreg/bcreg20110629b1.pdf.

[35] See Alan Frankel, "Towards a Competitive Card Payments Marketplace," in *Reserve Bank of Australia, Payments System Review Conference*, Proceedings of a Conference held in Sydney on November 29, 2007; Also see Alan Frankel and Allan Shampine, "Economic Effects of Interchange Fees," *Antitrust Law Journal*, 3 (2006): 627 – 673.

[36] An exception is Calvano who, in a submission to the Federal Reserve Board, noted that it was unlikely that a drastic reduction in interchange fees was optimal. See Emilio Calvano, " Note on the Economic Theory of Interchange," Economic Theory of Interchange Fees, February 22, 2011, available at http://www.federalreserve.gov/SECRS/2011/March/20110308/R-1404/R-1404_030811_69122_621890579792_1.pdf

[37] E. Glen Weyl, "A Price Theory of Multi-sided Platforms," *American Economic Review* 100:4 (2010): 1642–72.

mand conditional on a modest fraction of customers carrying cards. The merchant stands to lose a sale—and the margin on that sale—if a consumer cannot pay or decides they do not want to pay unless they can do with their preferred method. Indeed, some of the economics literature that finds that there may be a market failure in the setting of interchange fees argues that merchants do not have any choice but to accept the card.[38]

If consumers have a more elastic demand than merchants then it would not be possible for payment systems overall to earn as much revenue or profit if the price to merchants were, indirectly through interchange fee regulation, regulated to zero or a very low level. We can reasonably assume that the payments system would have been maximizing private profits before government intervention to lower interchange fees. After price caps are imposed on the merchant side of the business we would expect that there would be an attempt to increase fees to the consumer side of the business. However, since consumers have relatively elastic demand we would not expect that the payments systems overall would be able to fully replace revenue and profit after increasing prices and reducing service offering. Total profits would tend to decline since the revenue base would fall and because average profits are likely to be lower as well.

The reduction in revenue and profits would tend to reduce the overall level of investment in innovation in payment card systems and ultimately the amount of innovation that would take place. Most economic models of investment in research and development find that the optimal investment depends on sales. For example, all else equal a business that is considering investing in process improvements will obtain greater returns if it can average the fixed costs of its research and development efforts across a larger business. An entrepreneur, and its venture backers, would, to take another example, realize a greater return if the sales and profit potential is greater. Those sales and profits would be smaller after imposing the constraint that it is not possible to earn significant revenues and profits from the side of the market with more inelastic demand.

This process can be illustrated with a simple example based on a textbook model of innovation.[39] Consider a situation that is initially competitive, with a large number of issuers setting price equal to marginal cost and earning zero economic profit. Suppose one of these firms is considering investing in an innovation that would lower its costs. If it makes the investment, it will gain a temporary cost advantage over the other firms. While its advantage lasts, the innovative firm charges a price slightly below the old price (because the competitive threat of the other firms prevents it from charging any higher price), captures the entire market, and earns profits indicated by the shaded rectangle in the graph below.[40] The firm will make the investment if the net present value

---

[38] Özlem Bedre-Defolie and Emilio Calvano, "Pricing Payment Cards," *European Central Bank WP series (no 1139),* available at http://dl.dropbox.com/u/123685/Website/ppc.pdf.

[39] Based on Jean Tirole, *The Theory of Industrial Organization,* Cambridge, MA: The MIT Press, 1988; a similar argument applies to many of the other models of innovation presented in this chapter. This particular model was chosen for simplicity.

[40] This assumes that the cost reduction is not too large (called a non-drastic innovation). If the cost reduction is large enough that the post-innovation monopoly price is lower than the pre-innovation marginal cost (called a drastic innovation), then the innovating firm will charge the monopoly price. This does change the conclusion that the reduction of interchange will reduce the incentive to innovate, but does complicate the graphical presentation.

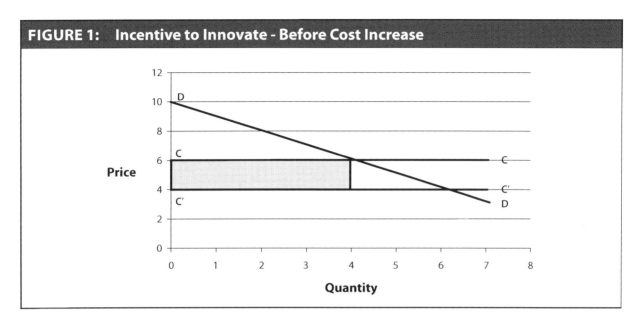

FIGURE 1: Incentive to Innovate - Before Cost Increase

of these profits (taken over the expected duration of its cost advantage) is greater than the cost of the investment.

Now suppose government regulations reduce issuers' interchange revenue, raising both the pre-innovation marginal cost and the post-innovation marginal cost (but with the same difference between the cost levels). This shifts the rectangle upward, as shown in the second graph below. Since demand slopes down, this reduces the incentive to innovate. The magnitude of the reduction

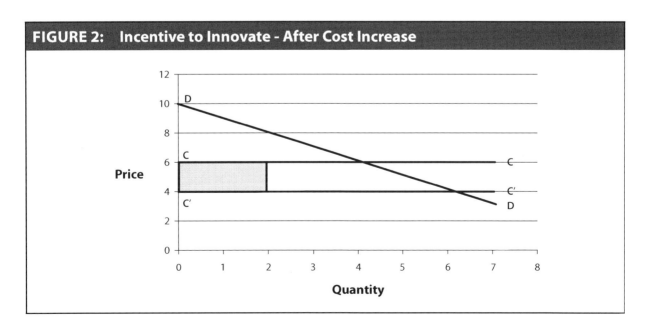

FIGURE 2: Incentive to Innovate - After Cost Increase

is determined by the elasticity of demand. The more elastic the demand curve, the greater the reduction in the size of the rectangle.[41]

Although we can be confident that investment in innovation would decline as a result of switching from the merchant-pays to the consumer-pays model it is difficult to forecast the degree of the decline. That depends on how elastic the demand by consumers is and how clever banks, networks, and other members of the payment card systems are in raising fees for consumers and mitigating the losses from the merchant side. However, two sources of evidence should make us concerned that depressing effects of regulation on innovation could be significant.

First, empirical studies have found regulated industries tend to be relatively less innovative. An early survey of the effects of regulation found mixed evidence of the effect of regulation on innovation.[42] Some heavily regulated industries had high productivity growth (electric power, telecommunications, airlines, and trucking), whereas others had low productivity growth (railroads, and pharmaceuticals). One study estimated that 15 percent of the productivity slowdown of the 1970s in the US could be explained by increased regulation.[43] More recent research has found more substantial evidence of the negative effects of regulation on productivity growth.[44] In particular, price regulation in the pharmaceutical industry has been found to deter the launch of new drugs.[45] It is difficult to be separate out cause and effect for these studies—perhaps industries that are regulated are ones that would have less innovation anyone. Nevertheless, the studies are consistent with the view that there is a negative effect of regulation on innovation.

The experience of the check-based payments system that has been subject to price regulation, for all intents and purposes, in the US since 1914[46] provides a second source of evidence and also raises some concerns. As a result of a combination of common law and Federal Reserve Board regulation, there are significant constraints on the ability of financial institutions to charge individuals who cash checks—there is on par payment so banks have to pay the face value of the check.[47]

---

[41] This discussion is based on the issuer incentive to innovation. However, the point applies more generally to the payments ecosystem. By constraining the price on the inelastic side of the ecosystem the overall prospects for revenue and profit must decline overall.

[42] Paul L. Joskow and Nancy L. Rose, "The Effects of Economic Regulation," in Handbook of Industrial Organization, ed. Richard Schmalensee, *Handbook of Industrial Organization*, Oxford: North-Holland, 1989.

[43] Gregory B Christainsen and Robert H. Haveman, "Public Regulations and the Slowdown in Productivity Growth," *American Economic Review*, 71 (1981): 320-325.

[44] John W. Dawson and John J. Seater, "Federal Regulation and Aggregate Economic Growth," Working Paper, December 2008, available at http://econ.appstate.edu/RePEc/pdf/wp0902.pdf; Simeon Djankov, Caralee McLiesh, and Rita Maria Ramalho, "Regulation and Growth," Economic Letters, 92:3 (2006): 395-401; Giuseppe Nicoletti, Stefano Scarpetta and Philip R. Lane, "Regulation, Productivity, and Growth: OECD Evidence," *Economic Policy*, 18:36 (2003): 9-72.

[45] Margaret K. Kyle, "Pharmaceutical Price Controls and Entry Strategies," *Review of Economics and Statistics*, 89:1 (2007): 88-99; Abdulkadir Civan and Michael T. Maloney, "The Effect of Price on Pharmaceutical R&D," *B.E. Journal of Economic Analysis and Policy*, 9:1 (2009): 15.

[46] Stephen Quinn and William Roberds, "The Evolution of the Check as a Means of Payment: An Historical Survey," *Federal Reserve Bank of Atlanta Economic Review*, 93:4 (2008): 1-28.

[47] Howard H. Chang, David S. Evans and Daniel D. Garcia Swartz, "An Assessment Of The Reserve Bank of Australia's Interchange Fee Regulation," 4:4 (2005): 328-358.

While there are apparently no systematic studies of innovation in the checking business, two tendencies are apparent in the US. First, there has been a great deal of process innovation to reduce the cost of handling paper checks. This was born of necessity given the exponential growth in the use of checks over time. Second, there seems to have been little innovation that has benefited merchants or consumers. For most to the last century there was little progress in how consumers wrote checks and managed their checkbooks; only recently have they benefited from online banking which has made it easier to use funds in a checking account. For most of the last century there as little progress in how merchants authenticated and handled checks. Recently merchants have been able to use electronic capture and some third-party check verification systems have arisen. For many consumers paying with a check at a store in the United States in 2011 would not appear to be much different than paying with a check at a store in 1911.

B. Impact on Starting a New System

A price cap on interchange fees would tend to have two implications for entrepreneurs seeking to start a new four-party system.

First, for the reasons just discussed the regulation would reduce the expected overall profitability of the new system. The system would not be able to earn as much profits under the constraint that it cannot charge the side of the market that has inelastic demand. Therefore entrepreneurs would be less motivated to start a system under these circumstances. Suppose, for example, that American Express was told in 1957 that as a result of government regulation imposed following complaints from merchants that it was not possible to have a merchant discount of more than 50 basis points at a time when Diners Club was charging more than 500 basis points. We would expect that even if American Express recognized that Diners Club and other systems would face the same price cap, American Express would forecast a smaller revenue and profit for its business. That is because it, as well as the other systems, would have to charge the more elastic consumer side of the business. As it was, American Express almost did not survive—it tried to sell itself to Diners Club and also considered shutting down by the early 1960s—even under the merchant-pays model.[48]

Second, the price cap would interfere with the ability of the system to use the relative prices to merchants and cardholders to generate enough interest on the part of consumers and merchants to create critical mass. Putting aside the issue of how much money the system would make at maturity, most card systems appear to have started by providing incentives to consumers to get and want to use cards and then using the consumers amassed to motivate merchants to accept those cards for payment. Low prices to merchants as a result of low or zero interchange fees would increase merchant interest. But merchants would still need to incur costs to accept cards and would not do so unless the system had enough consumers. The system would therefore not have significant

---

[48] David S. Evans and Richard Schmalensee, *Catalyst Code: The Strategies Behind the World's Most Dynamic Companies*, Cambridge: Harvard Business School Press, 2007.

numbers of merchants to entice cardholders to join. Of course, the entrepreneur behind the system could seek other sources of funding for providing consumers with incentives to join. However, that could be very expensive and risky.[49]

The experience of ISIS illustrates the impact of inverting the business model from merchant to consumer pays.[50] ISIS announced in November 2010 its intention to create a new mobile payments network that would allow consumers to pay at physical points of sale using their mobile phones. As noted earlier, ISIS was a joint venture between three mobile carriers: ATT, Verizon and T-Mobile. ISIS also planned to use the Discover network to process transactions across its network, and Barclaycard US to issue its cards at launch. Consumer phones would have NFC-chips that would interact with merchant terminals to process these transactions, across the ISIS network.

The ISIS value proposition to consumers was the ability to transact at physical retail locations with a mobile phone and to use those phones to receive offers from merchants as inducements to shop in their stores, using cards that ran over the ISIS network. The proposition to merchants was lower acceptance fees since ISIS was planning to process transactions at a lower cost to that merchant than Visa or MasterCard was charging, presumably by using Discover's PULSE network[51] and by presumably persuading consumers to use a debit-like product. The combination of lower "swipe fees" and merchant offers was thought to be attractive enough for merchants to sign on, in spite of Discover's low market share.[52]

The ISIS business model was going to be funded in several ways: it was going to receive a commission on sales driven to merchants as a result of offers that were served to customers and from fees charged to merchants for processing payments across its network, even though those fees were said to be lower than those charged by MasterCard or Visa.

In May of 2011, ISIS abruptly announced a change in strategy, abandoning its ambition to be, in effect, the 5th payment network. It announced that it would reposition itself as a NFC-wallet, open to all issuers and networks. ISIS' spokesperson, Jaymee Johnson, stated that, "ISIS was forced to re-evaluate its strategy after financial reform legislation made it more difficult for companies like itself to make money off payment networks."[53] Johnson went on say that merchants were interested in the ISIS mobile network initially because it could deliver a mobile payments experience at a lower fee, but since Durbin was likely to so significantly reduce the fees associated with accepting cards, there was no future to the business model and the business the way it was initially conceived.

---

[49] Some of the advocates of interchange fee regulation recognize that interchange fees may be needed early on to solve this "chicken and egg problem". See Steven C. Salop et al, "Economic Analysis of Debit Card Regulation Under Section 920," Submitted To The Board of Governors of the Federal Reserve System Concerning Its Rulemaking Pursuant To Section 920 of the Electronic Fund Transfer Act, October 27, 2010.
[50] For some background see http://www.prepaid-press.com/wordpress/?page_id=4397.
[51] PULSE was purchased by Discover in 2005. PULSE is one of the leading EFT/ATM networks, processing debit transactions.
[52] Discover controls about 3.5 percent of all transactions, MasterCard and Visa together account for roughly 90 percent of transactions.
[53] See "Isis Explains Strategy Shift," Wireless Week, May 9, 2011, available at: http://www.wirelessweek.com/news/2011/05/Isis-Explains-Strategy-Shift.

ISIS was planning to enter, therefore, by differentiating itself from existing system by charging lower merchant fees. The government-imposed price caps largely eliminated that source of differentiation by forcing the four-party debit card systems to have low interchange fees and therefore likely low merchant fees. One could argue that ISIS provided value only because it was bypassing systems with inefficiently high interchange fees. However, by restricting competition on an important dimension government imposed price caps likely reduce the prospects for entry and differentiated-product competition.

The possible introduction of new card schemes in Europe also illustrates how low interchange fee caps could affect the decision to invest in new possibly innovative card schemes. Monnet, Payfair, and EAPS[54] have been considering starting pan-European card systems partly in response to European regulations that mandate the development of a single European payments area (SEPA). The SEPA initiatives are designed to encourage the development of an integrated European payments system. In payment cards Europe has multiple schemes in most countries and these schemes do not interoperate well across borders. A possible result of SEPA, however, is the erosion of the domestic schemes and their replacement with cross-border schemes. That provides a business opportunity for new entry especially given that the only cross-border schemes are MasterCard and Visa.

At least two considerations come to bear on launching a new scheme. The first is the long run question of whether the new system could earn enough profits overall (which would then need to be paid to issuers, acquirers, the network and other participants) to warrant the investment and risk. To the extent that reduced interchange fees, for the reasons discussed above, reduce revenue and profits they would likely also reduce the return on investment for a new system. The second is the shorter run question of whether it is possible for a new system to achieve the critical mass necessary for ignition.[55] This presents a practical business problem. Interchange fee setting by a pan-European system would likely be viewed by the Commission in the same way as it viewed price setting by MasterCard and Visa. If so that would mean it would be faced possibly with a similar price cap in order to have an acceptable regime. However, in order to persuade banks that currently issue cards with domestic schemes to shift some or all of their volume to a new scheme the new scheme would, in many countries, be competing with domestic schemes that offer a higher interchange fee. It would therefore be difficult to attract cardholders and as a result hard to obtain merchant acceptance.

Part of the problem with a new scheme is that it would be required to compete with incumbent systems that have been able to use interchange fee revenues to recruit bank issuers and consumers over many decades. Even if all schemes were subject to the same price cap—zero

---

[54] The Euro Alliance of Payment Schemes (EAPS) was formally announced in 2007 and is an international alliance of European bank and interbank networks designed to create a pan-European debit card system.

[55] See David S. Evans, "How Catalysts Ignite: The Economics of Platform-Based Start-Ups," in *Platforms, Markets and Innovation*, ed. A. Gawer, Cheltenham, UK and Northampton, MA: Edward Elgar, 2009; David S. Evans, "Launching New Payments Businesses: The Role of Critical Mass and Ignition Strategies," *Ignition Series eBook*, PYMNTS.com.

for example—the new scheme would be at a competitive disadvantage. It would lack a major tool for getting consumers on board but at the same time would not have a better price to offer merchants.[56]

C. Impact on the Direction of Innovation

Although the reduced profitability of four-party payment systems would likely reduce overall innovation there is no reason to believe that innovation would stop. In fact, the disruption in the existing business model would provide the opportunity and incentives to do things differently. However, interchange fee regulation would likely alter the direction of innovation.

Consider the following plausible scenario. Bank issuers do not impose transaction or other fees on cardholders because consumers have elastic demand; instead banks try to recover their losses through other fees related to the consumer's current account or through reduction in service. That seems like the most likely outcome in the US. As a result, for banks and for the system overall, not much revenue is based directly on transactions taking place. In addition, there is much less revenue coming from merchants directly. Getting an additional merchant or merchant location on board does not result in any direct increase in revenue since neither the merchant nor the cardholder would be paying transaction fees. The value only comes indirectly from increasing the value of the card brand to the consumer. In these circumstances we would expect that innovation will be directed towards products and services that can earn revenue as a result of consumers being more likely to take out a checking account, and purchasing complementary products, and possibly paying annual fees for the use of a debit or credit card. That is more or less what has happened in checking in the United States. There has been little consumer or merchant innovation surrounding checking account transactions as noted above. The innovation has occurred in the overall checking account services provided to merchants and consumers such as online banking and online bill pay as a way to lock in consumers to those services, and ultimately the checking accounts that they underpin. Eliminating monthly fees, being able to deposit checks at ATMS without putting them in envelopes, mobile banking and transactions alerts are just a few examples of how innovation is happening on top of checking accounts in the US.

D. Could Less Card Innovation be a Good Thing

Of course, one might argue that this redirection of innovative effort is a good thing. At least one theory of payment cards is that they are a clever way to extract money from merchants: card systems bribe consumers to sign up and use the card and then charge merchants who do not want

---

[56] Similar interchange fee caps on credit cards could have reduced the incentives of Discover to enter the US market in the mid 1980s. One part of its strategy was to secure merchant acceptance by offering lower merchant fees than the rates being charged by MasterCard, Visa, and American Express brands. A price cap would have limited the strategies available to it for obtaining merchant acceptance in competition with the established brands.

to lose sales from these consumers. Others have argued that payment card systems provide a subsidy to the wealthy that is paid for by a tax to the poor.[57]

Assessing the social value of payment cards versus other payment methods is beyond the scope of this paper. However, the view that we have too much use of payment cards and too much investment in payment card innovation has a couple of implications that would appear implausible on their face.

The first implication is that we should have more cash and check transactions. Much of the information in the world has moved from physical to digital media in the last 15 years. We would expect that the same would be true for payments, which is information all of which can be expressed digitally. In part it has. Check use has declined in a number of countries and cash use in some. Much of the growth of electronic payments has come from the use of debit and credit cards. Debit cards are the most popular non-cash electronic payment method in the US and the second-most popular method in Europe. Nevertheless, even in developed countries a large fraction—in many cases the majority—of consumer payments transactions are based on exchanging paper money, coins, or paper checks. It is hard to imagine that countries should have moved even more slowly from paper-based methods to electronic methods of payment than they actually have.

The second implication of objecting to the growth of debit and card cards is that given the government's reservations over the private-sector payments systems, perhaps, we should count more on the government for payments innovation. When Diners Club was created in 1950 general-purpose payments instruments were tightly controlled by the US government which controlled the cash and coins and largely controlled the checking account system through the Federal Reserve Board. Although the Federal Reserve Board is widely credited with making an intrinsically inefficient paper-based check system more efficient one would be hard pressed to look at the history of cash and checks—and more recently the ACH system—and argue that it has been a fountain of innovation. Looking around the world, whether it is M-Pesa in Kenya (a mobile phone based payments and banking system), PayPal's online wallet and recently introduced applications platform, DoCoMo's contactless mobile payments system in Japan, or Greendot's prepaid card products in the US, one does not typically see governments behind payments innovation. The inexorable rise in the use of debit and credit throughout the world after the introduction of Diners Club in the US and especially after the creation of the four-party system model, and the innovation surround those payment products, is best seen as a response to a lack of innovation by government-controlled payments systems. These private payments systems obtained traction with consumers and merchants because of the existence of transaction-cost problems that the government payment systems were not solving.

---

[57] Scott Schuh, Oz Shy, and Joanna Stavins, "Who Gains and Who Loses from Credit Card Payments? Theory and Calibrations," Public Policy Discussion Paper No. 10-03, August 31, 2010, available at http://www.bos.frb.org/economic/ppdp/2010/ppdp1003.pdf.

V. CONCLUSION

Consumers and merchants around the world have benefited over the last 60 years as a result payments innovation largely driven by for-profit payment card systems. There is no way to prove how much of this innovation—or alternative innovation—would have been possible under a consumer-pays model rather than the merchant-pays model that was actually used. However, given that the merchant-pays model is the one that entrepreneurs gravitated towards and that a consumer-pays model would have faced elastic demand from consumer it appears likely that society would have had considerably less innovation with the consumer pays model.

Interchange fee regulation has, or has proposed, forcing payment card systems to drop the merchant-pays model which would necessarily resulting in requiring them to flip their business models to consumers-pay. Such a radical change in business models, combined with the fact that it would impose price caps on the side of the market with inelastic demand and require recovery of costs and profits from the side of the market with elastic demand, must have material effects including on innovation. Forecasting innovation is difficult in the best of worlds but more so in the case of two-sided markets where theory is undeveloped.

Nevertheless, the most likely scenario is that investment in payments card innovation will decline overall and will shift towards the creation of value-added services for accounts that include payment cards as a feature. As we have already seen with the decision by the US joint venture of the three largest mobile carriers to drop its ambitious plans to start a new mobile-phone based payments system given the expected drop in debit-card interchange fees, it is likely that the inversion of the business model will result in the discouragement of the formation of new payment card systems or other systems for which payments is an essential attribute.

… chapter **7**

ECONOMIC ANALYSIS OF CLAIMS IN SUPPORT OF THE "DURBIN AMENDMENT" TO REGULATE DEBIT CARD INTERCHANGE FEES

By

David S. Evans, Howard H. Chang, and Margaret Weichert

I. INTRODUCTION AND SUMMARY

This paper examines the economic rationales for the imposition of price controls on the debit card industry.

Over the last several decades Congress has overturned laws that resulted in price controls in industries ranging from airlines to trucking.[1] It was widely recognized that government price setting causes more problems than it corrects. Consumers have benefited from lower prices, greater choice, and more competition as a result of the elimination of these controls.[2]

Bucking this trend, the U.S. Senate adopted the Durbin Amendment to the Dodd-Frank Act in 2010.[3] The final legislation included a seven-page section that requires the Federal Reserve Board to regulate the prices that banks and credit unions that issue debit cards to their checking account customers can receive from merchants when those customers pay merchants with these cards.[4] This so-called "interchange fee" is established by payment card systems such as Visa, MasterCard, Star, Pulse, and others that manage the networks that ultimately move money between merchants and cardholders.[5] Interchange fees have been a major source of revenue for banks and credit unions for providing debit cards.[6]

The Government Accountability Office ("GAO"), Congress's investigative arm, and the Federal Reserve Board staff conducted studies of interchange fee regulations during 2009.[7] Both reports

---

[1] Clifford Winston (1998), "U.S. Industry Adjustment to Economic Deregulation," Journal of Economic Perspectives, 12:3, pp. 89 – 110 ("Winston 1998").

[2] See Winston 1998.

[3] "US Senate Lawmakers Approve Durbin Interchange Amendment," Dow Jones Capital Markets Report, May 13, 2010

[4] See Sec. 1075 Reasonable Fees and Rules for Payment Card Transactions, from H.R.4173, the Dodd-Frank Wall Street Reform and Consumer Protection Act. Available at http://www.opencongress.org/bill/111-h4173/text .

[5] We adopt the oversimplified terminology used by proponents of the Durbin amendment that merchants pay interchange fees to issuers. In fact, merchants contract with acquirers to provide them with card services at specified prices and conditions. Payment card systems typically require merchant acquirers to pay an interchange fee to a card issuer when a consumer uses a card from that issuer to pay a merchant serviced by the acquirer. It is then up to the merchant acquirer to determine the extent to which it will seek to recover the costs of those interchange fees from the merchants. The largest merchants typically have contracts that specify that they pay the acquirer the applicable interchange fees, which can vary by transaction, plus additional fees for processing and other services ("interchange fee plus" contracts). Smaller merchants typically pay a "blended fee" that is the same for all cards (debit, credit, and prepaid) used at the merchant regardless of the applicable interchange fee on each transaction.

[6] So-called "three party" systems such as American Express and Discover charge a merchant discount that accounts for their role combined role as merchant acquirer and network and earn a considerable portion of their revenue from these merchant discounts. In recent years, these 3-party have also permitted financial institutions to issue cards in their systems (including, for Discover, signature debit cards) and to, in effect, share a portion of the merchant discounts with them.

[7] See "Credit Cards: Rising Interchange Fees Have Increased Costs for Merchants, but Options for Reducing Fees Pose Challenges," United States Government Accountability Office, November 2009 ("GAO 2009") and Robin A. Prager, Mark D. Manuszak, Elizabeth K. Kiser, and Ron Borzekowski (2009). "Interchange Fees and Payment Card Networks: Economic, Industry Development, and Policy Issues," Federal Reserve Finance and Economics Discussion Paper, 2009-23 ("Prager et al.").

expressed strong reservations about price regulations. In addition, the U.S. Department of Justice stated that it was opposed to regulation of interchange fees and that attempts to legislate lower credit card interchange fees may harm consumers.[8]

Although Congress had held hearings on various aspects of credit and debit interchange fees, there were no hearings concerning the proposal to impose price controls and relatively little discussion of the proposal. As a result, there are two primary sources of explanations of the economic rationales for regulation of the debit card industry. First, there are the statements by Senator Durbin and other congressional proponents of the legislation that were made during the abbreviated Senate floor discussion and in other venues prior to passage of the bill. Senator Durbin, in particular, has been a vocal defender of the law in the months after its adoption. Second, the Federal Reserve Board established a rulemaking procedure for developing its regulations, during which trade groups representing merchants have submitted comments that articulate the rationales they see for the price controls.

A review of these statements finds that the proponents of debit interchange fee regulations have advanced several major justifications for government intervention.[9] The trade associations and their supporters in Congress claim that:

- MasterCard and Visa have engaged in price fixing in violation of the antitrust laws.

- Interchange fees have increased over time, resulting in merchants incurring costs that force them to increase prices to consumers.

- Canada and some other countries have zero interchange fees on domestic debit cards so that the merchant does not pay anything to the cardholder's bank when she swipes.

- Consumers would save more than $1 billion a month from reduced prices if merchants did not have to pay these fees, and small businesses, in particular, would benefit if they did not have to pay interchange fees.

Upon close review, we find that these claims are not supported by serious evidence or analysis, are factually incorrect, or are misleading.[10]

- Despite knowing that payment card systems have been setting interchange fees for four decades, no U.S. antitrust authority has ever charged these systems with price fixing violations of the antitrust laws. The courts have in fact rejected that allegation thus far.

---

[8] Letter dated June 23, 2008 from the U.S. Department of Justice to Congressman Lamar Smith, available at http://www.electronicpaymentscoalition.org/downloads/letter_DOJ.pdf ("DOJ June 2008 Letter").
[9] See below for citations for these claims.
[10] See below for discussion and support.

- It is not true that the interchange fee rates established by card systems have increased materially over time. As documented by Federal Reserve Board economists, the rates that merchants pay when cardholders swipe have been roughly steady for most payment card networks for the last six years; in fact the average debit card interchange fee has declined over the last decade.

- It is true that Canadian merchants generally pay a zero interchange fee for debit cards, but what has been left unsaid by the price control proponents is that Canadian consumers pay more and get less for their debit cards than American consumers. Canadians effectively cannot use their debit cards to make purchases over the Internet, and they pay higher fees for using their cards and for checking account services in general, compared to American consumers.

- The claim that consumers will benefit ignores the likelihood that merchants will not pass along what are penny cost savings for the typical products they sell fully or quickly to consumers. One large merchant has acknowledged the business reality that these cost savings will go to its bottom line.

- Most small businesses do not accept debit cards and will not benefit from the price controls. They will in fact be harmed because their checking account fees will go up.

II. DEBIT CARD PRICE FIXING AND ANTICOMPETITIVE PRACTICES

According to Senator Durbin, "This system of price-fixing by Visa and MasterCard on behalf of thousands of banks has gone entirely unregulated."[11] The Merchants Payments Coalition, represented by the law firm of Constantine Cannon, claims that "Visa and MasterCard conspired with their members to fix prices and leverage their power in the credit card market to dominate the debit market."[12] One of the economists retained by the merchants has stated that MasterCard and Visa have monopoly power over merchants, which have no choice but to accept cards.[13]

---

[11] Senator Durbin's April 12, 2011 Letter to Jamie Dimon.
[12] See the February 22, 2011 submission to the Federal Reserve by Constantine Cannon on behalf of the Merchant Payments Coalition at p. 1. We also note that to the extent the merchants believe the increases in PIN debit interchange fees were the result of what they claim were MasterCard and Visa's actions in leveraging power in the credit card market into the debit card market, they had the opportunity to seek redress in the settlements of the class action litigation that they negotiated with MasterCard and Visa.
[13] See James C. Miller, "Addressing the Debit-Card Industry's Market Failure," February 2001, appended to the February 22, 2011 submission to the Federal Reserve by the Retail Industry Leaders Association, at p. 3 ("Miller Report").

A. The View of U.S. Antitrust Authorities and Other Regulators

These are serious allegations. Price fixing is subject to criminal penalties under Section 1 of the Sherman Act. Monopolistic practices are unlawful under Section 2 of the Sherman Act. The U.S. Department of Justice is responsible for taking companies that engage in these practices to court. The Federal Trade Commission also has the power to attack price fixing and monopolistic practices.

The U.S. Department of Justice and Federal Trade Commission have scrutinized the practices of the payment card systems for about four decades. They have known during this period of time that all of the four-party payment card systems were setting interchange fees. Merchants have complained about these fees on numerous occasions during this period and have even brought antitrust lawsuits against the card systems. Yet neither antitrust authority has ever concluded that setting interchange fees was unlawful price fixing or a monopolistic practice.

Under current U.S. case law, interchange fees are not considered to be a violation of the antitrust laws against price fixing or monopolistic practices and in fact have been found to be lawful and necessary. Visa was sued in the 1980s for engaging in price fixing in establishing an interchange fee. The Eleventh Circuit Court of Appeals affirmed a lower court ruling that these fees were reasonable and essential for a payment card system.[14] The Court found that "[a]n abundance of evidence was submitted from which the district court plausibly and logically could conclude that the [interchange fee] on balance is procompetitive because it was necessary to achieve stability and thus ensure the one element vital to the survival of the VISA system—universality of acceptance."[15] Other courts have reviewed and reached similar decisions rejecting antitrust claims regarding interchange fees.[16]

Merchants are trying to get the U.S. courts to reach a different decision, as is their right. Various groups of merchants filed antitrust lawsuits against MasterCard and Visa, and these lawsuits, most of which were consolidated into a single proceeding in 2005, remain pending. At this point in time, however, no court has ruled on any substantive aspect of the merchants' price fixing claims.

The U.S. Department of Justice, a research report by Federal Reserve Board economic staff, and the General Accountability Office of the U.S. Congress have all examined the desirability of interchange fee regulation and, despite knowing the market structure of this industry and how payment systems set interchange fees, have all cautioned against regulation.

The Federal Reserve Board is the primary regulator focused on payments and payment systems in this country, and has extensive experience overseeing Federal Reserve Bank payments services. It has also been aware that the payment card networks set interchange fees. The Board has not advocated regulation of these fees. The Federal Reserve Board staff released a detailed report on interchange fees

---

[14] *National Bancard Corp. (NaBanco) v. Visa U.S.A., Inc.*, 779 F.2d 592 (11th Cir. 1986) ("*NaBanco v. Visa U.S.A., Inc.*").
[15] *NaBanco v. Visa U.S.A., Inc.*, 779 F.2d 592, 605.
[16] See *Reyn's Pasta Bella v. Visa U.S.A.*, 259 F. Supp. 2d 992 (N.D. Cal. 2003) and *Kendall v. Visa U.S.A. Inc.*, Slip. Op., 2005 WL 2216941 (N.D. Cal. 2005).

in May 2009.[17] While the staff acknowledged that market-set interchange fees might not maximize economic efficiency, the report explained that it was uncertain whether interchange fees were set higher than they should be and that regulation of these fees was subject to a number of practical problems.[18] The Federal Reserve Board staff research report strongly rejected cost-based regulation.

The GAO was directed under the Credit Card Accountability Responsibility and Disclosure Act of 2009 ("CARD Act") to conduct a study of credit card interchange fees and was also asked by members of the Senate Small Business Committee to review the market for interchange fees.[19] The GAO found that proposals to regulate credit card interchange fees would have uncertain effects on consumers, as the extent to which merchants would pass on cost savings was uncertain, cardholder fees could increase, and it would be very difficult to determine the optimal level of interchange fees that effectively balances the costs and benefits among the networks, issuers, merchants, and consumers.[20]

During the congressional debate over credit card interchange fees, the U.S. Department of Justice was asked for its views regarding proposed legislation that would have provided antitrust immunity to merchants to form a buyer cartel to negotiate interchange fees with MasterCard and Visa.[21] The Justice Department concluded "[C]redit card networks forced by regulation to collect less from merchants may well respond by charging more to cardholders in fees, or reducing card rewards programs and other features that are attractive to consumers." It noted that, "Notwithstanding the best of intentions and goals, the regulator will be imperfect in its attempt to replicate the terms that would be reached in a free market."[22]

The merchants disagree with the conclusions of the U.S. Department of Justice, the Federal Reserve Board staff research report, and Government Accountability Office. They are pursuing a private antitrust case against MasterCard and Visa. The arguments they have made in favor of the Durbin Amendment echo their claims in this private litigation. But, as noted above, no federal antitrust authority or court has to date agreed with their claims that MasterCard and Visa are engaging in anticompetitive behavior in establishing interchange fees.

B. The Role of Interchange Fees in Payment Systems

Payment systems must have rules in place concerning what happens when a consumer that has been issued a card by a bank pays a merchant that has agreed to accept a card. The merchant has to know how much it is getting when the consumer pays with the card and the bank that issued the card has to know how much it needs to pay to the merchant. The merchant that takes the card and

---

[17] Prager et al.
[18] Ibid.
[19] The GAO did not address debit card interchange fees. However, many of its conclusions are relevant to debit as well as credit card interchange fees.
[20] See GAO 2009, at pp. 44-46.
[21] See the DOJ June 2008 Letter.
[22] Ibid.

the bank that issued the card also have to know what happens if, for example, there is fraud or the consumer disputes the charge. Some of the merchant trade associations have argued that the payment systems should have an interchange fee of zero, which would require banks to pay the merchant 100 cents on the dollar. Other proponents of regulation have argued that the interchange fee should be set at a level that reimburses the bank for some of its costs. Regardless, though, it is necessary for payments systems to "fix" some interchange fee, whether it is zero or some other amount. It is not practical to have a system in which the many banks that issue cards negotiate individually with the many merchants that accept cards. That is what the Eleventh Circuit concluded in 1986 when it found that interchange fees were lawful and necessary for the survival of the four-party payment system.

All four-party payment systems set interchange fees. In doing so, these payment systems face a number of competing economic factors. Higher interchange fees encourage more banks to issue cards on their system. These higher fees encourage banks to provide increased benefits to consumers to get and use cards, which in turn increases the amount of transactions going through the system. Lower interchange fees encourage more merchants to accept cards.[23] The ATM networks were able to persuade merchants to install PIN pads at the point-of-sale to route transactions through their systems by charging very low interchange fees in the 1990s, and all payment card systems reduced interchange fees to supermarkets, fast food retailers, and other merchant categories to persuade merchants in these categories to accept cards. Ultimately, the interchange fee is an element of the competition that takes place among different card brands. Payment card systems must set interchange fees with an understanding of what merchants are willing to pay to accept cards and what banks need to issue cards or consumers to use cards. They also have to pay attention to the level of interchange fees that competing payment systems have established, as well as the cost, value, and features of all other payment methods available to consumers and merchants including cards from three-party systems, cash, checks, and store cards. The fact that payment card systems have established interchange fees mainly in the 1-2 percent range in the United States reflects the fact that higher fees would discourage merchant acceptance and lower fees would not provide enough inducement to banks to issue cards or consumers to use them.

In the United States there is competition among at least five payment systems for debit card transactions on a national basis.[24] That contrasts with many countries, including Canada, in which

---

[23] These statements do not account for the feedback effects between merchants and consumers. Lower interchange fees encourage merchants to take cards given the demand by consumers to use those cards at merchants; to the extent a lower interchange fee reduces the demand by consumers to use cards to pay for goods and services with those cards—because banks for example issue fewer cards or promote them less heavily—then merchant demand will fall as well.

[24] There are two major signature debit systems, Visa and MasterCard, and Discover has announced signature debit issuers on its system. Interlink, Star, Pulse, NYCE, and Maestro are PIN debit systems that we understand operate on an effectively national basis. Interlink is owned by Visa and Maestro is owned by MasterCard, so we do not count them as additional systems. In addition, there are approximately 15 other PIN debit systems, including, Jeanie, Accel, Shazam, Credit Union 24, AFFN, and Alaska Option that operate on at least a regional basis; they may in fact operate on a national basis but we have not verified that they do.

there is only one national debit card scheme. Banks can typically enable consumers to use their cards using a signature or a PIN.[25] They can choose between MasterCard and Visa for signature and between Interlink (owned by Visa), Star (First Data), Pulse (Discover Card), NYCE (FIS), and Maestro (MasterCard) for PIN. They can then encourage their consumers to use signature or PIN when they pay with their debit cards. Merchants can decide which payment card systems to accept. They can also decide whether to install PIN pads at the point of sale so that consumers can pay with a PIN and thereby use the PIN debit network(s) the bank has chosen to put on the card. In the past some merchants have provided various kinds of encouragement to consumers to use their PINs rather than signature since PIN had lower interchange fees.

The competition among debit card systems has resulted in systems choosing somewhat different interchange fees as they balance merchant, issuer and cardholder demand. Payment card systems also engage in negotiations with a number of large merchants concerning their rates. These negotiations result in such merchants receiving significant discounts off of the interchange fees they would otherwise pay.[26] Generally, there is significant variation in the interchange fees across systems, merchant size, and merchant categories.[27] This variation is what one would expect from competition among systems over banks, merchants, and cardholders.[28]

The Durbin Amendment requires the Federal Reserve Board to regulate debit interchange fees and as a result the Board has proposed price controls on these payment systems. Rather than having interchange fees determined by the market forces described above, the Federal Reserve Board was mandated to devise standards for how much banks that issue cards can receive in interchange fees. On December 16, 2010, the Board proposed two alternatives. Under one alternative, debit card issuers could not receive interchange fees of more than 12 cents, compared to an average market rate of 44 cents as of 2009. A second proposal would place the cap at 7 cents but allow banks to demonstrate on the basis of cost that they should receive a fee of up to 12 cents. In effect, the setting of interchange fees would be taken out of the hands of the payment card systems and put

---

[25] We use "signature" and "PIN" as shorthand. In fact, the industry has evolved to be far more complex and the traditional lines between networks blurred, with a variety of authentication methods typically available on most cards such as "no signature required," remote/internet use with or without PIN or a designated password, so-called "PINless debit," contactless functionality, etc.

[26] See James M. Lyon (2006), "The Interchange Fee Debate: Issues and Economics," Federal Reserve Bank of Minneapolis, The Region, available at http://www.minneapolisfed.org/publications_papers/pub_display.cfm?id=3235. There may be other terms associated with these agreements, such as an agreement to promote a particular card brand.

[27] MasterCard's published debit card rate schedule, for instance, has 41 different categories; see http://www.mastercard.com/us/merchant/pdf/MasterCard_Interchange_Rates_and_Criteria.pdf, at pp. 74-89. Also, see http://usa.visa.com/download/merchants/april-2011-visa-usa-interchange-rate-sheet.pdf.

[28] One of the economists who submitted a report on behalf of the merchants has argued that this "price discrimination" demonstrates monopoly power. See the Miller Report at p. 3. In fact it is well known that this sort of price variation is routine in competitive markets and is not evidence of monopoly power. See William J. Baumol and Daniel G. Swanson (2003), "The New Economy and Ubiquitous Competitive Price Discrimination: Identifying Defensible Criteria of Market Power," *Antitrust Law Journal*, 3:70; and Illinois Tool Works Inc. v. Independent Ink, Inc., 126 S. Ct. 1281 (2006), rev'g 396 F.3d 1342 (Fed. Cir. 2005).

in the hands of the Board. The ability of debit card networks to compete for merchants and issuers using interchange fees would be largely eliminated and replaced with a rigid fee.

Senator Durbin has claimed that his amendment does not prevent banks from charging an interchange fee for the use of cards they issue to pay merchants so long as the networks do not set that fee. In his letter to the CEO of JPMorgan Chase, Jamie Dimon, the Senator says, "It is important to make clear that if Chase wants to set and charge its own fees in a competitive market environment, the amendment does not regulate those fees. The only regulated fees are those fees that banks let card networks fix on their behalf." [29]

In fact, it is clear that the purpose of the Durbin amendment, and its apparent effect given the Board's interpretation to date, is to have the Federal Reserve Board "fix prices" at a level that is most favorable to merchants and thereby replace the free-market price with a regulated price that mimics the price that a merchant cartel would seek to negotiate. Several points are noteworthy.

- It is hard to know what method Senator Durbin envisions for the "competitive market" to determine the interchange fee. Banks could negotiate with merchant acquirers or with banks. Either way, in a four-party system, bilateral negotiation would lead to a massive number of negotiations. That, in fact, is why it has been found to be efficient for the card system to establish this fee on behalf of participants in the system.

- We do not believe that it is clear that the Federal Reserve Board agrees that banks could bypass its regulations and negotiate their own fees. According to the Federal Reserve Board: "An issuer could not receive an interchange fee above the cap regardless of its allowable cost calculation."[30] The Board focuses on the magnitude of the receipt of interchange fees by the issuers regardless of how those interchange fees are determined.

- Although Senator Durbin might envision banks negotiating with acquirers over the interchange fee, we think it is more likely that he is conjecturing that banks would negotiate with merchants since the thrust of the legislation has been about merchant choices. Even if we focused on the largest 100 banks and the largest 10,000 merchants that would require 1,000,000 separate negotiations. Obviously smaller banks could not afford to negotiate with merchants.

---

[29] See Senator Durbin's April 12, 2011 Letter to Jamie Dimon.
[30] "Debit Card Interchange Fees and Routing; Proposed Rule," The Federal Reserve System, *Federal Register*, 75:248, December 28, 2010, at p. 81736, available at: http://edocket.access.gpo.gov/2010/pdf/2010-32061.pdf ("The Proposed Rules"). This statement is regarding the 7 cent "safe harbor" alternative (under which issuer could recover their variable costs of authorization, clearing and settlement, up to a 12 cent, by showing that their costs were greater than 7 cents). There is a similar statement in connection with the other alternative rule of a 12 cent cap on interchange fees: "Each issuer's supervisor would verify that an issuer does not receive interchange revenue in excess of the cap." See The Proposed Rules at p. 81738.

- It is unclear how bilateral negotiations among issuers and merchants could result in a valuable, or viable, payment card system for consumers, issuers, acquirers, or merchants. If the payment card system required merchants to accept the cards from all issuers—which is necessary to ensure consumers their cards would be accepted—then merchants would have no choice but to pay whatever fee the bank issuer demands since the merchant has to take the card for payment. If the payment card system prevented issuers from disabling their cards for individual merchants then the issuer would have to take whatever the merchant is willing to offer (either the system-set rate or the regulated rate), stop issuing debit cards, or start its own system. Yet if the payment system allowed merchants to refuse to accept cards from particular issuers consumers would lose, and if the payment system allowed issuers to disable particular merchants both consumers and merchants would face uncertainty.

In the end, the Durbin Amendment prevents the four-party card systems from establishing an interchange fee through competition and replaces it with government price controls.

III. TRENDS IN INTERCHANGE FEES

The proponents of debit card interchange fee regulations have claimed as evidence of monopoly power that the fees have increased over time. According to Senator Durbin, "Visa and MasterCard have incentive to constantly increase interchange rates and there is no countervailing market force to temper these fee increases. There is no naturally-occurring market force in today's interchange system that would ever lead rates to go down."[31] Others have pointed to increasing interchange fees as evidence of market failure.[32]

In fact, the published interchange fee rates have not changed much for most payment card systems. A May 2009 report by the Federal Reserve Bank summarized the interchange fee rates for the signature and PIN debit networks and the credit card networks from 2001 to 2008.[33] It showed no material increase between 2005 and 2009. A study prepared by an economist for the Merchants Payments Coalition presented similar estimates of interchange fee rates for the

---

[31] See Senator Durbin's April 12, 2011 Letter to Jamie Dimon.
[32] Steven C. Salop et al., Economic Analysis of Debit Card Regulation Under Section 920, Oct. 27, 2010, submitted to the Federal Reserve as part of prepared materials for a meeting between the Federal Reserve Staff and Merchants Payments Coalition on November 2, 2010, at p. 1 ("Salop et al.") and the February 22, 2011 submission to the Federal Reserve by Constantine Cannon on behalf of the Merchants Payments Coalition (including appended reports by James Miller and Steve Salop) ("Merchants Payments Coalition Report").
[33] Prager et al., at Figure 3.

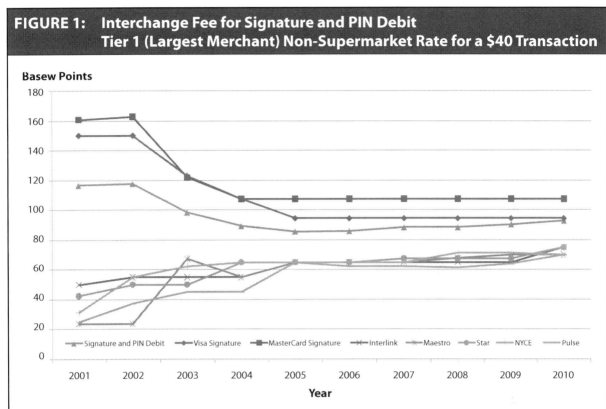

FIGURE 1: Interchange Fee for Signature and PIN Debit Tier 1 (Largest Merchant) Non-Supermarket Rate for a $40 Transaction

Source: Steven C. Salop et al., at Exhibit 1c, EFT Data Books 2002-2009, The Nilson Report
Notes: The combined signature and PIN debit interchange rate is a weighted average rate based on each network's share of the total debit purchase volume. Data was not available at the time of this report to calculate purchase volume shares for 2009 and 2010. The combined rate for those two years is based on 2008 purchase volume. Maestro's share of volume is reported as part of MasterCard Signature. Rate information for a number of PIN debit networks (representing approximately 10% of PIN volume) were not included in Salop et al.'s data. For the purpose of creating a combined signature and PIN rate we assumed the PIN networks included in Salop et al.'s analysis combine to make up the entire PIN volume.

signature and PIN debit networks.[34] We have reproduced these estimates above in Figure 1 for the past decade.[35]

Figure 1 shows that the average interchange fee for debit cards declined over the past decade, from about 1.17 percent to 0.91 percent taking a weighted average across signature and PIN debit.

---

[34] Salop et al., at Exhibits 1(a)-(d).
[35] Salop et al. presented four different estimates of interchange fees: largest non-supermarket merchants, largest supermarket merchants, smaller non-supermarket merchants, and smaller supermarket merchants. We believe the characterization of large non-supermarket merchants is not fully accurate. While MasterCard and Visa have tiered interchange rates that depend on merchant volume (as well as other factors), for at least some years, the PIN debit networks have had non-supermarket rates that depend on the size of the acquirer, not the size of the merchant. See "EFT Data Book," ATM & Debit News, September 15, 2005, at pg. 9 ("EFT Data Book, 2006 Edition"). It would therefore appear that even smaller merchants would qualify for the lower interchange tiers if they used a major acquirer. We have therefore reported the data series for what are called the largest merchant rates, as it is likely that major acquirers account for the majority of volume in the system. We have also chosen to report the interchange fee rates for non-supermarket merchants to be more broadly representative.

PIN debit interchange fees increased in the early part of the decade and then have been largely flat since with a slight uptick towards the end of the decade. Signature debit interchange fees declined in the early part of the decade and then have been flat since.[36] The data clearly show that (1) claims of "ever increasing" debit card interchange fees are incorrect, for debit overall or for either PIN or signature debit taken alone; and (2) average interchange fees for debit card transactions have actually declined in the past decade.[37] In fact, the weighted average debit interchange fee declined by about 20 percent over the decade and the weighted average debit interchange fee has been roughly constant since 2004.

Some of the discussions about increases in interchange fees confuse increases in the interchange fee rate with the total amount of fees that merchants pay for accepting debit cards. The total amount that merchants pay for debit cards has increased over time because this form of payment has become more popular with both consumers and merchants. Businesses spend more money on many inputs as their businesses expand and as inputs become more desirable so this is hardly unusual. Businesses, for example, are spending more money on information technology today than they were 10 years ago despite the fact that most information technology prices have declined.[38]

Consumers have come to like debit cards because of the convenience of paying with them rather than a check and because unlike credit cards, the money comes from their current funds and therefore does not present any risk that they will incur debt. The Federal Reserve Bank of Boston's 2009 Survey of Consumer Payment Choice found that 68 percent of consumers used debit cards, and the Federal Reserve Board Payments Study found that between 2000 and 2009 the proportion of non-cash transactions made with debit cards increased from 11 percent to 35 percent, making debit the preferred electronic payment option for consumers.[39] Since consumers are making more

---

[36] Signature debit card rates declined between 2002 and 2004 largely as a result of the settlement of the WalMart litigation. However, since that decline they have not increased materially.

[37] Merchant claims that debit card interchange fees have increased are based on comparing current rates to those in the mid to late 1990s, which was around the time debit cards started taking off in the United States. There were significant increases in PIN debit interchange fees between 1995 and 2005. The ATM networks initially set interchange fees very low to persuade merchants to spend money installing PIN pads. Like many businesses that engage in penetration pricing, they increased those rates over time. As Figure 1 shows, interchange fees for PIN debit have been essentially flat since 2005.

[38] See the Consumer Price Index, U.S. City Average Information Technology and Peripheral Equipment, Bureau of Labor Statistics, available at http://data.bls.gov/pdq/querytool.jsp?survey=cu, "Survey: IT spending to recover in 2010," Cnet, November 25, 2009, citing Goldman Sach's 2010 IT Spending Survey. .

[39] For the percentage of consumers with debits cards in 2009 see Kevin Foster, Erik Meijer, Scott Schuh, and Michael A. Zabek (2011), "The 2009 Survey of Consumer Payment Choice," Federal Reserve Bank of Boston, Public Policy Discussion Papers, at table 14, available at http://www.bostonfed.org/economic/ppdp/2011/ppdp1101.pdf ("2009 Survey of Consumer Payment Choice"). For the proportion of non-cash transactions in 2000 see "The 2010 Federal Reserve Payments Study: Noncash Payment Trends in the United States: 2000 – 2003," The Federal Reserve System, December 2004, at exhibit 2, available at http://www.frbservices.org/files/communications/pdf/research/2004PaymentResearchReport.pdf and for 2009 see "The 2010 Federal Reserve Payments Study: Noncash Payment Trends in the United States: 2006 – 2009," The Federal Reserve System, December 2010, at exhibit 8 http://www.frbservices.org/files/communications/pdf/press/2010_payments_study.pdf.

Table 1: Trends in Acceptance for Payment					
	Rarely Accepted	Occasionally Accepted	Often Accepted	Usually Accepted	Almost Always Accepted
Checks					
2008	1.6%	11.3%	31.5%	36.3%	19.3%
2009	3.8%	16.1%	27.7%	33.5%	19.0%
Debit Cards					
2008	1.4%	1.6%	12.4%	36.6%	47.9%
2009	2.0%	0.8%	12.6%	32.0%	52.8%

transactions with debit cards, the total fees that a merchant pays with cards has also increased, even if the amount per transaction has been relatively stable. Much of this increase has come from consumers replacing check payments with debit cards. It is beyond the scope of this paper to discuss all of the benefits to merchants from reduced check use (such as the advantages of guaranteed payment found with debit cards). However, they have been well documented elsewhere.[40]

Merchants are paying more debit card fees because of two decisions that have made it easier for people to swipe and harder for people to pay with checks. Many merchants have installed point-of-sale equipment that makes it very easy for consumers to pay with a credit or debit card, and they have installed equipment that makes it very easy for consumers to pay by entering their PINs..[41] Merchant innovations include self check-out lanes and automated fuel dispensers, which take advantage of the speed and efficiency of card payments while helping reduce merchant infrastructure costs. Indeed, both merchants and consumers appear to have a much stronger preference for debit card payments over check payments. From the consumer's perspective, merchants are making it difficult for consumers to pay with checks. Over half of consumers report that debit cards are almost always accepted, while less than one-fifth of consumers report that for checks.[42] As shown in Table 1, just between 2008 and 2009 the fraction of consumers who reported that checks were rarely or occasionally accepted increased from 13.9 percent to 19.9 percent; the fraction of consumers who reported that debit cards were rarely or occasionally accepted decreased from 3.0 percent to 2.8 percent. Over the last decade merchants have also expressed their preference for debit payments. Entire merchant categories such as fast food have embraced debit cards, thereby increasing the use of these cards and the total fees received by the banks for providing debit cards

---

[40] See, for example, Daniel D. Garcia-Swartz, Robert W. Hahn, and Anne Layne-Farrar (2006), "The Move Toward a Cashless Society: A Closer Look at Payment Instrument Economics," Review of Network Economics, 5:2.

[41] See EFT Data Book, 2006 Edition and "First Data Survey Finds Consumers Want Variety of Electronic Payment Choices," Payment News, July 4, 2005 citing First Data's Consumer Usage Study, available at http://www.paymentsnews.com/2008/02/gartner-says-co.html.

[42] 2009 Survey of Consumer Payment Choice.

as a method of payment. Despite the heated rhetoric in the political arena about the cost of acceptance, efforts to use the courts and regulation to pay less, and assertions that they have no choice, actual merchant behavior shows a desire to encourage electronic payments.

IV. ZERO INTERCHANGE FEE COUNTRIES AND FOREIGN REGULATION

Senator Durbin has argued that Canada and other countries have zero interchange fees yet vibrant debit card markets. He says that, "[M]any other countries enjoy vibrant debit systems with interchange fees strictly regulated or prohibited entirely" and that "banks … can easily continue to offer debit card services without the excessive subsidy of high interchange fees."[43] He also points to Canada as an example: "Do you know what the interchange fee is in Canada? It is zero. The same companies that are offering debit cards here in the United States do not charge an interchange fee in Canada."[44] The Merchants Payments Coalition and their economic expert also highlight the fact that seven of the eight countries with the highest debit card penetration have zero interchange fees.[45]

In total, eight countries have been identified by the proponents of debit card price controls as having zero interchange fees. They are Canada, Denmark, Finland, Iceland, the Netherlands, New Zealand, Norway, and Luxembourg. We do not believe one could seriously infer anything by cherry picking eight countries from the more than 120 countries around the world and concluding they should provide the model for the American debit card system. These countries are small and together account for only 1.2 percent of the world's population. The largest one, Canada, has one-ninth the population of the United States, and the smallest, Luxembourg, has about the same population as Fresno, California. In many of them, there are only a handful of banks providing checking account services and they have a monopoly debit card system owned by these banks.[46]

---

[43] Senator Durbin's April 12, 2011 Letter to Jamie Dimon.

[44] Richard Durbin, "Swipe Fee Reform," March 16, 2011, available at http://durbin.senate.gov/public/index.cfm/statementscommentary?ID=4cc823e7-c232-44f2-bfc0-b80b31e2561a. It should be noted that U.S. debit card systems—such as MasterCard, Visa, Star and NYCE—are not part of the Interac system in Canada, and that Visa's debit interchange fees in Canada is above zero (we have not confirmed the MasterCard rate).

[45] See Steven C. Salop et al. and the Merchants Payments Coalition Report.

[46] For instance, in Canada the top five banks (Royal Bank of Canada, Toronto Dominion Bank, Bank of Nova Scotia, Bank of Montreal, Canadian Imperial Bank of Commerce) account for 85 percent of the total bank assets, see http://www.osfi.gc.ca/osfi/index_e.aspx?ArticleID=554 and the organization that operates Canada's debit card system was founded by four of these top five banks (see "Interac: Changing for the Future," Interac, 1997, available at http://neumann.hec.ca/~p119/gif/interac1.pdf). For information on Dankort in Denmark, see Payment Systems in Denmark, Denmarks NationalBank, September 2005, available at http://www.nationalbanken.dk/DNUK/Publications.nsf/d8a9f2b39990e07880256a3e004157b5/1e8fec8f259e61ffc125706c003d4409/$FILE/kap08.html, and for information on Interpay and bank concentration in Netherlands see Fumiko Hayashi and Stuart E. Weiner (2005), "Competition and Credit and Debit Card Interchange Fees: A Cross-Country Analysis," Federal Reserve Bank of Kansas City, available at http://www.kansascityfed.org/publicat/psr/rwp/Weiner-HayashiWorkingPaper11-30-05.pdf.

There is no logical basis for pointing to these countries— rather than China, France, Singapore or many other countries around the world that have debit card interchange fees similar to those in the US—as models for our county. The economic submissions that claim that the existence of countries with a zero interchange fee demonstrates that the US should follow this model, or regulate its fees, are simply not credible.

Although we do not believe that comparisons with countries that differ in so many dimensions[47] from the United States are reliable, we have investigated the experience of these countries in some detail. The results should provide significant caution to those who advocate sharply reducing interchange fees paid by merchants. All of these countries offer only PIN based debit cards to their citizens and it is not possible to use those cards in most places to purchase goods over the Internet or in other situations in which the consumer cannot tap her PIN into a terminal. These cards are therefore largely useless for modern e-commerce, which is growing rapidly around the world. Citizens of these countries cannot use their debit cards to buy books on Amazon, play games on Facebook, buy applications on their smart phones, or to pay almost anywhere else on the Internet; they have to turn to credit cards and other payments, such as PayPal, that can link directly to their checking account.

We have conducted a detailed analysis of Canada, which is the largest of these zero-interchange fee countries, the one most proximate to the US, and the one most frequently mentioned by the merchant associations as a model for the US. Let us begin with some background detail on Canada. It has a population of 34 million people, of whom approximately half are concentrated in 10 metropolitan areas.[48] Five banks account for 85 percent of the total bank assets in Canada,[49] and there are a total of 77 banks in the country.[50] Canada had one of the highest rates of check use in the world up until 1995.[51]

The Canadian banks decided jointly in 1984[52] to establish a PIN debit network, in part to defray the very high costs of check use they were incurring. They agreed on a zero interchange fee to encourage merchants to install the necessary technology. Until recently Interac has been the only debit card scheme in Canada.[53]

---

[47] Aside from being very small economies these countries differ from the United States in a number of ways that influence the economics of the debit card business. These include consumer credit card penetration, the intensity of competition in retail banking, and the presence of monopoly acquirers and/or processors owned by issuers (which may provide payments from merchants to issuers that are equivalent to interchange fees).

[48] See "Canada's population estimates," Statistic Canada, available at http://www.statcan.gc.ca/daily-quotidien/110324/dq110324b-eng.htm and "Population and dwelling counts, for census metropolitan areas and census agglomerations, 2006 and 2001 censuses," Statistics Canada, available at http://www12.statcan.ca/english/census06/data/popdwell/Table.cfm?T=201&S=3&O=D&RPP=150.

[49] "Financial Data – Banks," Office of the Superintendent of Financial Institutions Canada, as of February 28, 2011, available at http://www.osfi.gc.ca/osfi/index_e.aspx?ArticleID=554.

[50] There were 77 deposit taking financial institutions regulated by the Office of the Superintendent of Financial Institutions Canada listed on April 23, 2011, http://www.osfi-bsif.gc.ca/osfi/index_e.aspx?DetailID=568.

[51] "Statistics on Payment Systems in the Group of Ten Countries," Bank for International Settlements, December 1998, available at http://www.bis.org/publ/cpss29.pdf.

[52] "About Us," Interac, available at http://www.interac.ca/about.php.

[53] Visa and MasterCard started offering signature debit in Canada in 2009.

The debit cards offered by Canadian banks are very different from the debit cards offered by American banks.

- Until 2004 Canadian consumers could use their cards only to pay in Canada. Starting in 2004, they could use them to pay at merchant locations in the United States that were connected to the NYCE debit card system—only about 1.5 million of the over 8 million locations that accept signature debit. Today, it is not possible for Canadians to use their cards at all outside of Canada and the United States. By contrast, Americans can pay with their debit cards anywhere in the world where MasterCard and Visa are accepted.

- Canadians by and large cannot use their cards to pay for goods and services at the vast number of merchants and content providers on the Internet. Americans can use their debit cards to pay for Internet purchases as well as use them with PayPal and other electronic wallets used in eCommerce.[54] Through 2004 it was not possible for Canadians to pay with their debit cards for Internet purchases or for card-not-present transactions such as telephone and mail orders. Today, it is possible for Canadians to pay with their cards at 600 Internet merchants[55] -- but not by simply entering their debit card number as people do in the United States. Internet consumers selecting the Interac Online payment option are redirected to their financial institution's website where they log in to their online bank account and select the amount to debit. Consumers are then redirected back to the merchant's website where they receive the confirmation details of the transaction.[56]

- Many Canadians have to pay to use their cards. The fees are as much as CDN$0.60 to CDN$0.65 per transaction for consumers that have exceeded their monthly threshold for accounts without unlimited transactions.[57] Most Americans pay nothing to use their cards. We discuss this in more detail below.

Canadian retail banks offer two main types of checking accounts, which offer different pricing for "consumer debits"—transactions that debit the checking account, including debit card transactions,

---

[54] A 2010 Javelin study reports that debit's share of online purchases grew from 26% in 2008 to 28% in 2009 and debit cards ranked only behind credit cards as the most common payment method selected by consumers, see http://www.marketingcharts.com/topics/e-commerce/consumers-favor-credit-cards-online-12090/. The Federal Reserve Bank of Boston reported in their 2009 Survey of Consumer Payments that debit cards were the most commonly used payment method for Internet payments – accounting for 36% of all transactions. See 2009 Survey of Consumer Payment Choice, at Table 22, available at http://www.bostonfed.org/economic/ppdp/2011/ppdp1101.pdf .

[55] That is a very small fraction of Internet merchants. Based on a review of these merchants they do not include many of the largest Internet merchants including Amazon, Wal-Mart, E-bay, etc. Many of the merchants appear to be relatively small websites. A full list of merchants accepting Interac Online is available at http://www.interac.ca/consumers/productsandservices_ol_search.php.

[56] "Products and Services," Interac, http://www.interac.ca/consumers/productsandservices_ol_main.php.

[57] Canadian and US dollars have a roughly equivalent exchange rate. As of May 6, 2011, a CDN$1.00 dollar could be exchanged for US$1.035.

but also including checks, ATM withdrawals, and Internet bill payments. There is a basic account which has a monthly service fee and transaction fees for consumer debits in excess of a monthly threshold. There is also a premium account which has a higher monthly service fee than the basic account and allows users to make an unlimited number of consumer debits at no extra charge.

Table 2 shows the features and pricing for basic and unlimited transaction accounts at the top five Canadian banks.[58] The table reports the average cost per debit card transaction based on 20, 30, and 40 consumer debits per month. Depending on the consumer's bank, the type of account, and the number of debit transactions in the month, the average cost per debit transaction is between CDN$0.27 and CDN$0.65.[59]

With this information in hand it is useful to compare the cost of debit cards and checking accounts for Americans and Canadians. Americans almost never pay for using a debit card.[60] In 2009, prior to changes in Regulation E and the passage of the Durbin Amendment, 76 percent of U.S. checking accounts were free of monthly service fees, and the minimum balance needed to qualify for free checking was only about $185. Therefore the typical American did not pay anything for paying with a debit card and did not pay anything significant for having a checking account so long as she had sufficient funds.[61] The Canadian Bankers Association reports that 30 percent of accounts pay no service fees; however, the minimum account balance for a "free" account was usually CDN $1,000.[62] Thus the typical Canadian pays between CDN $131 and

---

[58] Table 2 reports a hypothetical effective cost per debit transaction by allocating total monthly service fees and per transaction fees across the total number of debit transactions. We note that the table does not reflect that unlimited transaction accounts may also offer some services and fee waivers (such as fee waivers on number of out of network ATM transactions, waivers on email money transfers, check imaging, and discounts on other banking services) that are additional to the features of the basic transaction accounts. For example, at Bank of Montreal unlimited checking account customers receive one free non-BMO ATM transaction per month, AIR MILES rewards on debit card purchases (1 per $40 spent), check imaging, and two free Interac email money transfers per month (see http://www.bmo.com/pdf/plans_en.pdf) and at RBC Royal Bank unlimited account customers receive two free Interac email money transfers per month, a fee waiver of CDN$3 per month for overdraft protection, a CDN$35.00 rebate on certain eligible credit cards, check imaging, two free cross border transactions per month, and three free non-RBC ATM transactions per month (see http://www.rbcroyalbank.com/products/deposits/banking-compare.html).

[59] The cost to the consumer will depend on the number of consumer debits she makes. For example, the cost per debit for a consumer making only 1 or 2 transactions a month will be very high, about CDN$2 or more even on the basic plans, while the cost per debit for consumer making hundreds of monthly debit will be low on a per transaction basis on the unlimited plans, under CDN$0.05. We believe the range of consumer debit reported in Table 2 covers usage by typical Canadian consumers. The cost to the consumer will also depend on how accurately she is able to choose the plan that is lowest cost and how much her usage patterns changes from month to month. These calculations assume that that monthly fee is entirely related to the number of debit transactions; they could tend to inflate the average cost per transaction to the extent the fee includes other services provided by the banks for which it would charge a fee.

[60] They do pay overdraft fees when they do not have enough funds in their account.

[61] A minority of consumers paid overdraft fees for when they paid but did not have sufficient funds in their account. See "NSF, Overdraft-Protection Fees Drawing Greater Fire," US Banker, September 2007, available at http://www.americanbanker.com/usb_issues/117_9/-329016-1.html and "FDIC Study of Bank Overdraft Programs," FDIC, November 2008, available at http://www.fdic.gov/bank/analytical/overdraft/FDIC138_Report_Final_v508.pdf.

[62] Banks and Consumers, Canadian Bankers Association, http://www.cba.ca/en/media-room/50-backgroundeers-on-banking-issues/127-banks-and-consumers.

Table 2: Monthly Checking Accounts Fees at the Top 5 Canadian Banks

Bank	Account Type	Monthly Fee	Number of Debits Included	Additional Transactions Fee	20 Transactions		30 Transactions		40 Transactions	
					Total Cost	Effective Cost Per Transaction	Total Cost	Effective Cost Per Transaction	Total Cost	Effective Cost Per Transaction
RBC Royal Bank	Basic	$4.00	15	$0.60	$7.00	$0.35	$13.00	$0.43	$19.00	$0.48
	Unlimited	$10.95	Unlimited	n/a	$10.95	$0.55	$10.95	$0.37	$10.95	$0.27
Bank of Montreal	Basic	$4.00	10	$0.60	$10.00	$0.50	$16.00	$0.53	$22.00	$0.55
	Unlimited	$13.95	Unlimited	n/a	$13.95	$0.70	$13.95	$0.47	$13.95	$0.35
Toronto Dominion Bank	Basic	$3.95	10	$0.65	$10.45	$0.52	$16.95	$0.57	$23.45	$0.59
	Unlimited	$12.95	Unlimited	n/a	$12.95	$0.65	$12.95	$0.43	$12.95	$0.32
CIBC	Basic	$3.90	10	$0.65	$10.40	$0.52	$16.90	$0.56	$23.40	$0.59
	Unlimited	$12.95	Unlimited	n/a	$12.95	$0.65	$12.95	$0.43	$12.95	$0.32
Bank of Nova Scotia	Basic	$3.95	12	$0.65	$9.15	$0.46	$15.65	$0.52	$22.15	$0.55
	Unlimited	$12.95	Unlimited	n/a	$11.95	$0.60	$11.95	$0.40	$11.95	$0.30

Sources:
RBC Royal Bank: http://www.rbcroyalbank.com/products/deposits/banking-compare.html
Bank of Montreal: http://www.bmo.com/pdf/plans_en.pdf
Toronto Dominion Bank: http://www.tdcanadatrust.com/accounts/accounts-fees.pdf
CIBC: http://www.cibc.com/ca/chequing-savings/chequing-accts.html
Bank of Nova Scotia: http://www.scotiabank.com/cda/files/d2d/d2dcb_e.pdf

$167 a year for a premium account and CDN $84 and $125 a year for a basic account with 240 debit transactions annually.

V. CONSUMERS AND SMALL BUSINESS WOULD NOT BENEFIT

Senator Durbin has said the amendment would benefit consumers.[63] The merchant trade associations have made similar claims that consumers would save more than $1 billion a month.[64] These figures correspond to the average amount of debit interchange fee revenue that merchants

---

[63] See "Durbin: Interchange Reform will Take Effect as Planned on July 21," Congressional Documents and Publications, March 29, 2011, available at http://durbin.senate.gov/public/index.cfm/pressreleases?ID=c9a55fa4-c91a-4ec5-b2ac-cdbde32826ef and also see 157 Cong. Rec. S1780 (daily ed. Mar. 17, 2011) see the statement of Sen. Dick Durbin, available at http://www.gpo.gov/fdsys/pkg/CREC-2011-03-17/html/CREC-2011-03-17-pt1-PgS1778.htm.

[64] According to the National Association of Convenience Stores "[d]elaying swipe fee reform has consequences that will cost merchants and their customers $1 billion each month…" See "Durbin Amendment in Danger of Delay," Convenience Store Decisions, March 17, 2011 quoting National Association of Convenience Stores Senior Vice President of Government Relations Lyle Beckwith. And, "[t]he consequences of inaction are clear; the dominant networks (and their banks) will continue to impose supracompetitive interchange fees on all merchants — more than $1 billion per month of fees that are ultimately borne by consumers." See the "Merchants Payment Coalition Submission to the Board of Governors of the Federal Reserve System," Merchants Payment Coalition, February 23, 2011, available at http://www.federalreserve.gov/newsevents/files/MPC_Consumer_Meeting_20110223.pdf

would not pay if the Federal Reserve Board's proposal to reduce interchange fee rates to 12 cents per transaction were implemented. The claim that consumers would save more than $1 billion a month is based on two false assumptions.[65]

The first false assumption is that merchants would reduce the prices they charge consumers by the full amount of any savings they receive. Economic studies of how merchants respond to cost changes demonstrate that merchants would not reduce prices quickly or fully in response to the reduction in debit interchange fees. Debit interchange fees would fall by about $0.016 cents for a $10 purchase. Studies have found that merchants typically do not reduce prices in response to small cost changes. Prices are sticky. Merchants will eventually reduce prices, but other economic studies have found that they reduce prices only by about 40-70 percent of the reduction in cost. While it is likely under economic theory that merchants in highly competitive segments will eventually be forced to pass through the cost savings in the form of lower prices, many merchants that accept debit cards do not operate in highly competitive markets. For example, based on the Federal Trade Commission's definitions of grocery store and big box retailer markets, which account for a significant portion of debit card use, consumers in many metropolitan areas have a choice between few competitors in these industries.[66] In fact, big box retailer Home Depot's CFO reported in providing guidance on their earnings estimate that the company expected that the bottom line benefit to the company would be $35 million a year.[67]

The second false assumption is that banks and credit unions will not raise the fees for checking accounts and debit cards as a result of the revenues they will lose. To the extent banks and credit unions raise fees, such increased fees would offset any savings consumers receive from lower merchant prices. The average bank or credit union would lose roughly $60 of revenue from the average consumer checking account.[68] Banks and credit unions reduced checking account fees and dropped debit card transaction fees as the use of debit cards by consumers increased dramatically (and therefore interchange fee revenues increased also) during the 2000s. As they lose these revenues, that process will work in reverse. Retail banking is the

---

[65] For more details see David S. Evans, Robert L. Litan, and Richard Schmalensee, "Economic Analysis of the Effects of the Federal Reserve Board's Proposed Debit Car Interchange Fee Regulations on Consumers and Small Businesses," Submission to the Board of Governors of the Federal Reserve System, February 22, 2011 ("Evans et al.").

[66] In Staples/Office Depot the FTC argued and a court agreed that these office superstores faced little competition from other stores that sold office supplies and that the geographic markets were local. In 15 metropolitan areas, Staples and Office Depot were the only competitors. The FTC has also reviewed a number of supermarket mergers and in the course of doing so determined that there is a relevant product market for large supermarkets that can provide a full array of grocery and related products to consumers and that this market includes the grocery portion of supercenters. Based on examining data for a number of cities and admittedly casual inspection, it appears that most people have the choice between a few supermarkets as defined by the antitrust authorities. A downtown resident of Boston, Massachusetts would find 4 supermarket chains within the city limits (5 if we included Whole Foods, which the FTC would not); based on the experience of one of the authors, most people would find only one or two of these convenient to use on a regular basis for major shopping.

[67] "Event Brief of Q4 2010 Home Depot Inc Earnings Conference Call – Final," CQ FD Disclosure, February 22, 2011.

[68] See Evans et al., at p 28.

kind of highly competitive business in which economists would expect that firms would pass on most of the cost savings to consumers in the form of lower prices and most of cost increases in the form of higher prices. The history of banking in the last decade reflects this, as do the announcements by banks that they are increasing their fees in anticipation of the debit card interchange fee reductions.

Evans, Litan and Schmalensee have estimated that banks would likely increase their fees to consumers over the first 24 months of the proposed regulations by far more in total than merchants would decrease their prices to consumers. In fact, they estimate that merchants would receive a windfall of between $17.2-$19.9 billion dollars in the first 24 months the rules are in effect, depending on which proposal the Federal Reserve Board adopted of the two advanced in December 2010.

Senator Durbin has also claimed that small businesses would benefit from the legislation.[69] But this is not true. Virtually all small businesses have checking accounts with debit cards. They will pay more for these accounts as a result of banks losing debit card interchange fee revenue, which is usually greater for small business accounts than for consumer accounts. Although precise statistics are not available, most small businesses do not accept debit cards for payments and therefore would not benefit from reduced debit card interchange fees.[70] We tend to think of small businesses as the local shopkeepers, many of whom do take debit. But most small businesses are manufacturers, tradespeople, or in other lines of work that do not involve being paid with credit or debit cards. Only 10 percent of small businesses are in retail where card payments are most common. Therefore, most small businesses would lose as a result of the Durbin Amendment.

VI. CONCLUSION

The Durbin Amendment goes against the views expressed by the General Accountability Office, a Federal Reserve Board staff research report, and the Antitrust Division of the U.S. Department of Justice—all of which effectively raised red flags about the possible adverse effects of interchange fee regulation on consumers. It was adopted with surprisingly little discussion given that it results in the imposition of price controls and the elimination of the free market for a significant American industry. The trade groups that promoted this legislation obviously had the interests of merchants

---

[69] "Durbin Responds to OCC Chief on Interchange, Meets with Small Business About Benefits of Reform," Congressional Documents and Publications, March 10, 2011, available at http://durbin.senate.gov/public/index.cfm/pressreleases?ID=6886cb40-cd16-4d83-a0d4-5363324a9abc.

[70] As discussed in Evans, Litan and Schmalensee, because small businesses that accept payment cards have blended fee contracts with their merchant processors, and have little bargaining power with these processors, it is likely that these small businesses will not receive the full benefits of the reduction in interchange fees or receive these benefits quickly.

in mind in shifting the costs of debit cards from merchants to consumers. However, they have also claimed that imposing price controls on the debit-card industry would serve the public interest. We disagree. The best evidence shows that the imposition of the price controls described by the Federal Reserve Board on December 16, 2010 would cost consumers billions of dollars over the next two years. If Canada is any example, a dramatic reduction in interchange may well result in consumers here also paying more, but getting less.

CONCLUSION

There are two competing stories about interchange fees.

One is that there is a market failure in the payment card industry that results in payment card systems setting fees that are too high. Price regulation is needed to reduce these fees. Doing so will improve social welfare by getting consumers and merchants to make the right choices when it comes to payment instruments.

As the essays in this volume document, there is an almost complete lack of empirical support for imposing price regulation. It is true that economic theory shows that profit-maximizing payment card systems would ordinarily not choose the socially optimal price both for market power reasons and because of features of multi-sided platforms. But economic theory would show market failures by these terms in many industries. The imposition of regulation requires more.

Yet there is simply no empirical evidence on the key economic questions that one would want answers to before imposing regulation and for deciding what the regulated interchange fee should be. There are no credible empirical estimates of the socially optimal interchange fee and thus no way to know the magnitude of the difference between the socially optimal and privately set interchange. Without knowing that magnitude it is not possible to decide whether the market failure significant enough to warrant regulation. Nor are there credible empirical estimates of what the socially optimal interchange fee is, and therefore no basis for deciding on the regulated fee. A central proposition of the case for regulation is that interchange fees result in consumers using electronic payments too much. There is, however, no credible evidence that consumers are using cash and checks too little and electronic payments too much.

The other story is also about a market failure but one that stems from the political and legal process. It is one in which merchants, through lobbying efforts and the courts, have organized what is, in effect, a buyer cartel that is seeking to lower prices to its members. In a two-sided industry, a buyer cartel on one side of the platform results in shifting the costs of the platform to the other side. The results in Australia are consistent with this waterbed effect: consumers ended up paying higher card fees and there is no evidence—simply assertions based on flawed economics—that merchants passed enough of the savings onto consumers to offset these higher fees. The evidence on pass-through rates points in the same direction in the US. It will remain to be seen whether the facts bear out the prediction made in Chapter 5 that debit-card interchange fee regulation in the US will result in a massive transfer of wealth from consumers to merchants.

CONTRIBUTORS

Howard Chang
Principal with Global Economics Group

Robert E. Litan
Vice President for Research and Policy at the Kauffman Foundation, Senior Fellow in Economic Studies at Brookings

Abel Mateus
Professor, University of New Lisbon; Director at Global Economics Group; and former First President of the Portuguese Competition Authority

Richard Schmalensee
Howard W. Johnson Professor of Economics and Management and Dean Emeritus, MIT Sloan School of Management

Daniel D. Garcia Swartz
Senior Consulting Economist at CompassLexecon

Margaret Weichert
Principal at Market Platform Dynamics

ABOUT THE AUTHOR

David S. Evans is the Chairman of the Global Economics Group and the Founder of Market Platform Dynamics. He teaches economics and antitrust at the University of Chicago Law School, where is a Lecturer, and at the University College London, where he is a Visiting Professor. He received his Ph.D. in economics from the University of Chicago.

BIBLIOGRAPHY

Ackerberg, Daniel A., and Gautam Gowrisankaran (2003) "Quantifying Equilibrium Network Externalities in the ACH Banking Industry," mimeo, University of Arizona, October.

Ahlborn, Christian, Howard H. Chang, and David S. Evans (2001) "The Problem of Interchange Fee Analysis: Case without a Cause?" *European Competition Law Review*, vol. 22, no. 8 (August), pp. 304-312.

American Express (2005) American Express Company Annual Report 2004. February.

Armstrong, Marcia (1991) "Retail Response to Trade Promotion: An Incremental Analysis of Forward Buying and Retail Promotion," unpublished doctoral dissertation, School of Management, University of Texas at Dallas.

Armstrong, Mark (2004) "Competition in Two-Sided Markets," mimeo, University College London.

Armstrong, Mark (2004, 2005) "Two-Sided Markets: Economic Theory and Policy Implications." mimeo, University College, London, April.

Armstrong, Mark (2004) Simon Cowan, and John Vickers (1994) Regulatory Reform – Economic Analysis and British Experience. Cambridge, Massachusetts: MIT Press.

Armstrong, Mark (2004) and Julian Wright (2004) "Two-Sided Markets, Competitive Bottlenecks and Exclusive Contracts," mimeo, University College London, November.

ANZ (2003) *Annual Report*.

Australian Bureau of Statistics (2001) *2001 Census Basic Community Profile and Snapshot*. http://www.abs.gov.au/ausstats/abs@census.nsf/4079a1bbd2a04b80ca256b9d00208f92/7dd97c937216e32fca256bbe008371f0!OpenDocument

Australian Bureau of Statistics (2003) *Year Book Australia*. http://www.abs.gov.au/Ausstats/abs@.nsf/Lookup/361F400BCE3AB8ACCA256CAE00053FA4

Australian Bureau of Statistics (2005) *Household Final Consumption Expenditure*. March.

Australian Prudential Regulation Authority (2005) *Monthly Banking Statistics*. July. http://www.apra.gov.au/Statistics/loader.cfm?url=/commonspot/security/getfile.cfm&PageID=9124

Balto, David A (2000) "The Problem of Interchange Fees: Costs without Benefits?" *European Competition Law Review*, vol. 21, no 4 (April), pp. 215-224.

Baxter, William F. (1983) "Bank Exchange of Transactional Paper: Legal and Economic Perspectives," *Journal of Law and Economics*, vol. 26, no. 3 (October), pp. 541-588.

Bayot, Jennifer (2003) "Credit Card Rewards Turn From Nouns to Verbs," *The New York Times*, September 21.

Bergman, Mats A. (2005) "Two-Sided Network Effects, Bank Interchange Fees, and the Allocation of Fixed Costs." Mimeo, Swedish Competition Authority, January.

Besley, Timothy and Harvey Rosen (1999) "Sales Taxes and Prices: An Empirical Analysis," *National Tax Journal*, 52: 157-178.

Bolt, Wilko, and Alexander F. Tieman (2004a) "Skewed Pricing in Two-Sided Markets: An IO Approach," De Nederlandsche Bank, Amsterdam, Working Paper No. 13, October.

Bolt, Wilko, and Alexander F. Tieman (2004b) "A Note on Social Welfare and Cost Recovery in Two-Sided Markets,", De Nederlandsche Bank, Amsterdam, Working Paper No. 24, December.

Borenstein, Severin, C. Cameron, and R. Gilbert (1997) "Do Gasoline Prices Respond Asymmetrically to Crude Oil Price Changes?" *Quarterly Journal of Economics* 112: 305-339 (February).

Brammall, Bruce (2002) "Watchdog Fears ANZ Card Hikes," *Herald Sun*, November 5.

Brammall, Bruce (2003) "Bank May Ditch Reward Scheme," *Herald Sun*, February 20.

Bulow, Jeremy and Paul Pfleiderer (1983) "A Note on the Effect of Cost Changes on Prices," *Journal of Political Economy*, 91: 182-185.

Bureau of Transportation Statistics (2000) "Airport Activity Statistics of Certificated Air Carriers: Summary Tables 2000," Table 1, online: http://www.bts.gov/publications/airport_activity_statistics_of_certificated_air_carriers/2000/tables/table01.html.

Caillaud, Bernard, and Bruno Jullien (2003) "Chicken and Egg: Competition among Intermediation Service Providers," *Rand Journal of Economics*, vol. 34, no. 2 (Summer), pp. 521-552.

Cannex Australia (2004) *Card reforms in Australia: Monitoring of market effects*, October.

Carlton, Dennis W. (1986) "The Rigidity of Prices," *American Economic Review*, 76: 637-58.

Carlton, Dennis W., and Alan S. Frankel (1995a) "The Antitrust Economics of Credit Card Networks," *Antitrust Law Journal*, vol. 63, no. 2 (Winter), pp. 643-668.

Carlton, Dennis W., and Alan S. Frankel (1995b) "The Antitrust Economics of Credit Card Networks: Reply to Evans and Schmalensee," *Antitrust Law Journal*, vol. 63, no. 3 (Spring), pp. 903-915.

Chakravorti, Sujit (2003) "Theory of Credit Card Networks: A Survey of the Literature," *Review of Network Economics*, vol. 2, no. 2 (June), pp. 50-68.

Chakravorti, Sujit, and Alpha Shah (2003) "Underlying Incentives in Credit Card Networks," *Antitrust Bulletin*, vol. 48, no. 1 (Spring), pp. 53-75.

Chakravorti, Sujit, and Roberto Roson (2004) "Platform Competition in Two-Sided Markets: The Case of Payment Networks," Federal Reserve Bank of Chicago, Working Paper 2004-09, July.

Chakravorti, Sujit, and Ted To (2003) "A Theory of Credit Cards," mimeo, Federal Reserve Bank of Chicago, July.

Chakravorti, Sujit, and William R. Emmons (2003) "Who Pays for Credit Cards?" *Journal of Consumer Affairs*, vol. 37, no. 2 (Winter), pp. 208-230.

Chang, Howard H., and David S. Evans (2000) "The Competitive Effects of the Collective Setting of Interchange by Payment Card Systems," *Antitrust Bulletin*, vol. 45, no. 3 (Fall), pp. 641-677.

Chang, Howard H., David S. Evans, and Daniel Garcia Swartz (2005) "An Assessment of the Reserve Bank of Australia's Interchange Fee Reforms," Working Paper, May.

Chevalier, Michel and R. Curhan (1976) "Retail Promotions as a Function of Trade Promotions: A Descriptive Analysis," *Sloan Management Review*, 18: 19-32.

Cornell, Andrew (2004) "Deal Highlights Change in Card Market," Australian Financial Review, July 12.

Cornell, Andrew. 2005. "American Express Aims for Expansion," *Australian Financial Review*, April 18.

Cotterill, Ronald (1998) "Estimation of Cost Pass Through to Michigan Consumers in the ADM Price Fixing Case," Food Marketing Policy Center, University of Connecticut, Research Report No. 39.

Cotterill, Ronald (2000) "Dynamic Explanations of Industry Structure and Performance," presented at the USDA Conference "The American Consumer and the Changing Structure of the Food System," May 3-5, 2000.

Cruickshank, Don (2000) "Annex D3: Interchange Fees for Credit and Debit Cards," UK Banking: A Report to the Chancellor of the Exchequer, UK: HM Treasury (March), pp. 247-272.

De Grauwe, Paul, and Laura Rinaldi (2002) "A Model of the Card Payment System and The Interchange Fee," in Clemens Esser and Michael H. Stierle, eds., *Current Issues in Competition Theory and Policy*, Berlin: VWF.

Enders, Walter (2004) *Applied Econometric Time Series*. John Wiley and Sons: New York.

Euromonitor International (2005a) "Department Stores in Australia," October.

Euromonitor International (2005b) "Grocery Stores, Food Retailers and Supermarkets in Australia," October.

Euromonitor International (2005c) "Superstores and Warehouse Clubs in Australia," October.

European Commission (2002) "Commission Decision of 24 July 2002 Relating to a Proceeding Under Article 81 of the EC Treaty and Article 53 of the EEA Agreement," *Official Journal of the European Communities*, vol. 318 (November 22), pp. 17-36.

European Commission (2003) "Statement on Mastercard." Midday Express Press Release, October 30.

Evans, David S. (2003a) "Some Empirical Aspects of Multi-Sided Platform Industries," *Review of Network Economics*, vol. 2, issue 3 (September), 191-209.

Evans, David S. (2003b) "The Antitrust Economics of Multi-Sided Platform Markets," *Yale Journal on Regulation*, vol. 20, no. 2 (Summer), pp. 325-381.

Evans, David S., Andrei Hagiu, and Richard Schmalensee (2004) "A Survey of the Economic Role of Software Platforms in Computer-Based Industries," CESifo Working Paper No. 1314, October.

Evans, David S., and Richard Schmalensee (1995) "Economic Aspects of Payment Card Systems and Antitrust Policy toward Joint Ventures," *Antitrust Law Journal*, vol. 63, no. 3 (Spring), pp. 861-901.

Evans, David S., and Richard Schmalensee (2005a) *Paying with Plastic: The Digital Revolution in Buying and Borrowing*. Second Edition. MIT Press: Cambridge, MA.

Evans, David S., and Richard Schmalensee (2005b) "The Economics of Interchange Fees and Their Regulation: An Overview," paper presented at a Conference *Interchange Fees in Credit and Debit Card Industries: What Role for Public Authorities?* Federal Reserve Bank of Kansas City, Santa Fe, New Mexico, May 4-6.

Evans, David S., and Richard Schmalensee (2005c) "The Industrial Organization of Markets with Two-Sided Platforms," *NBER Working Paper Series*, No. 11603, September.

Food Marketing Institute. 1998. A Retailer's Guide to Electronic Payment System Costs, Washington, DC: Food Marketing Institute.

Frankel, Alan S., 1998. "Monopoly and Competition in the Supply and Exchange of Money," Antitrust Law Journal, vol. 66, no. 2 (Winter), pp. 313-361.

Gabszewicz, Jean J. and Xavier Y. Wauthy. 2004. "Two-Sided Markets and Price Competition with Multi-homing," mimeo, Belgium: Center for Operations Research and Economics, Catholic University of Louvain.

Gans, Joshua S., and Stephen P. King. 2003a. "Approaches to Regulating Interchange Fees in Payment Systems," Review of Network Economics, vol. 2, no. 2 (June), pp. 125-145.

Gans, Joshua S., and Stephen P. King. 2003b. "The Neutrality of Interchange Fees in Payment Systems," Topics in Economic Analysis and Policy, vol. 3, no. 1, online: http://www.bepress.com/bejeap/topics/vol3/iss1/art1/.

Gans, Joshua S., and Stephen P. King. 2003c. "A Theoretical Analysis of Credit Card Reform in Australia," Economic Record, v. 79, issue 247 (December), pp. 462-472.

Garcia Swartz, Daniel D., Robert W. Hahn, and Anne Layne-Farrar. 2004. "The Economics of a Cashless Society: An Analysis of the Costs and Benefits of Payment Instruments," AEI-Brookings Joint Center for Regulatory Studies, Related Publication 04-24, September.

Goldberg, Pinelopi and Michael Knetter (1997) "Goods Prices and Exchange Rates: What Have We Learned?" *Journal of Economic Literature*, 35: 1243-1272.

Goldberger, Arthur S. (1991) *A Course in Econometrics.* Harvard University Press: Cambridge, Massachusetts.

Graeme, James (2003) "Loyalty is No Longer Paying Off," *Sunday Telegraph*, May 4.

Greene, William H (1993) *Econometric Analysis.* Macmillan: New York.

Guthrie, Graeme, and Julian Wright. 2003. "Competing Payment Schemes," mimeo, National University of Singapore, September.

Hagiu, Andrei. 2004a. "Two-Sided Platforms: Pricing and Social Efficiency," Research Institute for the Economy, Trade and Industry Discussion Paper Series 04-E-035, Research Institute for the Economy, Trade and Industry, Tokyo, December.

Hagiu, Andrei. 2004b. "Two-Sided Platforms: Pricing and Social Efficiency – Extensions," Research Institute for the Economy, Trade and Industry Discussion Paper Series 04-E-036, Research Institute for the Economy, Trade and Industry, Tokyo, December.

Hamilton, James (1994) *Time Series Analysis.* Princeton University Press: Princeton, NJ.

Hanna, Jim (2002) "Fed: Consumers to Save $500m-Plus Under Credit Card Shake-Up," *AAP Newsfeed*, August 27.

Hansen, Bruce (2001) "The New Econometrics of Structural Change: Dating Breaks in U.S. Labor Productivity," *Journal of Economic Perspectives*, 15: 1065-1076.

Hayashi, Fumiko. 2004. "A Puzzle of Payment Card Pricing: Why Are Merchants Still Accepting Card Payments?" mimeo, Federal Reserve Bank of Kansas City, December.

Hayashi, Fumiko, Richard Sullivan, and Stuart E. Weiner. 2003. A Guide to the ATM and Debit Card Industry, Federal Reserve Bank of Kansas City.

Horan, Matthew (2003) "Banks Up Card Fees Yet Again," *Sunday Telegraph*, September 21.

House of Representatives Standing Committee on Economic Economics, Finance and Public Administration (2005) *Official Committee Hansard*. August 12. http://www.aph.gov.au/hansard/reps/commttee/R8516.pdf

HSN Consultants. 1987. The Nilson Report, no. 406 (June).

HSN Consultants. 1991. The Nilson Report, no. 510 (October).

HSN Consultants. 1992. The Nilson Report, no. 522 (April).

HSN Consultants. 2001a. The Nilson Report, no. 737 (April).

HSN Consultants. 2001b. The Nilson Report, no. 738 (April).

HSN Consultants. 2003. The Nilson Report, No. 783, March.

Huber, Peter J. (1964) "Robust Estimation of a Location Parameter," *Annals of Mathematical Statistics*, 35: 73-101.

Humphrey, David, Magnus Willesson, Ted Lindblom, and Göran Bergendahl. 2003. "What Does it Cost to Make a Payment?" Review of Network Economics, vol. 2, no. 2 (June), pp. 159-174.

Hunt, Robert M. 2003. "An Introduction to the Economics of Payment Card Networks," Review of Network Economics, vol. 2, no. 2 (June), 80-96.

IMA Market Development AB. 2000. "Study Regarding the Effects of the Abolition of the Non-discrimination Rule in Sweden: Final Report, Results and Conclusions," mimeo, Lerum, Sweden, February.

ITM Research. 2000. "The Abolition of the No-discrimination Rule." mimeo, Amsterdam, March.

Jackson, William, III (1997) "Market Structure and the Speed of Price Adjustments: Evidence of Non-monotonicity," *Review of Industrial Organization*, 12: 37:57.

Johnston, Jack (1983) *Econometric Methods*. McGraw-Hill: New York.

Jullien, Bruno. 2004. "Two-Sided Markets and Electronic Intermediaries," CESifo Working Paper No. 1345, November.

Karrenbrok, Jeffrey D. (1991) "The Behavior of Retail Gasoline Prices: Symmetric or Not?" *Federal Reserve Bank of St. Louis Review*, 73: 19-29.

Katz, Michael L. (2001) "Network Effects, Interchange Fees, and No-Surcharge Rules in the Australian Credit and Charge Card Industry," Commissioned Report in *Reform of Credit Card Schemes in Australia*, Reserve Bank of Australia, August.

Katz, Michael L., and Harvey S. Rosen (1998) *Microeconomics.* Irwin/McGraw-Hill: Boston, Massachusetts.

Katz, Michael L. 2001. Reform of Credit Card Schemes in Australia II, Commissioned Report: Network Effects, Interchange Fees, and No-Surcharge Rules in the Australian Credit and Charge Card Industry, Reserve Bank of Australia, August.

Konkurrencestyrelsen. 2005. "Konkurrencestyrelsens Undersøgelse af Dankortgebyret," ISA/1107-8900-003/bjs/fab/lkf, Copenhagen, February.

Lipsey, R.G., and Kelvin Lancaster. 1956. "The General Theory of the Second Best," Review of Economic Studies, vol. 24, no. 1 (October), pp. 11-32.

Littlechild, Stephen. 2003. "Reflections on Incentive Regulation," Review of Network Economics, vol. 2, no. 4 (December), pp. 289-315.

McFarland, Lyndal. 2005. "Update: Australia's Virgin Blue Outlook Clouded by Fuel," CNN Money, May 18, online: http://money.cnn.com/services/tickerheadlines/for5/200505180450 DOWJONESDJONLINE000368_FORTUNE5.htm.

Macfarlane, I.J. 2005. "Gresham's Law of Payments," Talk to AIBF Industry Forum 2005, Sydney, 23 March.

Manenti, Fabio M., and Ernesto Somma. 2003. "Plastic Clashes: Competition among Closed and Open Systems in the Credit Card Industry," mimeo, Università di Padova, October.

Maxwell, Miranda (2005) "Tough Leader Wanted for Australia's Telstra," *Reuters*, May 10. http://www.reuters.com/newsArticle.jhtml?type=reutersEdge&storyID=8443245

McKinnon, Michael (2001) "Credit Card Profit Under Fire," *Courier Mail*, April 27.

Megginson, William L., and Jeffrey N. Netter. 2001. "From State to Market: A Survey of Empirical Studies on Privatization," Journal of Economic Literature, vol. 39, no. 2 (June), pp. 321-389.

National Bancard Corporation v. Visa U.S.A., Inc. 1982. "Defendant's Trial Brief," Southern District of Florida, April 12.

National Bancard Corporation v. Visa U.S.A., Inc. 1984. 596 F. Supp. 1231 (S.D. Fla.).

National Bancard Corporation v. Visa U.S.A., Inc. 1986a. 779 F.2d 592 (11th Cir.).

National Bancard Corporation v. Visa U.S.A., Inc. 1986b. 479 U.S. 923.

Network Economics Consulting Group (2005) *Early Evidence of the Impact of Reserve Bank of Australia Regulation of Open Credit Card Schemes.* May.

Newmark, David, and Steven Sharpe (1992) "Market Structure and the Nature of Price Rigidity: Evidence from the Market for Consumer Deposits," *Quarterly Journal of Economics*, 107: 657-680.

Office of Fair Trading. 2003a. "MasterCard Interchange Fees: Preliminary Conclusions," London, OFT634, February.

Office of Fair Trading. 2003b. "UK Payment Systems: An OFT Market Study of Clearing Systems and Review of Plastic Card Networks," London, OFT658, May.

Peltzman, Sam (2000) "Prices Rise Faster than they Fall," *Journal of Political Economy*, 108: 466-502.

Perron, Pierre (1989) "The Great Crash, the Oil Price Shock, and the Unit Root Hypothesis," *Econometrica*, 57: 1361-1401.

Poirier, Dale J. (1976) *The Econometrics of Structural Change*. North Holland: Amsterdam.

Poirier, Dale J. and Steven G. Garber (1974) "The Determinants of Aerospace Profit Rates 1951-1971," *Southern Economic Journal*, 41: 228-238.

Poterba, James (1999) "Retail Price Reactions to Changes in State and Local Sales Taxes," National Tax Journal, 49: 165-176.

Reserve Bank of Australia (2001) *Reform of Credit Card Schemes in Australia I: A Consultation Document*. December.

Reserve Bank of Australia (2002) *Reform of Credit Card Schemes in Australia IV: Final Reforms and Regulation Impact Statement*. August.

Reserve Bank of Australia (2004) *Payment System Board Annual Report 2004*.

Reserve Bank of Australia (2005a) *Banking Fees in Australia*.

Reserve Bank of Australia (2005b) *Additional Credit Card Statistics*. online: http://www.rba.gov.au/Statistics/Bulletin/C01hist.xls.

Reserve Bank of Australia (2005b) "Credit and Charge Card Statistics," May, online: http://www.rba.gov.au/PaymentsSystem/AustralianPaymentsSystem/ExcelFiles/RPS.xls.

Reserve Bank of Australia (2005c) *Additional Credit Card Statistics*. online: http://www.rba.gov.au/PaymentsSystem/PaymentsStatistics/ExcelFiles/RPS.xls.

Reserve Bank of Australia (2005d) *Market Shares Of Credit And Charge Card Schemes*. online: http://www.rba.gov.au/Statistics/Bulletin/C02hist.xls

Reserve Bank of Australia and Australian Competition and Consumer Commission (2000) *Debit and Credit Card Schemes in Australia: A Study of Interchange Fees and Access*. October.

Rochet, Jean-Charles (2005) "The Interchange Fee Mysteries – Discussion of 'Economic Rationale for Interchange Fees' by D. Evans and R. Schmalensee," presented at a Conference *Interchange Fees in Credit and Debit Card Industries: What Role for Public Authorities?* Federal Reserve Bank of Kansas City, Santa Fe, New Mexico, May 4-6.

Bibliography

Rochet, Jean-Charles. 2003. "The Theory of Interchange Fees: A Synthesis of Recent Contributions," Review of Network Economics, vol. 2, no. 2 (June), pp. 97-124.

Rochet, Jean-Charles and Jean Tirole (2002) "Cooperation among Competitors: Some Economics of Payment Card Associations," *The RAND Journal of Economics*, 33: 1-22.

Rochet, Jean-Charles, and Jean Tirole. 2003a. "An Economic Analysis of the Determination of Interchange Fees in Payment Card Systems," Review of Network Economics, vol. 2, no. 2 (June), pp. 69-79.

Rochet, Jean-Charles and Jean Tirole (2003) "Platform Competition in Two-Sided Markets," *Journal of the European Economic Association*, 1: 990-1029.

Rochet, Jean-Charles, and Jean Tirole. 2004a. "Defining Two-Sided Markets," mimeo, Industrial Economic Institute: Toulouse, France, January.

Rochet, Jean-Charles, and Jean Tirole. 2004b. "Two-Sided Markets: An Overview." Mimeo, Industrial Economic Institute: Toulouse, France, March.

Rysman, Marc. 2004. "An Empirical Analysis of Payment Card Usage," mimeo, Boston University, January.

Schiff, Aaron. 2003. "Open and Closed Systems of Two-Sided Networks," Information Economics and Policy, vol. 15, no. 4 (December), pp. 425-442.

Schmalensee, Richard (2003) "Interchange Fees: A Review of the Literature," *Payment Card Economics Review*, 1: 25-44.

Schmalensee, Richard (2002) "Payment Systems and Interchange Fees," *Journal of Industrial Economics*, 50: 103-122.

Schwartz, Marius, and Daniel R. Vincent. 2004. "The No Surcharge Rule and Card User Rebates: Vertical Control by a Payment Network," mimeo, Georgetown University.

Small, John, and Julian Wright. 2000. "Decentralized Interchange Fees in Open Payment Networks: An Economic Analysis," mimeo, University of Aukland, December.

Stavins, Joanna. 1997. "A Comparison of Social Costs and Benefits of Paper Check Presentment and ECP Truncation," New England Economic Review, (July/August), pp. 27-44.

Stigler, George J., and James K. Kindahl (1970) *The Behavior of Industrial Prices*. National Bureau of Economic Research: New York.

Swedish Bankers' Association. 2004. "Banks in Sweden—Facts about the Swedish banking market." September.

Tirole, Jean. 1988. The Theory of Industrial Organization, Cambridge, Massachusetts: MIT Press.

Tyagi, Rajeev K. (1999) "A Characterization of Retailer Response to Manufacturer Trade Deals," *Journal of Marketing Research*, 36: 510-516.

United States Census Bureau. 2004. "2002 Economic Census: Industry Series," online: http://www.census.gov/econ/census02/guide/INDSUMM.HTM.

United States Department of Commerce Bureau of Economic Analysis. 2003 "Imputations in the National Income and Product Accounts," September 29.

United States Department of Commerce Bureau of Economic Analysis. 2004 "Gross Domestic Product: Implicit Price Deflator," November 30.

Van Raalte, Chris, and Harry Webers. 1998. "Spatial Competition with Intermediated Matching," Journal of Economic Behavior and Organization, vol. 34, no. 3 (March), pp. 477-488.

Vickers, John. 2005. "Public Policy and the Invisible Price: Competition Law, Regulation, and the Interchange Fee, paper presented at a Conference Interchange Fees in Credit and Debit Card Industries: What Role for Public Authorities? Federal Reserve Bank of Kansas City, Santa Fe, New Mexico, May 4-6, 2005

Visa International. 2001. International Country Overviews, October.

Viscusi, W. Kip, John M. Vernon, and Joseph E. Harrington, Jr. 2000. Economics of Regulation and Antitrust, Cambridge, Massachusetts: MIT Press.

Walters, Rockney G. (1989) "An Empirical Investigation into Retailer Response to Manufacturer Trade Promotions," *Journal of Retailing*, 65: 253-272.

Weiner, Stuart E., and Julian Wright. 2005. "Interchange Fees in Various Countries: Developments and Determinants," paper presented at a Conference Interchange Fees in Credit and Debit Card Industries: What Role for Public Authorities? Federal Reserve Bank of Kansas City, Santa Fe, New Mexico, May 4-6, 2005.

Winston, Clifford, and Steven A. Morrison. 1986. The Economic Effects of Airline Deregulation, Washington, DC: The Brookings Institution.

Wolters, Timothy. 2000. ""Carry Your Credit in Your Pocket": The Early History of the Credit Card at Bank of America and Chase Manhattan," Enterprise and Society, vol. 1, no. 2 (June), pp. 315-354.

Wright, Julian. 2000. "An Economic Analysis of a Card Payment Network." Mimeo, NECG and University of Auckland, December.

Wright, Julian. 2003a. "Optimal Card Payment Systems," European Economic Review, vol. 47, no. 4 (August), pp. 587-612.

Wright, Julian. 2003b. "Pricing in Debit and Credit Card Schemes," Economics Letters, vol. 80, no. 3 (September), pp. 305-309.

Wright, Julian. 2003c. "Why Do Firms Accept Credit Cards?" mimeo, University of Auckland.

Wright, Julian. 2004a. "The Determinants of Optimal Interchange Fees in Payment Systems," Journal of Industrial Economics, vol. 52, no. 1 (March), pp. 1-26.

Wright, Julian. 2004b. "One-sided Logic in Two-sided Markets," Review of Network Economics, vol. 3, no. 1 (March), pp. 44-64.

Made in the USA
Columbia, SC
04 March 2018